HTML5 Quick
Markup Reference

Wallace Jackson

Apress®

HTML5 Quick Markup Reference

Wallace Jackson
Lompoc, California, USA

ISBN-13 (pbk): 978-1-4302-6535-1   ISBN-13 (electronic): 978-1-4302-6536-8
DOI 10.1007/978-1-4302-6536-8

Library of Congress Control Number: 2016944265

Managing Director: Welmoed Spahr
Lead Editor: Steve Anglin
Technical Reviewer: Chád Darby
Editorial Board: Steve Anglin, Pramila Balan, Louise Corrigan, Jonathan Gennick,
    Robert Hutchinson, Celestin Suresh John, James Markham, Susan McDermott,
    Matthew Moodie, Jeffrey Pepper, Ben Renow-Clarke, Gwenan Spearing
Coordinating Editor: Mark Powers
Copy Editor: Kim Burton-Weisman
Compositor: SPi Global
Indexer: SPi Global
Artist: SPi Global

Distributed to the book trade worldwide by Springer Science+Business Media New York, 233 Spring Street, 6th Floor, New York, NY 10013. Phone 1-800-SPRINGER, fax (201) 348-4505, e-mail orders-ny@springer-sbm.com, or visit www.springeronline.com. Apress Media, LLC is a California LLC and the sole member (owner) is Springer Science + Business Media Finance Inc (SSBM Finance Inc). SSBM Finance Inc is a Delaware corporation.

For information on translations, please e-mail rights@apress.com, or visit www.apress.com.

Apress and friends of ED books may be purchased in bulk for academic, corporate, or promotional use. eBook versions and licenses are also available for most titles. For more information, reference our Special Bulk Sales–eBook Licensing web page at www.apress.com/bulk-sales.

Any source code or other supplementary materials referenced by the author in this text are available to readers at www.apress.com/9781430265351. For detailed information about how to locate your book's source code, go to www.apress.com/source-code/. Readers can also access source code at SpringerLink in the Supplementary Material section for each chapter.

Printed on acid-free paper

This book is dedicated to affordable software developers and all the members of the open source software community who work so diligently to make professional application development software, as well as audio, 2D, video, and 3D content development tools, freely available to new media application developers, so that we can utilize these tools to achieve our creative dreams and our financial goals.

I also dedicate this book to my superstar father, Parker Jackson, my family, my life-long friends, my content production facility's neighbors, and my production team partners, for all their help, assistance, and those relaxing beautiful sunset BBQs underneath pink clouds on Point Conception.

Contents at a Glance

Contents

About the Author

Wallace Jackson has been writing for several leading multimedia publications about production for the media content development industry, after contributing an article about advanced computer processing architectures for the centerfold (a removable "mini issue" insert) of the original issue of *AV Video Multimedia Producer* magazine, distributed at the SIGGRAPH trade show.

Wallace has written for a number of popular publications, regarding his work in interactive 3D and new media advertising campaign design including *3D Artist* magazine, *Desktop Publisher Journal*, *CrossMedia*, *Kiosk*, *AV Video Multimedia Producer*, and *Digital Signage* magazine, as well as many other publications.

Wallace Jackson has authored more than twenty Apress book titles, including several titles in the ever popular Apress *Pro Android* series, Java and JavaFX game engine development titles, digital image compositing titles, digital audio editing titles, digital video editing titles, digital illustration titles, VFX special effects titles, digital painting titles, Android 6 new media content production titles, and now JSON and HTML5 titles.

In the current book covering HTML5 markup Wallace focuses on the tags, or elements, which comprise the HTML5 and HTML 5.1 standard, and uses them to demonstrate HTML5 content production as well as HTML5 application and document design fundamentals, to beginners who want to become savvy regarding HTML5 workflows and how to pull new media content production assets into HTML5.

Wallace is currently the CEO of MindTaffy Design, the new media advertising agency which specializes in new media content production and digital campaign design and development, located by La Purisima State Park, in Northern Santa Barbara County, on the Point Conception Peninsula, halfway between their clientele in Silicon Valley to the North, and Hollywood, The OC, West Los Angeles, and San Diego to the South.

Mind Taffy Design has created open-source, technology-based (HTML5, JavaScript, Java 9, JavaFX 9, and Android 6.0) digital new media i3D content deliverables for more than a quarter century, since January of 1991.

The company's clients consist of a significant number of international brand manufacturers, including IBM, Sony, Tyco, Samsung, Dell, Epson, Nokia, TEAC, Sun Microsystems (Oracle), Micron, SGI, KDS USA, EIZO, CTX International, KFC, Nanao USA, Techmedia, EZC, and Mitsubishi Electronics, among others.

Wallace received his undergraduate degree in business economics from the University of California at Los Angeles (UCLA) and his graduate degrees in MIS/IT, business information systems design and implementation from the University of Southern California (USC).

Wallace also received post-graduate degrees from USC in entrepreneurship and marketing strategy and completed the USC Graduate Entrepreneurship Program. Wallace earned his degrees while at USC's nighttime Marshall School of Business MBA Program, which allowed him to work full-time as a COBOL and RPG-II programmer.

You can visit Wallace's blog at www.wallacejackson.com or you can view his multimedia production content at www.iTVset.com or www.MindTaffy.com. You could also follow Wallace Jackson on Twitter at @wallacejackson, or connect with him on LinkedIn at www.LinkedIn.com/in/wallacejackson.

About the Technical Reviewer

Chád ("Shod") Darby is an author, instructor, and speaker in the Java development world. As a recognized authority on Java applications and architectures, he has presented technical sessions at software development conferences worldwide (in the United States, UK, India, Russia, and Australia). In his fifteen years as a professional software architect, he's had the opportunity to work for Blue Cross/Blue Shield, Merck, Boeing, Red Hat, and a handful of start-up companies.

Chád is a contributing author to several Java books, including *Professional Java E-Commerce* (Wrox Press), *Beginning Java Networking* (Wrox Press), and *XML and Web Services Unleashed* (Sams Publishing). Chád has Java certifications from Sun Microsystems and IBM. He holds a BS in computer science from Carnegie Mellon University.

You can visit Chád's blog at www.luv2code.com to view his free video tutorials on Java. You can also follow him on Twitter at @darbyluvs2code.

Acknowledgments

I would like to acknowledge all my fantastic editors, and their support staff at Apress, who worked those long hours and toiled diligently on the book, to make this the preeminent *HTML5 Quick Markup Reference* manual currently available in the marketplace.

I would like to thank the following people:

Steve Anglin, for his work as the acquisitions editor for the book, and for recruiting me to write development titles at Apress, covering widely popular open source content-development platforms (Android, Java, JavaFX, HTML5, CSS3, JS, JSON, etc.).

Matthew Moodie, for his work as development editor on the book, and for his experience and guidance during the process of making the DVE Fundamentals book one of those fantastic digital video editing, compositing and special effects titles.

Mark Powers, for his work as the coordinating editor for this book, and for his constant diligence in making sure that I either hit my chapter delivery deadlines or far surpassed them.

Chád Darby for his work as the technical reviewer on this book and for making sure that I didn't make technical mistakes.

Introduction

HTML5 Quick Markup Reference is intended for the HTML5 content developer. As HTML5 now powers not only web browsers, but also, smartphones, iTV Sets, gaming consoles, tablets, smart watches, notebooks, laptops, e-books, and more. This book is for digital artisans, digital videographers, multimedia producers, digital illustrators, HTML5 OS or application developers, HTML5 website developers, all social media campaign developers, HTML5 game producers, HTML5 effect compositors, user interface design architects, user experience designer architects, and anyone else interested in generating the superior-quality HTML5 content experience that the public is looking for.

The book covers HTML5 and new HTML5.1 concepts, elements, editing, new media assets, publishing, programming, styling and real-time rendering. This equates to creating the most advanced multimedia-capable HTML5 content applications, including genres including digital images, digital audio, digital video, digital illustration or scalable vector graphics (SVG), Interactive 3D, or WebGL and WebGL 2, as well as Web 3.0 (Semantic Web Search).

Each chapter builds upon the knowledge learned in the previous chapter. Thus, later chapters in the book have readers creating more advanced HTML5 content using canvas, objects, applets, templates, ruby, or iframes. There are also appendices covering how to download, and set-up, open source HTML5 content production integrated development environments (or IDEs), using the leading NetBeans, Eclipse, and IntelliJ software packages. I also cover how to download, and install, leading new media content development software packages (all free) in Appendix D.

In Chapter 1, you look at the history of HTML5, the future of HTML5, and the topics covered in the book.

In Chapter 2, you look at the HTML5 tags used for your top-level document definition, as we start at the top, or HEAD, of your HTML document, and work downwards, in this title.

In Chapter 3 you look at those HTML5 elements that greatly affect search engine optimization, or SEO, including your META and TITLE tags. These are contained at the top, or in the HEAD of a HTML5 document, building on what was learned in Chapter 2.

Chapters 4 covers referencing external assets from an HTML5 document or application using the LINK element. You look at how to "externalize" your CSS3 and JavaScript assets, as a data footprint optimization technique.

Chapter 5 explores the SCRIPT (JavaScript) and STYLE (cascading style sheet) tags, in the HEAD of the HTML5 document. JavaScript and CSS3 are discussed in detail.

Chapter 6 introduces the concept of global attributes, or parameters, allowed for use by every tag (element) across HTML5.

Chapter 7 covers "hypertext," which differentiates HTML5, and look at document navigation using an ANCHOR tag or element.

Chapter 8 delves into using new media assets with HTML5, including digital image, digital video, digital audio, digital illustration, interactive 3D, and similar leading-edge content.

Chapter 9 covers HTML5 content hierarchy and organization of HTML5 documents, as well as the effect of this hierarchy for search engine optimization (SEO) strategies and techniques.

Chapter 10 introduces new semantic content elements, which allow HTML5 to merge into this new Web 3.0, or "semantic search," era, which is now upon us. These tags allow HTML5 developers to make their HTML5 content compatible with Web 3.0.

Chapter 11 gets into publishing HTML5 text-based content, as well as how to use tags (elements) to "style" text content. This chapter covers what many consider the "core" tags in HTML5, including paragraph, bold, italics, underline, and more.

Chapter 12 outlines the HTML5 phrase tags, which allow you use special types of text in a semantic context with your HTML5 documents, websites, e-books, iTV shows, games, and applications.

Chapter 13 takes a look at HTML5 elements which allow you to create bulleted, numbered and other ordered lists of data or information in your HTML5 documents. These tags are also "core" tags in HTML and can be used for user interface design as well.

Chapter 14 covers another popular topic for HTML5 content developers, specifically, tables, and these many table related elements which are supported in HTML5 for tabular information designs.

Chapter 15 delves into interactive HTML5 form design, and the many complexities involved with client-side form markup and how to talk to these, using server-side forms processing languages and databases, which store the information culled using these forms.

Chapter 16 explores the positioning of content for HTML5, using the division and span elements, in combination with CSS3.

Chapter 17 covers scripting in HTML5 in greater detail by using the JavaScript programming language in combination with a SCRIPT element in both the HEAD and the BODY of HTML5 documents.

Chapter 18 looks at CSS styles in HTML5 in greater detail by using cascading style sheets, in combination with the STYLE element, in both the HEAD and the BODY of your HTML5 documents.

Chapter 19 gets into HTML5 real-time rendering done using the CANVAS element. This allows developers to create games, interactive 2D or i2D content, as well as interactive 3D or i3D content, using an advanced real-time drawing surface, also found in the Android 7 OS, as well as in other advanced operating systems.

Chapter 20 deals with the different ways to "plug in" or embed external content into HTML5 documents using Java applets or other types of "objects" new in HTML5.

Chapter 21 covers frames in HTML, including the iFrame element still supported in HTML5. This element allows you to seamlessly embed content from another website or application inside of your current HTML5 website or application.

Chapter 22 covers Ruby annotations, small text elements, attached to main text, usually to indicate the pronunciation or meaning of your corresponding characters. These annotations are often used in Japanese, Korean, and Chinese publications.

Finally, Chapter 23 explores the new tags introduced in HTML 5.1 to bridge the HTML5 content markup language from a web browser centric platform over into the new HTML5 operating systems that are running popular consumer electronics devices today, such as smartphones running Firefox OS and iTVs running Opera OS.

If you are interested in producing cutting-edge, Web 3.0 compatible, HTML5 content, and you want to learn all your basic HTML5 element fundamentals, as well as how new media assets can work together with HTML5 design or publishing elements, this is the *HTML5 Quick Markup Reference* manual that you can use to begin your journey to new experiences with HTML5 content.

Indeed, the *HTML5 Quick Markup Reference* manual gives you comprehensive HTML5 design element knowledge that transitions you from an HTML5 neophyte to an HTML5 design professional.

CHAPTER 1

■ ■ ■

HTML5 History: The Past and Future of HTML Markup

Let's get started by taking a look at the history of markup languages, of which HTML—now in its fifth revision, called HTML5—is the most popular and widely utilized. This year (2016) portends the release of another version of HTML5 called HTML 5.1, which supports using HTML5 not only for all of the popular browsers, but also for the new HTML5 operating systems that have recently appeared as competitors to Android, iOS, and Windows Mobile. The browser manufacturers—specifically Opera, Mozilla Firefox, and Google Chrome—realized that they could enhance their browser code, add icons, and run HTML5 on top of the Linux kernel and compete with the other consumer electronics operating systems. Now Firefox OS is on Panasonic iTV Sets and Alcatel-Lucent smartphones, and the Opera HTML5 OS is on Sony Bravia iTV Sets. HTML 5.1 adds features more in line with HTML5 OS requirements.

This book provides a reference to all of those HTML5 tags and their parameters, attributes, characteristics, and configuration options, of which there are currently 120 or more. I organize these as logically as possible, starting at the top of the HTML5 document with the metatags for search engine optimization (SEO), styling (CSS), or interactivity (JavaScript), and logically stratify chapters covering tags used for writing (text), forms, lists, multimedia, and similar document features and attributes.

Besides the history and future of HTML, this chapter overviews the markup (coding) format or syntax for tag and parameter usage, so that understand the rest of the book as we cover the 120 HTML5 tags used to implement document features, along with the parameters they support.

Finally, I outline the rest of the book to show you how I organize and reference the 120 HTML tags in the HTML5 specification into logical topical areas, which build on each other in an orderly fashion.

The History of HTML: Reveal Codes Tags

The first time I ever encountered tags, which are used for formatting text values, was using a word processing software package called WordPerfect for the Data General MV-7800XP mini-computer. This software had a handy feature called **Reveal Codes** that was accessed using F3, the third function key along the top of the keyboard. Using this

© Wallace Jackson 2016
W. Jackson, *HTML5 Quick Markup Reference*, DOI 10.1007/978-1-4302-6536-8_1

feature showed **Control Codes** surrounding formatted text values, so the bolded word **Important** looked like <b>Important<b> when you pressed the F3 Reveal Codes key. Pretty cool feature!

A system called **ENQUIRE** is another HTML predecessor. In 1980, the physicist **Tim Berners-Lee**, prototyped ENQUIRE, a system for CERN researchers to utilize and share text-based documents. In 1989, Berners-Lee proposed an Internet-based hypertext system. He specified HTML and wrote the browser and server software in late 1990. Berners-Lee and CERN data systems engineer Robert Cailliau collaborated, however, the project was never adopted by CERN.

The first publicly available HTML description was a document called "HTML Tags," first mentioned on the Internet by Berners-Lee in late 1991. The document described 18 elements. Except for the hyperlink tag, they were all influenced by SGMLguid, an in-house Standard Generalized Markup Language (SGML) documentation format developed at CERN. Eleven of the original tag formatting elements remain active in HTML5 today. They are covered in this book.

Berners-Lee also considered HTML's markup tags to be an application of SGML. HTML was formally defined as being such by an Internet Engineering Task Force (IETF), in the mid-1993 publication of the first proposal for an HTML specification called "Hypertext Markup Language (HTML)". It was released as an Internet specification by Tim Berners-Lee and Dan Connolly. There was also "SGML Document Type Definitions," which define HTML syntax and grammar. Similarly, Dave Raggett's competing Internet draft, "HTML+ (Hypertext Markup Format)" released later in 1993, suggested standardizing already-implemented features, such as tables and fill-able forms.

After these early HTML and HTML+ drafts expired in early 1994, the IETF created the HTML Working Group, which completed the HTML 2.0 draft in 1995. This was the first HTML specification, intended as the defacto standard against which all future HTML implementations should be compared. Further development of HTML under these auspices of the IETF was stalled, by competing interests.

Since 1996, the HTML specifications have been maintained, with input from commercial software vendors, by the World Wide Web Consortium, also known as the W3C. In 2000, HTML4 became an international standard, ISO/IEC 15445:2000. HTML5 was released in Q4 of 2014 and HTML 5.1 is scheduled for release at the end of 2016, which is why it is covered in this book.

What Is HTML5? A Definition and Syntax

HTML is the markup language that web browsers, and more recently, operating systems, use to interpret and compose text, images, and other material into visual or audible content pages for widespread human consumption, as well as by cats who watch HTML5 iTV Sets.

Default characteristics for each item represented using HTML5 markup tags and their parameters are defined in the browser. These characteristics can be altered or enhanced by the web page designer's use of CSS or JavaScript, although these are not covered in this reference book.

HTML markup—as well as other markup languages, such as SGML and XML—uses **tags** to surround document components that you wish to enhance. For instance, to make text **bold**, you use the HTML **<b> tag** in the following fashion:

```
<p><b>This text will be bold.</b> And this text will not be bold.</p>
```

The ending tag has a **backslash** before the letter or letters that define the tag; it tells the engine (code) that is **parsing** the document to turn off that feature. A <p> paragraph tag tells the HTML5 rendering engine that you're going to insert a paragraph (<p>) of text; a bold (<b>) tag tells it when you want to turn bolding on and off.

Tags need to be nested in the proper order, so the bold tag should be contained (nested) inside of your paragraph tag, as seen in the preceding HTML5 markup example.

The first tag, which turns the feature on, can also have optional parameters, or features for configuring how you want that tag to behave. Here's an example of the use of parameters:

```
<a title="Anchor Tag" href="http://www.apress.com">APRESS WEBSITE LINK</a>
```

This anchor (<a>) tag provides a way to link to the Apress website from within a different website. The **title** parameter shows users a title when they mouseover the link. The **http** parameter provides the website address, or URL.

More Syntax for HTML5: Using Comments

Since this entire book is essentially an HTML5 markup reference that uses the basic syntax (markup encoding structure) covered in the previous section, I'll address how comments are handled in HTML5 now; that way, we can get all of the syntax issues out of the way along with the history and future of HTML5 content development.

HTML5 comment tags are similar to comment tags for other programming languages such as Java 9 and JavaScript. They start with the **left pointing chevron** (<) and then the **exclamation point** (!) character, followed by **two hyphens** (dashes, or minus signs) and then you insert your comment text, and end with another two dashes, and finally a right-facing chevron (>) character. Here is an example of a comment in HTML5:

```
<!-- This is an example of how a comment is constructed in HTML5 -->
```

Next, let's take a look at where HTML5 is going, so that you know just how valuable this quick markup reference book is going to be to your new media content deliverable work process.

The Future of HTML: HTML5 OS and HTML 5.1

HTML was only for use in browsers until Google acquired Android and started to dominate the consumer electronics device marketplace, which it continues to do today, with over 100 manufacturers using Android for iTV Sets, smartphones, tablets, e-book readers, set-top boxes, and even personal computers. Not wanting to be left out of this lucrative market, HTML5 browser manufacturers morphed their browsers into HTML5

OS products by adding features such as icons, and connecting their code and technology to the latest Linux OS kernel, which powers the popular Android OS and many other popular operating systems.

HTML is now used not only for production of content for popular browser software, but also with consumer electronics devices, which means that tags have to be added, since there is a more advanced usage (operating systems) for HTML5 and future versions of HTML, such as HTML 5.1.

An impending solution for adding the OS-related features is HTML 5.1, which continues to add advanced features with new media content development support. OS user interfaces support the new <dialog> tag. HTML5.1 also supports menuing with dialogs by using the new <menu> and <menuitem> tags, which we'll cover in a special chapter on HTML 5.1.

Next, let's take a look at how we're going to cover these tags.

HTML5 Quick Reference: Tag Categories

This book goes over HTML5 tags from the highest level of the document in a "top down" fashion. We start with the tags that define the areas of your HTML5 document and the tags found at the top of your document, which define SEO (meta tags) and external documents (such as CSS and JS documents and favicons), which are linked to an HTML5 document from external file resources. The first four chapters cover the tags that define your HTML5 document's infrastructure.

Chapters 2 through 9 cover the basics, such as **hypertext** (linking to other URLs), **new media** assets such as imagery, audio, and video, and the **document content hierarchy** and **heading levels**.

Chapters 10 through 15 cover text-based elements such as paragraphs, lists, forms, and tables, which contain most of the text-based content found in HTML5 documents and apps today. These chapters are a bit longer because there are quite a few tags related to these areas in HTML.

Chapters 16 through 20 cover more advanced topics, such as document positioning, divisions, document styles, CSS3, document interactivity, JavaScript, document rendering using the canvas, and document objects.

Chapters 21 through 23 cover infrequently used tags, and HTML 5.1. I also include several appendices, which cover how to set up an HTML5 IDE, as well as how to obtain advanced open source new media content development packages, so that you can develop your entire HTML5 projects using a single content development workstation.

Summary

This chapter looked at HTML's history, future, definition, syntax, commenting, and summarized how this book plans to categorize and reference the 120 tags that currently comprise the HTML5 and HTML 5.1 feature set.

In the next chapter, you learn about the top-level document tags, such as <html>, <head>, and <body>, and how they define the overall structure of the HTML5 content document.

CHAPTER 2

■ ■ ■

HTML5 Documents: Top-Level Document Definition

In this chapter, let's continue by taking a look at the topmost level of HTML5, the **<html>** tag, which defines and contains your HTML5 document, the **<head>** tag, which defines how it is configured, and the **<body>** tag, which handles the contents. These are the highest-level tags in the HTML5 markup schema. All three tags need to be in your HTML5 document, in the proper order and used for the proper purposes.

I also go over the markup (coding) format and syntax for your HTML5 document level tags, and their optional parameter. We look at how to define your document type using a **<!DOCTYPE>** tag, and at the different types of HTML documents. We focus on HTML5 for this reference book, as you may have noticed, from the title, but I also cover older incarnations, such as HTML4 and XHTML for context sake.

The HTML5 Document Definition Tags

This chapter explains the tags used to define your HTML document type, document root, document header, and document content. We start with the first tag, the **<!DOCTYPE doctype>** declaration, which defines your document type, and then we progress downward to the tags that are **nested** inside of the <html> tag, including the <head> and <body> tags.

The !DOCTYPE Tag: Defines HTML Document Type

The first tag in the HTML5 document is the **<!DOCTYPE html>** tag, which has no closing tag because it simply defines the version of HTML5 that you are using for your HTML document. You would think that it would be <!DOCTYPE html5>, but **html** actually means HTML5. Don't ask me why— I do not know.

© Wallace Jackson 2016
W. Jackson, *HTML5 Quick Markup Reference*, DOI 10.1007/978-1-4302-6536-8_2

The following HTML5 markup structure is an example of a document declaration and nested top-level tags :

```
<!DOCTYPE html>
  <html>
    <head>
            <!-- HTML5 Document Header Attributes (Tags) Go In Here -->
    </head>
    <body>
            <!-- HTML5 Document Body Content (Tags) Will Go In Here -->
    </body>
  </html>
```

Older HTML document types, such as HTML4 or XHTML 1.1, are declared with either "strict" or "transitional" document types. HTML5 has done away with the document type differences; therefore, it is much simpler. Let's take a quick look at XHTML and HTML4 next, in case you have to write HTML for legacy (old) systems and clients running older operating systems and browsers.

The XHTML Document Types: XHTML 1.0

XHTML, or **Extensible** HTML, is an older and stricter type of HTML document definition that is based on **XML**. XHTML is the XML implementation of HTML. It is **stricter** because tags must be opened, closed, and nested in an orderly fashion so that the parser can correctly interpret them. The XHTML document type also requires the <!DOCTYPE> tag, whereas the HTML5 document type does not, so some HTML5 documents simply start with the <html> tag instead of the <!DOCTYPE html><html> tag sequence. All of the major HTML5 browsers correctly parse XHTML document types; however, you want to use HTML5 because of the superset of features and tags that are provided in it (as I'll outline in this book). Since XHTML is still used in a wide range of document content and applications, I'll cover it in this section so that you know how to declare XHTML document types, if you wish.

If you are using the older XHTML document type for some reason, you declare the document type as follows:

```
<!DOCTYPE html PUBLIC "-//W3C//DTD XHTML 1.0 Transitional//EN
            http://www.w3org/TR/xhtml1/dtd/xhtml1-transitional.dtd">
  <html>
    <head>
            <!-- XHTML Document Header Attributes (Tags) Go In Here -->
    </head>
    <body>
            <!-- XHTML Document Body Content (Tags) Will Go In Here -->
    </body>
  </html>
```

The "strict" XHTML document type is less flexible. You should declare this document type using the following HTML syntax and markup:

```
<!DOCTYPE html PUBLIC "-//W3C//DTD XHTML 1.0 Strict//EN
            "http://www.w3org/TR/xhtml1/dtd/xhtml1-strict.dtd">
  <html>
    <head>
          <!-- XHTML Document Header Attributes (Tags) Go In Here -->
    </head>
    <body>
          <!-- XHTML Document Body Content (Tags) Will Go In Here -->
    </body>
  </html>
```

The "frameset" XHTML document type allows you to define your HTML documents using discrete areas called **frames**. You should declare an XHTML frameset document type using the following HTML syntax and markup:

```
<!DOCTYPE html PUBLIC "-//W3C//DTD XHTML 1.0 Frameset//EN
            "http://www.w3org/TR/xhtml1/dtd/xhtml1-frameset.dtd">
  <html>
    <head>
          <!-- XHTML Document Header Attributes (Tags) Go In Here -->
    </head>
    <body>
          <!-- XHTML Document Body Content (Tags) Will Go In Here -->
    </body>
  </html>
```

Frames are no longer recommended for use in HTML5. You can now use **divisions** with the **<div>** tag. Divisions can be used much like layers in Photoshop or GIMP. They are far more flexible and can be moved (animated).

Next, let's take a look at the HTML 4.01 document type.

The HTML4 Document Types: HTML 4.01

HTML4 was released on December 18, 1997. HTML 4.01 was released on April 24, 1998. There were two major versions prior to HTML4: HTML 3.2 and the original HTML 2.0 specification. HTML4 added greater multimedia support, cascading style sheets, Java scripting languages, printing capabilities, and support for disabled users. It started internationalization (language) support as well. HTML4 conforms to the **ISO 8879 SGML** specification. HTML4 documents use a much more complex !DOCTYPE tag implementation, using SGML's **Document Type Definition** (DTD) declaration syntax along with the repository URL reference.

If you are using the older HTML4 document type for some reason, you declare the document type as follows:

```
<!DOCTYPE html PUBLIC "-//W3C//DTD HTML 4.01 Transitional//EN
                "http://www.w3org/TR/html4/loose.dtd" >
  <html>
   <head>
          <!-- HTML4 Document Header Attributes (Tags) Go In Here -->
   </head>
   <body>
          <!-- HTML4 Document Body Content (Tags) Will Go In Here -->
   </body>
  </html>
```

Transitional HTML 4.01 is more forgiving because it supports more tags, parameters, and syntax formats; whereas strict HTML is more like XML or XHTML and has many more rules that need to be closely followed. You declare a HTML4 document type as follows:

```
<!DOCTYPE html PUBLIC "-//W3C//DTD HTML 4.01 //EN
                "http://www.w3org/TR/html4/strict.dtd" >   <html>
   <head>
          <!-- HTML4 Document Header Attributes (Tags) Go In Here -->
   </head>
   <body>
          <!-- HTML4 Document Body Content (Tags) Will Go In Here -->
   </body>
  </html>
```

The HTML 4.01 frameset DTD or document type definition looks like the following <!DOCTYPE> tag:

```
<!DOCTYPE html PUBLIC "-//W3C//DTD HTML 4.01 Frameset//EN
                "http://www.w3org/TR/html4/frameset.dtd" >   <html>
   <head>
          <!-- HTML4 Document Header Attributes (Tags) Go In Here -->
   </head>
   <body>
          <!-- HTML4 Document Body Content (Tags) Will Go In Here -->
   </body>
  </html>
```

Again, frames is an outdated document design approach, so don't design with it unless you absolutely have to on an HTML legacy project. Next, let's take a look at the <html> tag.

The HTML Tag: Defining the Root of the Document

The <html> tag tells the browser (and now the OS) that this is an HTML document, especially in the absence of the <!DOCTYPE> tag that you frequently see in HTML5 markup. An <html> tag anchors (or roots) the document and contains all the other tags.

This is an example of the HTML tag with child tags inside it:

```
<html xmlns="http://www.w3.org/1999/xhtml">
        <head>
                <!-- HTML5 Document Header Attributes (Tags) Go In Here -->
        </head>
        <body>
                <!-- HTML5 Document Body Content (Tags) Will Go In Here -->
        </body>
</html>
```

Notice the xmlns parameter, which references the **XML Naming Schema** address and defaults to **www.w3.org/1999/xhtml**.

In HTML5 added a second new parameter for a **manifest** that allows developers to add a URL for a custom document cache location for off-line browsing. The following is an example (Replace the www.apress.com website with your own cache address location URL):

```
<html xmlns=http://www.w3.org/1999/xhtml manifest="http://www.apress.com">
        <head>
                <!-- HTML5 Document Header Attributes (Tags) Go In Here -->
        </head>
        <body>
                <!-- HTML5 Document Body Content (Tags) Will Go In Here -->
        </body>
</html>
```

Your default CSS3 settings for this HTML tag should look like the following CSS3 style sheet definition, used in most browser and operating system implementations:

```
html       { display:block; } <!-- Display content using a block format -->
html:focus { outline:none;  } <!-- Do not outline content when selected -->
```

Next, let's look at the <head> tag and learn how it allows you to set up and configure what your document can do.

The HEAD Tag: Configuring the HTML5 Document

The HTML5 <head> tag contains over a half dozen child tags that are used to configure your HTML5 document and define what it can do and how it is found on the Internet. These child tags include the <title>, <style>, <script>, <meta>, <link>, <base>, and <noscript> tags. The <title> tag puts a name at the top of the browser, tab, and page.

The <script> tag defines the JavaScript configuration. The <style> tag defines the style sheet (CSS3) configuration. The <link> tag links to external file resources. The <meta> tag allows you to add metadata. The <base> tag defines the default URL for all link targets in your HTML5 document. The <head>structure looks like this:

```
<html>
    <head>
            <title>
            <script>
            <style>
            <link>
            <meta>
            <base>
            <noscript>
    </head>
</html>
```

The <head> tag previously had a **profile** attribute, which specifies a URL to a document containing a set of rules for the <meta> tag content attributes. It is important to note that this particular parameter is not supported in HTML5, so I am not covering it in this book.

The <head> child tags are covered in their own chapters, so let's look at the <body> tag next. Then we can move on to some of the lower-level tags used in HTML5.

The BODY Tag: Containing the Document Content

The <body> tag contains most of the tags covered in this book. All six <body> tag attributes (parameters) that were supported in HTML4 and have been removed from HTML5 support, but I cover them in this section anyway, for the sake of comprehensive coverage. An **alink** parameter is used with a color value to define the color of active links in the body of the document. The **vlink** parameter is used with a color value to define the color of visited links. Finally, the **link** parameter is used with a color value to define the color of links that have not been visited.

You can control background color with the **bgcolor** parameter. You can install a background image with the **background** parameter. Finally, you can specify the color for the text in an HTML4 document with a **text** parameter, which is used with a color value to define the color for content text in the body of your document. In HTML5, you use CSS3 to provide your body styling. We look at this a bit later on with the <style> tag and cascading style sheets.

Your default CSS3 settings for the <body> tag should look like the following CSS3 style sheet definition (in most browser and operating system implementations):

```
body       { display: block; margin: 8px; }
body:focus { outline:none; }
```

Most HTML5 documents use the basic <!DOCTYPE html> and <html>, <head>, and <body> tags without any parameters, other than class or id parameters (which are covered later on), like this basic HTML5 document with a TITLE, and P (paragraph) text installed in the <head> and <body> sections of the document:

```
<!DOCTYPE html>
   <html>
     <head>
             <title>Website Title Goes Here</title>
     </head>
     <body>
             <p>Website Text Paragraph Content.</p>
     </body>
   </html>
```

From here, we get into some of the tags that you use to control your content and the way that your document is referenced on the Internet.

Summary

In this chapter, you learned about the top-level HTML5 document tags, including the <!DOCTYPE>, <HTML>, <HEAD>, and <BODY> tags. Notice that the tag names can be in lowercase or uppercase letters, so use whatever tag style you prefer for your markup.

In the next chapter, you start looking at the document tags inside the <HEAD> parent tag, which influences SEO, including the <title>, <meta>, and <base> tags, and learn how to use them to optimize the search engine configuration for your HTML5 document.

CHAPTER 3

▩ ▩ ▩

HTML5 Search Engine Optimization: Title and Meta

Let's continue here in Chapter 3 by looking at the tags that are the most important for **search engine optimization**, also referred to as **SEO**. SEO is the practice of optimizing your website ranking in search engines. SEO tags are found at the document definition and configuration level. These tags are contained in the document HEAD, and were covered briefly in Chapter 2. The SEO-centric tags include your **<title>** tag, which defines and contains your document title and keywords, as well as the **<meta>** tags, which define how the HTML5 document is listed in the various search engines. These two tags, along with the **<base>** tag, are the most important tags to use for SEO in the HTML5 markup schema, besides the paragraph and heading tags that contain the actual text content and keywords that the search engines use to index and rank your HTML5 documents. We cover these tags later on in the book, along with the <body> tag.

In this chapter, I also go over the markup (coding) format and syntax for HTML5 document-level SEO tags, with their various parameters. We look at how to define your document title using the <title> tag and at the different types of metadata that you can advise the search engines with regarding a <meta> tag or a collection of <meta> tags, as is more commonly used. We'll also look at the **<base>** tag because it also relates to SEO.

The HTML5 HEAD Tags Important for SEO

This chapter covers three high-level <head> tags used to define how you want the search engines to index your HTML document title, description, and content. We'll start with the <title> tag, which defines your document title, and then progress downward to tags that are inside the <head> tag, including the <meta> and <base> tag.

The TITLE Tag: Defining the HTML5 Document Title

The first tag in the <head> section of your document definition is usually the **<title>** tag, which contains your HTML5 document title between the opening tag and the closing tag. The <title>tag is one of the key tags that a search engine algorithm looks at to determine

© Wallace Jackson 2016
W. Jackson, *HTML5 Quick Markup Reference*, DOI 10.1007/978-1-4302-6536-8_3

what the content is within your document. These SEO algorithms are referred to as **bots** because the code that they use simulates AI, or artificial intelligence, and so they seem to be functioning like search engine robots.

The following HTML5 markup structure is an example of a document <title> declaration for the HTML5 document and the top-level tags it is nested:

```
<!DOCTYPE html>
   <html>
    <head>
         <title>Title, Using Important Search Term Keywords</title>
    </head>
    <body>
         <!-- HTML5 Document Body Content (Tags) Will Go In Here -->
    </body>
   </html>
```

Document titles should be descriptive and contain **keywords** that describe the content and help the search engine bots define how to index the website or HTML5 app. For instance, my iTVclock.com website title has keywords for iTV Sets and watch faces (smartwatch designs in Android) using the following HTML5 markup and syntax:

```
<!DOCTYPE html>
  <html lang="en">
    <head>
    <title>iTV Clocks for iTV Sets | 3D Watch Faces for iTV Sets</title>
    </head>
    <body>
    <!-- iTV Clock's HTML5 Document Body Content (Tags) Will Go In Here -->
    </body>
   </html>
```

As you can see, the domain name (iTV Clock) and important keywords (iTV Sets and Watch Faces) are in the descriptive title, so that the search engine bots know iTV clock is for iTV Sets and that they relate to the (Android) watch faces API because these iTV clocks will also be for sale as Android watch faces for your smartwatch. Also, notice that I used the **lang="en"** parameter in the HTML tag. This tells the HTML5 rendering engine that the page uses the English language.

Next, let's look at the <meta> tag, which is used to define content type, author, keywords, and description.

The META Tag: Defining Document Characteristics

The <meta> tag allows you to provide **metadata**, or data about your document that is not visible to the document viewer (reviewer), but which tells the search engine, browsers, and HTML5 operating systems about descriptive, SEO, robot, author, and copyright characteristics in your HTML5 document.

Metadata contained in the <meta> tags takes the form of **name-value** data pairs, much like JSON data definitions. If you want to learn more about JSON, reference my book, *JSON Quick Syntax Reference* (Apress, 2016).

There can be more than one <meta> tag. They go in the <head> section of the HTML5 document. There must be both a **name** and a **content** parameter—one cannot exist without the other, so if you have a **name="name"**, you must have a **content="data value."**

The <meta> tag format for the iTV Clock website has the following HTML5 markup syntax, with the six primary <meta> tags most often utilized within the document's <head> section:

```
<!DOCTYPE html>
  <html lang="en">
    <head>
      <title>iTV Clocks for iTV Sets | 3D Watch Faces for iTV Sets</title>
      <meta name="description" content="Use your iTV Set as a Clock!">
      <meta name="keywords" content=" iTV Clock, iTV Set, Watch Faces">
      <meta name="robots" content="index, follow">
      <meta name="copyright" content="Copyright 2014 through 2016">
      <meta name="author" content="Wallace Jackson">
      <meta charset="UTF-8">
    </head>
    <body>
      <!-- iTV Clock's HTML5 Document Body Content (Tags) Will Go In Here -->
    </body>
  </html>
```

The description metatag contains the description used in the search engine listing result. The keywords metatag offers a keyword list to the search engine robot. The robots metatag suggests how your site should be indexed. The copyright and author metatags secure your HTML5 document's copyrights.

There is also a <meta> tag parameter called **charset** that is used to define the character set for your document, which for most HTML5 documents and applications is either **UTF-8** or **UTF-16**. Universal Text Format 8-bit uses **256** character representations and Universal Text Format 16-bit uses **65,536** character representations. UTF-16 clearly represents a wider range of languages than UTF-8, although UTF-8 represents languages that use an alphabet character set, such as English, French, Spanish, Italian, Portugese, and German.

Before the simplified HTML5 **charset="utf-8"** parameter, a <meta> tag to define the character set (for HTML 4.0 and prior) looked as follows:

```
<meta http-equiv="Content-Type" content="text/html" charset="utf-8"> (HTML4)
```

Table 3-1 lists 17 name:content data value pairs used in the <meta> tag format for HTML5 documents and applications.

Table 3-1. *Meta Tag name:content Data Value Pairs and Their Uses*

Name Value	Content Value	Purpose or Usage
description	A description for the HTML document	Your search engine listing description content control
keywords	Your keyword list	SEO keyword suggestions
robots	index and follow	SEO robot instructions
copyright	Copyright dates	Document copyright dates
author	Author name	Document author(s) names
webauthor	Author name	Document author(s) names
charset	Character set used	Generally UTF-8 or UTF-16
abstract	Document summary	Abstract of content summary
revisit-after	Period (i.e., 9 days)	Robot revisit instructions
language	Name of language	Language used for document
distribution	global, local, IU	Global, local or internal distribution for document
expires	Date (1 Jan 2017)	Document content expiration
generator	Name of software	Document content generator
reply-to	E-mail address	Document contact information
no-email-collection	An anti-spam link	metatags.info/nospamharvest
rating	Intended audience	general, mature, restricted
googlebot	noodp	Use page description in ODP

You can use the **http-equiv** parameter to define your HTTP header for the information (values) of your content parameter. This metatag is used to add certain non-standard values to your HTML5 website header, so let's cover some of those standard http-equiv values used in website.

Table 3-2 lists 13 of the http-equiv:content data value pairs used inside the <meta> tag format for HTML5 documents and applications.

Table 3-2. *Meta Tag name:content Data Value Pairs and Their Uses*

http-equiv	Content Value	Purpose or Usage
content-type	Media Type, CharSet	Define MIME type and charset
cache-control	Set cache settings	Defines caching parameters
cookie	Defines cookie file	Define cookie name and dates
content-disposition	Define applications	Defines file name extension
imagetoolbar	Shows image toolbar	Control display (IE) toolbar
MSThemeCompatible	Use WinXP UI theme	Sets WinXP UI theme for site
picslabel	Label image content	Allows imagery to be labeled
pragma	Sets HTTPS caching	Ensure HTTPS page not cached
Resource-Type	Defines resources	Define a page resource type
refresh	Time before refresh	Redirect after a time period
Content-Script-Type	Scripting language	Define a scripting language
Content-Style-Type	Style Sheet language	Define a style sheet language
window-target	Specify window name as a window target for HTML5 document rendering / parsing	Sets the window name for the webpage to be rendered in; generally used to break out of a frameset

Next, let's look at the **<base>** tag and how it allows you to define a base target URL for your HTML5 document.

The BASE Tag: Configuring a URL for a Document

The HTML5 <base> tag is has no ending tag. It uses the HREF parameter to define the default URL and therefore the default "target" parameter for all links in the document. If I were to add the <base> tag to the iTV Clock HTML5 website, the resulting markup structure would look like this:

```
<!DOCTYPE html>
  <html lang="en">
    <head>
      <title>iTV Clocks for iTV Sets | 3D Watch Faces for iTV Sets</title>
      <meta name="description" content="Use your iTV Set as a Clock!">
      <meta name="keywords" content=" iTV Clock, iTV Set, Watch Faces">
      <meta name="robots" content="index, follow">
      <meta name="copyright" content="Copyright 2014 through 2016">
      <meta name="author" content="Wallace Jackson">
      <meta charset="UTF-8">
```

```
  <base href="http://www.iTVclock.com">
  </head>
  <body>
   <!-- iTV Clock's HTML5 Document Body Content (Tags) Will Go In Here -->
  </body>
 </html>
```

There can only be a single <base> tag defined in the HTML5 document; it needs to be defined within the HEAD section of the document. The order of the child tags within the <head> tag does not matter, in case you are wondering.

More of the <head> child tags are covered in the next two chapters. Let's move on to the other HTML5 tags that are child tags of the <body> tag.

Summary

In this chapter, you learned about the HTML5 document tags for search engine optimization (SEO) contained in the <HEAD> tag, including the <TITLE>, <META>, and <BASE> tags. Again, notice that your tag names can be either lowercase or uppercase letters, so use whichever tag style you prefer in your HTML5 markup syntax.

The next chapter discusses the LINK document tags inside the <HEAD> parent tag that influences linking to external assets, including favicons and cascading style sheets.

CHAPTER 4

■ ■ ■

HTML5 Referencing: Using External Links and Favicons

Let's continue by taking a look at the **<link>** tag. This important tag is used to connect external files, documents, and resources such as HTML5 icons, or favicons (these are used in the browser tabs), to your HTML5 documents and applications. This tag is also found at the **HEAD** document definition and configuration level, just like the tags covered in the previous chapters.

In this chapter, I also go over the markup (coding) format and syntax for HTML5 document-level <link> tags, including all of the various parameters. We'll look at how to define your external documents, profiles, and asset links using the <link> tag. We'll also look at many different types of link relationship data that you provide using the required **rel** parameter, one of the tag parameters used to reference external resources.

An HTML HEAD Tag to Link External Files

This chapter covers a single, high-level (in document HEAD) tag that is used to define how you want external files to be "linked" into your HTML5 document and its content. I call this "externalizing" HTML5 development assets, such as favicons and style sheets. There's a distinct advantage to doing this, which I explain in this section before we get into how to use the <link> tag and its parameters to externalize assets. If you externalize an asset as a file in an HTML5 document, it is **cached**, and therefore, only needs to be loaded **once**, in your index.html markup. Let's look at the advantage of this using your cascading style sheet (CSS3) asset as an example. If you externalize your style definitions for your HTML5 website or application, this code only needs to be loaded once, even though it is referenced using the same <link> tag on every page in your website. If the CSS file is 8KB and you have 101 pages on the website, this saves you 800KB of data transfer overhead!

© Wallace Jackson 2016
W. Jackson, *HTML5 Quick Markup Reference*, DOI 10.1007/978-1-4302-6536-8_4

The LINK Relationship: Types of External Assets

The only required parameter (also called an **attribute**) in a <link> tag is the **rel** or **relationship parameter**, which tells the HTML5 parsing (rendering) engine what type of document it links. The two most commonly used are icon and stylesheet, but we go over other rel parameter options during this section of the chapter. Table 4-1 shows the various rel parameter options currently supported for the <link> tag in HTML5.

Table 4-1. *Link rel Parameter Value and Purpose*

Rel Parameter Value	Rel Parameter Value Purpose
alternate	Link to an **alternate version** of the document
author	Link to put **Author Profile** in search results
help	Link to the **help document** for the HTML document
icon	Link external **icon (.ICO) resource** for document
license	Link to the **copyright information** for document
next	Link to **next document** in a series of documents
prefetch	Link to a target resource that should be **cached**
prev	Link to a **previous document** in a series of docs
search	Link to a **search tool** for the document
stylesheet	Link to an external **cascading style sheet** (.css)

Let's take a look at several of these in real-world use, starting with the HTML5 icon, popularly called a **favicon**. Let's also look at how to link to your external cascading style sheet and to an author profile URL.

Linking to an Icon: Using a Favicon in the Document Tab or App

One of the things you always want to do for an HTML5 website or HTML5 application is to have an **icon** to use for **visual branding** purposes. This is especially important for HTML5 iTV Sets, HTML5 tablets, and HTML5 smartphones, as icons launch your app!

An example of a document LINK declaration, for a favicon for the HTML5 document, along with the top-level <head> tag it is nested in, looks like the following HTML5 markup structure:

```
<!DOCTYPE html>
  <html lang="en">
    <head>
      <title>iTV Clocks for iTV Sets | 3D Watch Faces for iTV Sets</title>
      <meta name="description" content="Use your iTV Set as a Clock!">
      <meta name="keywords" content=" iTV Clock, iTV Set, Watch Faces">
      <meta name="robots" content="index, follow">
      <meta name="copyright" content="Copyright 2014 through 2016">
```

```
    <meta name="author" content="Wallace Jackson">
    <meta charset="UTF-8">
    <base href="http://www.iTVclock.com">
    <link rel="icon" href="itvclock.ico"> <!-- Link to icon resource -->
  </head>
  <body>
    <!-- iTV Clock's HTML5 Document Body Content (Tags) Will Go In Here -->
  </body>
</html>
```

As you can see, you also need to provide a URL with an **href** parameter. Since the itvclock.ico is in the same folder, I do not need any http, domain, or folder referencing. If I had this itvclock.ico on my iTVdesign.com website instead, this tag would then look like the following HTML5 markup syntax:

```
<link rel="icon" href="http://www.itvdesign.com/icon-folder/itvclock.ico">
```

I use GIMP 2.8.16 currently to create favicons using the **.ico** file name extension. Make sure that the graphic is **64 pixels** and **square**, 8-, 24-, or 32-bit color, and use a **File ► Export As** menu sequence to create it. If you need more background on this, see my book *Digital Image Compositing Fundamentals* (Apress, 2015).

Next, let's take a look at linking to your external CSS3 style sheet asset so that you can "externalize" your website or application styling into one highly optimized style sheet resource asset. This reduces the amount of code in each of the HTML5 documents (pages) because styling syntax has been removed into an external resource that can simply be linked to using a few characters of markup (in this case 60 characters or bytes).

Link to a Style Sheet: Using an External Style Sheet for CSS3 Style

One of the things you always want to do for an HTML5 website or application is to have a consistent visual appearance, or styling, for your HTML5 user interface design. This is also important for visual branding purposes and is equally important for HD and UHD iTVs, HD and UHD tablets, and HD smartphones.

Your style sheet link not only needs the rel and the href parameters, but also a type parameter, declaring your MIME type for the CSS file, which is text/css, just like it would be on the server-side of the MIME declaration for the CSS file on the server.

An example of a document LINK declaration for style sheet externalization for your HTML5 document, and the top-level tags the <link> tag is nested in looks like this:

```
<!DOCTYPE html>
  <html lang="en">
    <head>
      <title>iTV Clocks for iTV Sets | 3D Watch Faces for iTV Sets</title>
      <meta name="description" content="Use your iTV Set as a Clock!">
      <meta name="keywords" content=" iTV Clock, iTV Set, Watch Faces">
```

```
    <meta name="robots" content="index, follow">
    <meta name="copyright" content="Copyright 2014 through 2016">
    <meta name="author" content="Wallace Jackson">
    <meta charset="UTF-8">
    <base href="http://www.iTVclock.com">
    <link rel="icon" href="itvclock.ico">
    <link rel="stylesheet" type="text/css" href="itvclock.css">
  </head>
  <body>
    <!-- iTV Clock's HTML5 Document Body Content (Tags) Will Go In Here -->
  </body>
</html>
```

As you can see, it is common to have several <link> tags nested inside of your <head> tag. If your markup needs to be XHTML (XML) compliant, you add an orderly closing tag by inserting a **backslash** in front of the closing chevron, as is shown in the following markup syntax:

```
‹ link rel="stylesheet" type="text/css" href="itvclock.css" />
```

If you wanted to add a style sheet for printed media, you would add the **media** parameter into the style sheet's <link> tag to specify printed media (device hardware), as follows:

```
<link rel="stylesheet" type="text/css" href="itvclock.css" media="print" />
```

The media parameter has nine options, including the default **screen** option, including the **braille** or the **tty** options for the handicapped users, **aural** option for audio and speech synthesis, and hardware device options, for **printer** (printers), **projection** (projectors), **tv** (iTV) and **handheld** (smartphone, smartwatch, or tablets). You can also specify more than one media device by using Boolean operators **AND** (and), **NOT** (not), and **OR** (comma). If you want to specify values for the device, there are parameters to specify **width**, **height**, **orientation**, **resolution**, **aspect-ratio**, **color**, **color-index**, **monochrome**, and **scan** or **grid** values.

Next, let's take a look at your **rel="author"** parameter, and its option for linking to an external author profile.

Linking to an Author Profile: Putting a Face on a Search Listing

One of the more recent things that you are now able to do using the <link> tag for an HTML5 website or application is to have an author profile referenced via your HTML5 markup for personal branding purposes. This is especially important if you want your picture to appear in the search engine listing. I show you how to do this in this chapter with the <link> tag, as well as in Chapter 6 via the <a> (anchor) tag because the optimal way to implement it is using both a <head><link rel="author"></head> and <body><a rel="author"></body> markup structure (syntax) within your HTML5 document markup.

The following is an example of a document LINK declaration, for an author profile link:

```
<!DOCTYPE html>
  <html lang="en">
    <head>
      <title>iTV Clocks for iTV Sets | 3D Watch Faces for iTV Sets</title>
      <meta name="description" content="Use your iTV Set as a Clock!">
      <meta name="keywords" content=" iTV Clock, iTV Set, Watch Faces">
      <meta name="robots" content="index, follow">
      <meta name="copyright" content="Copyright 2014 through 2016">
      <meta name="author" content="Wallace Jackson">
      <meta charset="UTF-8">
      <base href="http://www.iTVclock.com">
      <link rel="icon" href="itvclock.ico">
      <link rel="stylesheet" type="text/css" href="itvclock.css">
      <link rel="author"
            href="https://plus.google.com/u/0/+WallaceJackson/about/p/pub"
            title="Wallace Jackson">
    </head>
    <body>
      <!-- iTV Clock's HTML5 Document Body Content (Tags) Will Go In Here -->
    </body>
  </html>
```

Notice that three key parameters were used: the required **rel=“author”**, an **href URL** for the Google+ account, and the **title** parameter containing the author name value.

Also, note how I spaced (formatted) the tag for enhanced readability, as extra white space (tabs and spaces) is allowed and is not processed by the HTML5 markup syntax parsing engine.

To do this thoroughly also requires an anchor tag with a **rel** parameter, which is covered in Chapter 6.

Next, let's look at the other nine parameters that the <link> tag supports, six of which work in HTML5 and three of which work in HTML4 and earlier.

The LINK Tag: The Optional Link Tag Parameters

The <link> tag has a number of optional parameters in addition to a required rel parameter. The most important is the **href** parameter, which allows you to specify a **URL location** for the external asset that is being linked to. You have seen this in use in the several <link> tag examples in this chapter, and the media parameter as well, so I will focus on the other four parameters supported in HTML5 during this section of the chapter. Other supported parameters for the <link> tag are seen in Table 4-2.

Table 4-2. *Link Tag Parameters*

Parameter Name	HTML5 Support	Parameter Purpose or Usage
href	Yes	**Location** (URL) for the linked asset
hreflang	Yes	The **language** used in a linked asset
rel	Yes	**Relationship** (type) of linked asset
media	Yes	**Device type** needed for linked asset
type	Yes	**Media type** used by the linked asset
sizes	Yes	**Pixel size** of a linked icon resource
crossorigin	Yes	Specify **cross-origin request** handling
rev	No	Relationship between linked documents
charset	No	Character encoding of a linked asset
target	No	Where a linked asset is to be loaded

The **hreflang** parameter specifies a language used by the externally linked asset or document. This <link> tag parameter is not as frequently implemented with HTML5 unless multiple language versions of an HTML5 document or an application have been created, and then it is needed.

The **type** parameter specifies what type of a file (asset) is being provided to the <link> tag. This is often called a **MIME type**, especially on the server-side for files supported by the server definition syntax.

A **sizes** parameter specifies the icon's dimensions in pixels (picture elements). It is often unutilized because icons are most often provided at 64 × 64 pixels.

The **crossorigin** parameter allows access to images, scripts, or styles that are on another server using the CORS (cross-origin resource sharing) standard. Setting this new parameter to anonymous restricts cross-sharing access between a server, and setting it to use-credentials sets the credentials flag to "true." User credentials can be shared using cookies, HTTP authentication, or client-side SSL certificates. It can be used with the <script> tag and with the <img> (image) tag, where it is more often utilized than with the <link> tag.

Next, let's look at the rest of the tags supported inside the <head> tag, and then we can look at **hypertext** (anchor tags).

Summary

This chapter talked about the HTML5 document <link> tag for linking external documents, profiles, and assets, which is also contained in the <head> tag. You looked at the required rel parameter, its values, and several examples. The rest of the optional parameters that apply to HTML5 markup, documents, and applications were also discussed.

In the next chapter, you look at the remaining <head> child tags, including the style, script, or noscript tags that influence linking to external JavaScript assets and apply exceptions to your externalized cascading style sheets.

CHAPTER 5

▓ ▓ ▓

HTML5 Processing: Using CSS and JavaScript

Let's finish up with the child tags of the parent <head> tag, which is itself a child tag of the <html> tag, by taking a look at the **<style>** tag for CSS3 document styling and the **<script>** tag for JavaScript (or JS) document scripting. We will also look at the **<noscript>** tag. These are the last of the tags contained in the **HEAD** section of the HTML5 document definition, so after this we focus on tags that are child tags of the **BODY** or content section. This is getting exciting. We are making excellent progress thus far!

In this chapter, I go over markup format and syntax for HTML5 document-level <style> and <script> tags, including all of their important parameters. We will look at how to define these external JavaScript documents using JS files, and how to use a <style> tag to insert exceptions to your externally linked CSS file for only that HTML5 document page. We also cover the <noscript> tag and how it defines alternate content for users who have disabled scripting languages in their browsers.

HTML HEAD Tags to Add Tag Processing

This chapter covers two high-level (in document HEAD) tags used to define how you want your HTML5 tags (markup) processed further to add desktop publishing like styling, pixel-precise positioning, special effects, animation, interactivity, and other types of "algorithmic" processing. This is done using the <style> tag for CSS3 processing, and the <script> tag for JavaScript processing.

The chapter title is "HTML5 Processing" because CSS and JS can further process HTML5. That said, this is not a book on CSS3 or JavaScript, just HTML5 markup (tags), so if you want to learn CSS3 styling or JS programming, be sure to buy a title from Apress. com that specifically covers those topics.

© Wallace Jackson 2016
W. Jackson, *HTML5 Quick Markup Reference*, DOI 10.1007/978-1-4302-6536-8_5

The SCRIPT Tag: Using JavaScript Programming

If you want to add advanced features to your HTML5 document, website, or application, you want to use JavaScript, which is actually based on the ECMAScript 262 standard. This is done using the **<script>** child tag in the <head> parent tag (section) of the HTML5 document. It contains JavaScript code inside of the <script> tag or uses the **src** parameter and optional (in HTML5, at least) **type** parameter to externally reference the JavaScript assets using a **JS** file. JavaScript is often referred to as JS, its abbreviation. I show you how to reference an external JavaScript asset in this chapter, as well as how to put JavaScript inside of your HTML5 document directly. Table 5-1 shows various parameter options, five of which are supported for this <script> tag in HTML5, and one of which is supported only in XHTML and HTML 4.

Table 5-1. *Supported <script> Tag Parameters*

Script Parameter	Script Parameter Purpose
src	Specify the URL for an **external JavaScript file**
type	Specify **optional media type** for external JS file
charset	Specify **character encoding** for external JS file
defer	Specifies to execute scripts **after HTML parsing**
async	Specified to execute scripts **asynchronously**
xml:space	Specifies whether white space in code should be preserved. This is not supported in HTML5.

You may be wondering when you should use external vs. internal JavaScript code. The rule of thumb is to use external JavaScript assets for global JavaScript code, which is used by every document in an HTML5 website; use internal JavaScript code for localized JavaScript functions, which are only used on that particular HTML5 page, document, or application.

If a function is used more than once, externalize it, so that it can be cached, and does not have to be served by your server more than one time, and can be accessed using your local storage device (cache), whenever it is needed by an HTML5 page.

Let's look at how I externalized JavaScript code, used in my iTVclock.com website to set the hands of the clocks.

The SRC Parameter: Externalizing JavaScript Program Assets

You can externalize JavaScript code just as you can with cascading style sheets, except that instead of the <link> tag, you use a **<script>** tag with its **src** (source file) parameter. It is important to note that the externalized JavaScript file must not contain the <script> tag, only the JavaScript code that would normally exist inside of the <script> tag were you to use the JavaScript internal to the HTML5 document approach.

An example of an HTML5 document <script> declaration for an external .js asset, along with the top-level <head> tag it's nested in, looks like the following HTML5 markup structure:

```
<!DOCTYPE html>
  <html lang="en">
    <head>
      <title>iTV Clocks for iTV Sets | 3D Watch Faces for iTV Sets</title>
      <meta name="description" content="Use your iTV Set as a Clock!">
      <meta name="keywords" content=" iTV Clock, iTV Set, Watch Faces">
      <meta name="robots" content="index, follow">
      <meta name="copyright" content="Copyright 2014 through 2016">
      <meta name="author" content="Wallace Jackson">
      <meta charset="UTF-8">
      <base href="http://www.iTVclock.com">
      <link rel="icon" href="itvclock.ico">
      <link rel="stylesheet" type="text/css" href="itvclock.css">
      <link rel="author"
            href="https://plus.google.com/u/0/+WallaceJackson/about/p/pub"
            title="Wallace Jackson">
      <script src="itvclock.js" type="text/javascript">
    </head>
    <body>
      <!-- iTV Clock's HTML5 Document Body Content (Tags) Will Go In Here -->
    </body>
  </html>
```

As you can see, I've provided an optional type parameter so that HTML4 browsers can also use this code. If I wanted this HTML markup to support XHTML, the tag would then look like the following XHTML markup syntax, using a proper closing tag:

```
< script src="itvclock.js" type="text/javascript" />
```

If I am only supporting HTML5 rendering engines, all I'd need to declare this external JavaScript asset is the following HTML5 markup syntax:

```
<script src="itvclock.js">
```

Next, let's look at how you can synchronize the loading of an external .js JavaScript asset, so that you can control how the JavaScript code is executed relative to the loading and parsing (execution) the HTML5 markup (tags) for your documents.

27

The ASYNC and DEFER Parameters: JavaScript Asset Execution

There are three ways to control how your JavaScript code is executed relative to the rendering (parsing) of your HTML5 markup (tags). If you don't specify any parameter to control synchronization, which is the default, the external JavaScript is downloaded and executed immediately, before the HTML5 content markup in the BODY of your document, since the <script> tag is in the <head> of the HTML5 document and thus processed first. There are also parameters to **defer** (process JavaScript after rendering) or to process **asynchronously**, at the same time the page is rendering.

Deferring JavaScript Processing: The <defer> Parameter

Let's look at an example of an HTML5 document <script> declaration for deferring the processing of an external .js asset. This is used if you need your HTML5 markup to be loaded and parsed before the JavaScript code is executed. The <script> tag, with the **defer** parameter enabled, should have the following HTML5 markup structure:

```
<!DOCTYPE html>
  <html lang="en">
    <head>
      <title>iTV Clocks for iTV Sets | 3D Watch Faces for iTV Sets</title>
      <meta name="description" content="Use your iTV Set as a Clock!">
      <meta name="keywords" content=" iTV Clock, iTV Set, Watch Faces">
      <meta name="robots" content="index, follow">
      <meta name="copyright" content="Copyright 2014 through 2016">
      <meta name="author" content="Wallace Jackson">
      <meta charset="UTF-8">
      <base href="http://www.iTVclock.com">
      <link rel="icon" href="itvclock.ico">
      <link rel="stylesheet" type="text/css" href="itvclock.css">
      <link rel="author"
            href="https://plus.google.com/u/0/+WallaceJackson/about/p/pub"
            title="Wallace Jackson">
      <script src="itvclock.js" type="text/javascript" defer="defer" >
    </head>
    <body>
      <!-- iTV Clock's HTML5 Document Body Content (Tags) Will Go In Here -->
    </body>
  </html>
```

As you can see, I've provided an optional type parameter so that HTML4 browsers can also use this code. If I wanted this HTML5 markup to support XHTML1, this <script> tag with the defer parameter enabled looks like the following XHTML markup syntax, which has the proper closing /> tag structure:

```
<script src="itvclock.js" type="text/javascript" defer="defer" />
```

If I am only supporting HTML5 rendering engines, all I'd need to have to declare this external JavaScript asset is the following HTML5 markup syntax with a defer parameter added:

```
<script src="itvclock.js" defer="defer">
```

Next, let's look at how to process the JavaScript code at the same time that your HTML5 markup is parsing.

Parallel JavaScript Processing: The <async> Parameter

Let's look at an example of an HTML5 document <script> declaration for paralleling the processing of an external .js asset. This is used if you need your HTML5 markup to be loaded and parsed **in parallel with**, or at the same time that your JavaScript code is executed. The <script> tag, along with the parent <head> tag that it is nested in, looks like the following HTML5 markup structure using the **async** parameter:

```
<!DOCTYPE html>
  <html lang="en">
    <head>
      <title>iTV Clocks for iTV Sets | 3D Watch Faces for iTV Sets</title>
      <meta name="description" content="Use your iTV Set as a Clock!">
      <meta name="keywords" content=" iTV Clock, iTV Set, Watch Faces">
      <meta name="robots" content="index, follow">
      <meta name="copyright" content="Copyright 2014 through 2016">
      <meta name="author" content="Wallace Jackson">
      <meta charset="UTF-8">
      <base href="http://www.iTVclock.com">
      <link rel="icon" href="itvclock.ico">
      <link rel="stylesheet" type="text/css" href="itvclock.css">
      <link rel="author"
            href="https://plus.google.com/u/0/+WallaceJackson/about/p/pub"
            title="Wallace Jackson">
      <script src="itvclock.js" type="text/javascript" async="async" >
    </head>
    <body>
      <!-- iTV Clock's HTML5 Document Body Content (Tags) Will Go In Here -->
    </body>
  </html>
```

As you can see, I've provided an optional type parameter so that HTML4 browsers can also use this code. If I wanted this HTML markup to support XHTML, the tag would then look like the following XHTML markup syntax, using a proper tag closing:

```
< script src="itvclock.js" type="text/javascript" async="async" />
```

If I am only supporting HTML5 rendering engines, all I'd need to have to declare this external JavaScript asset is the following HTML5 markup syntax, adding the async parameter:

```
<script src="itvclock.js" async="async">
```

Next, let's take a look at using the **charset** parameter.

The CHARSET Parameter: Using a Different JS Character Set

The <script> tag charset parameter specifies the character set that is being utilized in an external JavaScript asset. It is important to note that this only needs to be used if the character set for the external .js file is different from the character set used for the HTML5 markup syntax in your HTML5 document. Your <script> markup should look like this:

```
<!DOCTYPE html>
  <html lang="en">
    <head>
      <title>iTV Clocks for iTV Sets | 3D Watch Faces for iTV Sets</title>
      <meta name="description" content="Use your iTV Set as a Clock!">
      <meta name="keywords" content=" iTV Clock, iTV Set, Watch Faces">
      <meta name="robots" content="index, follow">
      <meta name="copyright" content="Copyright 2014 through 2016">
      <meta name="author" content="Wallace Jackson">
      <meta charset="UTF-16"> <!-- Document using UTF-16 Character Set -->
      <base href="http://www.iTVclock.com">
      <link rel="icon" href="itvclock.ico">
      <link rel="stylesheet" type="text/css" href="itvclock.css">
      <link rel="author"
            href="https://plus.google.com/u/0/+WallaceJackson/about/p/pub"
            title="Wallace Jackson">
      <script src="itvclock.js" type="text/javascript" charset="UTF-8" />
    </head>
    <body>
      <!-- iTV Clock's HTML5 Document Body Content (Tags) Will Go In Here -->
    </body>
  </html>
```

Next, let's take a quick look at an HTML <noscript> tag.

The NOSCRIPT Tag Advises Users: No JS Support

The <noscript> tag should always be implemented if you are using the <script> tag, but unfortunately, it is rarely used. It would come under the heading of "user error trapping," in my opinion, as some users turn JavaScript off in the browser or device, and need to be advised to turn the JavaScript capability back on for the application.

The following is an example of a document NOSCRIPT declaration for use of JavaScript assets, whether internalized or externalized:

```
<!DOCTYPE html>
  <html lang="en">
    <head>
      <title>iTV Clocks for iTV Sets | 3D Watch Faces for iTV Sets</title>
      <meta name="description" content="Use your iTV Set as a Clock!">
      <meta name="keywords" content=" iTV Clock, iTV Set, Watch Faces">
      <meta name="robots" content="index, follow">
      <meta name="copyright" content="Copyright 2014 through 2016">
      <meta name="author" content="Wallace Jackson">
      <meta charset="UTF-8">
      <base href="http://www.iTVclock.com">
      <link rel="icon" href="itvclock.ico">
      <link rel="stylesheet" type="text/css" href="itvclock.css">
      <link rel="author"
            href="https://plus.google.com/u/0/+WallaceJackson/about/p/pub"
            title="Wallace Jackson">
      <script src="itvclock.js" type="text/javascript" />
      <noscript>No JavaScript Support; Please Enable JavaScript!</noscript>
    </head>
    <body>
      <!-- iTV Clock's HTML5 Document Body Content (Tags) Will Go In Here -->
    </body>
  </html>
```

As you can see, it is common to have this tag after your <script> tag. Since it uses a proper closing tag, the markup is XHTML (XML) compliant.

Using SCRIPT Tags Internally: JavaScript Coding

It is also possible to include your JavaScript code alongside your HTML5 markup by surrounding it with <script> and </script> tags. You can also use comments to "hide" the JS code from the parsing engine, but the JavaScript rendering engine still sees the JavaScript code correctly. This is shown in the following example, where a simple Hello World JS app is in the comments inside the open and closing <script> tags (instead of the externalized .JS script loader):

```
<!DOCTYPE html>
  <html lang="en">
    <head>
      <title>iTV Clocks for iTV Sets | 3D Watch Faces for iTV Sets</title>
      <meta name="description" content="Use your iTV Set as a Clock!">
      <meta name="keywords" content=" iTV Clock, iTV Set, Watch Faces">
      <meta name="robots" content="index, follow">
      <meta name="copyright" content="Copyright 2014 through 2016">
```

```
<meta name="author" content="Wallace Jackson">
<meta charset="UTF-8">
<base href="http://www.iTVclock.com">
<link rel="icon" href="itvclock.ico">
<link rel="stylesheet" type="text/css" href="itvclock.css">
<link rel="author"
      href="https://plus.google.com/u/0/+WallaceJackson/about/p/pub"
      title="Wallace Jackson">
<script>
<!--
  Document.getElementById("JSapp".innerHTML="Hello World JavaScript";
-->
</script>
<noscript>No JavaScript Support; Please Enable JavaScript!</noscript>
</head>
<body>
<!-- iTV Clock's HTML5 Document Body Content (Tags) Will Go In Here -->
</body>
</html>
```

You should use this localized JavaScript approach with your JS functions, which exist only on that one HTML5 document, page, or application. Next, let's look at the CSS <style> tag.

The STYLE Tag: Styling HTML5 Markup Using CSS

The <style> tag has a fewer parameters, but includes the media and type parameters, and a new scoped parameter. The supported parameters are shown in Table 5-2.

Table 5-2. *Style Tag Parameters*

Parameter Name	New in HTML5?	Parameter Purpose or Usage
scoped	Yes	Style is locally scoped (to parent and children only)
media	No	Media/device style is targeted at
type	No	Media type specification of style tag

The **scoped** parameter specifies application only to the element (tag) being styled or "cascading" down to child tag elements, which is why it's called **cascading style sheet** (CSS). This parameter is not frequently implemented because most styles in HTML5 are applied globally across all pages in the document.

Here is an example of a <style> tag being used to apply a variation or exception from a global stylesheet externalized using the <link> tag.

```
<style> type=text/css><!-- #b (background-image:url(b.png);) --></style>
```

This HTML5 markup replaces the #b style for background-image styling with local styling that provides the current (proper) background image for this particular iTV Clock face. Doing this allows you to have a global style for background imagery and still replace a local background image style in any document that you want to vary from the global CSS style defined for the background image.

Notice that I use the comment trick (the same one used with JavaScript) to hide the CSS3 code from parsing engines, which would not understand it and would throw an error code. I do not cover CSS syntax in this book on HTML5 markup, but Apress has several titles on CSS.

```
<!DOCTYPE html>
 <html lang="en">
   <head>
     <title>iTV Clocks for iTV Sets | 3D Watch Faces for iTV Sets</title>
     <meta name="description" content="Use your iTV Set as a Clock!">
     <meta name="keywords" content=" iTV Clock, iTV Set, Watch Faces">
     <meta name="robots" content="index, follow">
     <meta name="copyright" content="Copyright 2014 through 2016">
     <meta name="author" content="Wallace Jackson">
     <meta charset="UTF-8">
     <base href="http://www.iTVclock.com">
     <link rel="icon" href="itvclock.ico">
     <link rel="stylesheet" type="text/css" href="itvclock.css">
     <link rel="author" title="Wallace Jackson"
           href=https://plus.google.com/u/0/+WallaceJackson/about/p/pub />
     <script><!--
      Document.getElementById("JSapp".innerHTML="Hello World JavaScript"; -->
     </script>
     <noscript>No JavaScript Support; Please Enable JavaScript!</noscript>
     <style> type=text/css><!-- #b (background-image:url(b.png);) --></style>
   </head>
   <body>
     <!-- iTV Clock's HTML5 Document Body Content (Tags) Will Go In Here -->
   </body>
 </html>
```

Next, let's look at the parameters that can be used by all HTML5 tags, and then we look at **anchor** tags, which are contained in the <head> (content) section of HTML5 document and application markup.

Summary

In this chapter, you learned about HTML5 document processing using JavaScript (JS) and cascading style sheets (CSS) with the <script> tag and <style> tag. You also looked at the <noscript> tag, which works in conjunction with the <script> tag. You saw how to use <script> internally in the HTML5 document, and how to use the <script> tag to override externalized CSS assets for localized style sheet changes.

In the next chapter, you learn about HTML5 global parameters.

CHAPTER 6

■ ■ ■

HTML5 Parameters: Using Global Tag Attributes

Before we start our extensive coverage of all of the child tags of the parent <body> tag, which is itself a child tag of the <html> tag, let's take a chapter here at the front of the book to cover the "global" parameters, which can be used by any of the tags in HTML5. These work with elements (tags) in the HEAD and BODY sections of the HTML5 document definition. In fact, a couple of them were covered in the first five chapters of this book!

In this chapter, I go over 16 parameters supported across all HTML5 document-level tags. I show you what these parameters do for your HTML5 documents and apps. Eight of these global parameters are new to HTML5 and the other eight work in previous versions of HTML as well. After this chapter, you'll be ready to learn all of the <body> tags!

HTML Global Parameters Across All Tags

This chapter covers those tag attributes, characteristics, or parameters that can be used with any tag in HTML5 and previous versions, such as HTML 4.01 and XHTML 1.1. It is logical to cover this before going into the plethora (around a hundred) of tags that are children of the <body> tag. I am doing this so that we can cover these global parameters in a single chapter.

Table 6-1 shows the 16 parameters. The first eight in the top half of the table only work in HTML5 browsers and operating systems. We cover these first, since HTML5 is the primary focus of this book. The bottom half of the table contains the eight parameters that work in HTML5 (due to backwards compatibility) and in earlier versions of HTML.

© Wallace Jackson 2016
W. Jackson. *HTML5 Quick Markup Reference*, DOI 10.1007/978-1-4302-6536-8_6

Table 6-1. *Supported Global HTML5 Tag Attributes*

Global Parameter	Global Parameter Purpose
contenteditable	Specify if an element **content is editable or not**
contextmenu	Specify **context menu** for the HTML5 element (tag)
data-<attribute>	Specify **custom data attributes** for your document
draggable	Specifies if an element is **draggable (or is not)**
dropzone	Specifies a **drop processing (copy, move or link)**
hidden	Specify **visibility (relevancy)** for each element
spellcheck	Specify **spelling and grammar check** for elements
translate	Specifies to execute scripts **after HTML parsing**
accesskey	Specify a **keystroke shortcut to focus an element**
class	Specify a **classname** for element in a style sheet
dir	Specify a **text reading direction** for an element
id	Specify a **unique ID** for element in a style sheet
lang	Specify the **language used** for that element
style	Allows **in-line CSS Style declaration for element**
tabindex	Specifies the **tabbing order** for that element
title	Specifies **extra information regarding** an element

Let's talk about the eight HTML5 global parameters first.

HTML5 Global Parameters: Advanced Attributes

The global attributes or parameters recently added to HTML5 are more advanced and add features more akin to devices, operating systems, and applications than to websites, as older versions of HTML were designed for. These parameters allow things such as drag and drop, editable content, context menus, custom data definition, spell-checking, and language translation.

The CONTENTEDITABLE Parameter: Can I Edit This Content?

The **contenteditable="boolean"** parameter (or attribute) allows you to specify whether or not you want your user to be able to edit the content inside of that element (tag) that the parameter is attached to (used inside of). When a contenteditable attribute is not set on an element, but is set on a parent tag of that element, a child element **inherits** the setting (true, false) from its parent element.

In fact, some browsers, including Opera and Firefox, set the inherit value as the default, whereas Chrome and Internet Explorer set the false value as the default. Thus, you could say there are three value options for this parameter, true, false, and inherit.

The following HTML5 markup is an example of creating an editable paragraph of text using a **<p>** tag (which is covered in Chapter 10):

```
<p contenteditable="true">Go ahead, edit this text if you're so inclined</p>
```

Next, let's look at context-sensitive menus in HTML5 with the contextmenu parameter.

The CONTEXTMENU Parameter: Context Sensitive Menuing

The **contextmenu="id"** parameter (or attribute) allows you to specify whether or not you want your user to be able to open a **context-sensitive menu** by right-clicking the content inside of that element (tag) to which the parameter is attached to. The contextmenu parameter value references the **ID** parameter of a **<menu>** tag element, which you define using **<menuitem>** child tags to define your menu options (items).

The following example shows a context-sensitive menu using the **<div>** tag (described in Chapter 14) in a document:

```
<div contextmenu="divmenu">
    <menu id="divmenu" type="context">
        <menuitem label="Menu Option 1"></menuitem>
        <menuitem label="Menu Option 2"></menuitem>
        <menuitem label="Menu Option 3"></menuitem>
    </menu>
</div>
```

You can attach context-menus to any HTML5 element; after all, this is a global parameter, so it can be attached to any HTML5 tag (document or app design element). Be sure that it is logical to attach a menu to your design element from a UI design standpoint; the user still has to right-click that element and expect that menu. Next, let's take a look at **custom data** constructs using the data parameter.

The DATA- Parameter: Custom Data Definitions for HTML5

The **data-name="datatype"** parameter (or attribute) allows you to specify **custom private data type definitions** to content inside of that element. The data-name parameter value allows you to add your data type name to the parameter itself, which is unique in HTML5 parameters, and references the **data type** used to define that particular tag's content.

It is logical to utilize in conjunction with **JSON** (JavaScript Object Notation) data object definitions, which you can research further in my *JSON Quick Syntax Reference* (Apress 2016) book.

To enhance the context-sensitive menu created using a **<div>** tag in the previous section, let's create a **data-car** data type definition and name each menu item (car models) with its country of origin. To accomplish this, modify your HTML5 tag markup to look like this:

```
<div contextmenu="carmenu">
    <menu id="carmenu" type="context">
        <menuitem data-car="german"   label="Mercedez Benz"></menuitem>
        <menuitem data-car="italian"  label="Lamborghini"></menuitem>
        <menuitem data-car="american" label="Corvette"></menuitem>
    </menu>
</div>
```

Next, let's take a look at the **draggable** design elements that you can create in HTML5, by using the draggable parameter.

The DRAGGABLE Parameter: Can I Drag This Element Around?

The **draggable="boolean"** parameter (or attribute) allows you to specify whether you want your user to be able to drag around the content inside of the tag on a display screen. There are actually three value options for this parameter, **true**, **false**, and **auto**. Using the auto option specifies the default draggable value for each particular browser.

The following HTML5 markup shows a draggable paragraph of text using a **<p>** tag:

```
<p draggable="true">You're able to drag this paragraph around the screen</p>
```

Next let's take a look at how to **drop** draggable elements in HTML5 by using the dropzone parameter. These two parameters are used in conjunction with each other, because to be able to drop an element, you have to be able to drag it in the first place!

The DROPZONE Parameter: What to Do When an Element Is Dropped

The **dropzone="action"** parameter (or attribute) allows you to specify the action that your HTML5 application implements once the user drags the content into place on the screen. There are three action value options for this parameter: **move**, **copy**, and **link**. The auto option specifies the default draggable value for each particular browser.

To create the dropzone area, attach a dropzone parameter to a <div> area using the **<div>** tag (see Chapter 14), as shown in the following HTML5 markup:

```
<div dropzone="move">Content Child Elements/Tags will be in here</div>
```

To create a copy of the dragged content in your dropzone area, use the **copy** option instead, as shown the following markup:

```
<div dropzone="copy">Content Child Elements/Tags will be in here</div>
```

This leaves your original dragged content intact and copies it to the new location. This is the least memory-efficient option because it duplicates the drag-and-drop content in system memory, which is inefficient. The solution is to use the **link** option, which displays the dropped content in a second location but references it from the original memory storing the original element. This is accomplished with the following HTML5 markup to link the new content in the division:

```
<div dropzone="link">Content Child Elements/Tags will be in here</div>
```

Next, let's look at how to **hide** elements in HTML5 using the hidden parameter.

The HIDDEN Parameter: Hide Element Content until it is Relevant

The **hidden="boolean"** parameter (or attribute) allows you to specify whether you want your element to be hidden from view. There are two value options for this parameter: **true** or **false**. Specifying the **hidden** tag sets the value to true; not specifying it sets the value to false. The following example creates a hidden paragraph of text using a **<p>** tag:

```
<p hidden>This paragraph will be hidden from the user's view</p>
```

Next, let's look at how to spell-check elements in HTML5, by using the **spellcheck** parameter.

The SPELLCHECK Parameter: Allow Spell-checking for Content

The **spellcheck="boolean"** parameter (or attribute) allows you to specify whether you want your text-based elements to have the spell-checking feature enabled. This is used in conjunction with the contenteditable attribute for text-capable elements, such as paragraphs, text areas, input fields, and the like.

To create an editable paragraph text that supports this spell-checking feature, use the **<p>** tag with the contenteditable and the spellcheck parameters both set to a value of **true**, as shown in the following HTML5 markup:

```
<p contenteditable="true" spellcheck="true">Paragraph with spellchecking</p>
```

Next, let's take a look at the language support in HTML5 using the translate parameter.

The TRANSLATE Parameter: HTML5 Global Language Support

The **translate="boolean"** parameter (or attribute) allows you to specify whether you want your text-based elements to be translated into different languages. Interestingly, instead of using true and false for the Boolean value, this parameter uses **yes** and **no**. The default (not specifying the translate parameter at all) is **yes** (translate this text element content), which equates to "support the localization of this content." Therefore, this parameter is primarily used to prevent a translation when you want the language for your HTML5 document to remain in the language that you originally created it in.

To create paragraph text that supports this translation feature, use the **<p>** tag with no translate parameter, or with the parameter set to a **yes** value, as shown in the following HTML5 markup:

```
<p>This Paragraph Will Be Translated by Default, to Localize the Content</p>
<p translate="yes">This Paragraph WILL Be Translated, for Localization.</p>
```

To create paragraph text that will never be translated, use the **<p>** tag with the **translate** parameter set to the **no** value, as follows:

```
<p translate="no">This Paragraph Will NOT Be Translated or Localized</p>
```

Next, let's take a look at global parameters supported across all versions of HTML, including HTML5 and HTML 5.1.

Pre-HTML5 Global Parameters: Legacy Attributes

The remaining eight parameters in Table 6-1 have been in HTML for quite a long time and are probably much more familiar to you. The style and lang parameters have been covered already, so let's go over the rest so that you can get into the tags that control content design and display in your HTML5 applications, websites, and documents.

The ACCESSKEY Parameter: Adding Keyboard Shortcut Keys

The **accesskey="key value"** parameter (or attribute) allows you to specify a **keyboard shortcut** for your elements. This is useful for hypertext anchor <a> tags (covered in Chapter 7), which allows your users to simply press a letter key on the keyboard to automatically access a website.

To create a keyboard shortcut for an anchor tag link, use an accesskey parameter inside of an <a> tag and assign it a key on the keyboard. Here's an example, using basic HTML5 markup:

```
<a href="http://www.Apress.com" accesskey="p">Publisher Website</a> <br>
<a href="http://www.WallaceJackson.com" accesskey="a">Author Website</a>
```

Next, let's take a look at how you attach HTML5 tags to cascading stylesheet (CSS) definitions using a class parameter.

The CLASS Parameter: Labeling Your Elements for Use with CSS

The **class="name"** parameter (or attribute) allows you to specify a **classname** for your tags. It is useful for any tags that can be styled using CSS3 or controlled using JavaScript, which includes the majority of the tags covered in this book.

To create a classname for a paragraph tag, use the class parameter inside of a <p> tag. To access this inside of a style tag, use the p.coloredtext dot notation. Here's a basic example using HTML5 markup with the high-level tags you've learned:

```
<html><head><style>
    p.coloredtext { color: red; }  <!-- CSS to set the p color to red -->
</style></head>
<body>
    <p class="coloredtext">This text will be displayed in a Red color.</p>
</body></html>
```

Next, let's look at how you define text direction (left to right, or LTR, and right to left, or RTL), using a dir parameter.

The DIR Parameter: Defining the Direction of your Text

A **dir="direction"** parameter (or attribute) allows you to specify the direction that you want your text-based elements to be read. This parameter uses **rtl** and **ltr** as options, as well as auto, which is the default for the browser. If you use auto, the browser tries to ascertain the correct direction based upon the content (the character set that it is utilizing).

To create paragraph text that supports this translation feature, use the **<p>** tag with no translate parameter, or with the parameter set to a **yes** value, as follows:

```
<p dir="rtl">This Paragraph Will Be Written from the Right To the Left!</p>
```

In HTML5, this parameter can be used with any tag, although it is only useful with some tags. In older versions of HTML, the parameter can't be used with <frame>, <iframe>, <frameset>, <param>, <script>, <base>, <br>, or <hr>.

Next, let's take a look at the id parameter.

The ID Parameter: Identifying Your Content Elements

The **id="name"** parameter (or attribute) allows you to specify an **id** to use as a handle. It is useful for any tags that can be styled using CSS3 or controlled using JavaScript.

To create an ID for a paragraph tag, use an id parameter inside of a <p> tag. To access this inside of a <script> tag, use the **document.getElementById()** function. Here's an example:

```
<html><body>
    <p id="helloworld">Click this button to change to: Hello World!</p>
    <button onclick="HelloWorldFunction()">Change Text, Please!</button>
    <script>
        function HelloWorldFunction() {
            document.getElementById("helloworld").innderHTML = "Hello World";
        }
    </script>
</body></html>
```

Next, let's take a look at how you specify language by using the lang parameter.

The LANG Parameter: Defining an Element's Language

The **lang="language"** parameter (or attribute) allows you to specify the language used in your text-based elements.

To create the paragraph text that supports this language specification feature, use the **<p>** tag with the lang parameter, set to the abbreviated value of the **language** used in your text element. An example of this is shown in the following HTML5 markup:

```
<p lang="es">Buenos Dias, Compadres!</p>
```

Next, let's take a look at the in-line stylesheet support in HTML5 using the style parameter.

The STYLE Parameter: Using In-Line Stylesheet Settings

The **style="css"** parameter (or attribute) allows you to specify "in-line CSS3" markup in an element (tag).

To create paragraph text that supports this stylesheet specification feature, use the **<p>** tag with the style parameter set to use **style markup**. The following is an example of how this is done using HTML5 markup:

```
<p style="color:green">This text will now use the green color!</p>
```

Next, let's take a look at controlling the way that your Tab key advances through your UI in HTML5 using the tabindex parameter.

The TABINDEX Parameter: Tab Key Advancement Ordering

The **tabindex="integer value"** parameter (or attribute) allows you to specify a **TAB key order** for your tags. It is useful for hypertext anchor <a>, allowing users to tab through each link in the order that you define. To create a tabbing order for an anchor tag link, use a tabindex parameter inside of an <a> tag and assign it a number. Here's an example using basic HTML5 markup:

```
<a href="http://www.Apress.com" tabindex="2">Publisher's Website</a>
<a href="http://www.WallaceJackson.com" tabindex ="1">Author's Website</a>
<a href="http://www.Luv2Code.com" tabindex ="3">Tech Reviewer Website</a>
```

Next, let's take a look at how you can define the pop-up tooltip text that your HTML5 tags show when your users do a mouse-over action on your user interface design elements.

The TITLE Parameter: Adding a Title to your Content Element

A **dir="direction"** parameter (or attribute) allows you to specify the direction you want your text-based elements to be read. This parameter uses **rtl** and **ltr** as options, as well as auto, which will be default for the browser. If you use auto the browser will try to ascertain the correct direction based upon the content (that is, what character set it is utilizing).

To create paragraph text which supports this translation feature use the **\<p>** tag with no translate parameter or with the parameter set to a **yes** value, as shown in the following HTML5 markup:

```
<p title="This will display on Mouse-Over">Mouse-Over Text for Tool Tip!</p>
```

In HTML5 this parameter can be used with any tag, though it is only useful with some tags. In previous versions of HTML, this parameter can't be used in \<meta>, \<base>, \<head>, \<html>, \<style>, \<param>, or \<script> tags.

Summary

This chapter explained global HTML5 parameters (also referred to as **attributes** or **characteristics**). In the next chapter, you're going to look at the HTML5 **anchor** \<A> or \<a> tag, which allows **hypertext** and **URL** references.

■ ■ ■

CHAPTER 7

HTML5 Navigation: Using an Anchor Tag for Hypertext

This chapter focuses largely on the **anchor** (<A> or <a>) tag, which added the differentiating hypertext features to HTML, or Hypertext Markup Language. The anchor tag originally supported URL links, allowing you to go to other websites, called **hypertext**, as well as anchors or page locators, allowing you to jump to different locations in the same URL (website). HTML5 now only supports URL linking with the <a> tag; however, I cover the legacy parameters for the <a> tag to be complete about this anchor tag element's coverage.

In this chapter, I go over a dozen parameters supported by HTML's anchor tag, seven of them are supported in HTML5, and five are also supported versions prior to HTML5.

HTML Anchor Tag Attributes: All Versions

This chapter covers the anchor or <a> tag used for hypertext, or linking across different HTML5 documents and applications, as well as a dozen anchor tag attributes, characteristics, or parameters. It is logical to cover this first, before we get into the plethora (around a hundred) of tags that are children of the <body> tag, because hypertext differentiates HTML5 and the anchor tag is commonly used to create navigation to other sections of a website. This is typically done by using CSS3 to style links so that they look like buttons. Table 7-1 shows the parameters used with the anchor <a> tag: the first two only work with HTML5, the next five work with all HTML versions, and the last five do not work with HTML5.

© Wallace Jackson 2016

W. Jackson, *HTML5 Quick Markup Reference*, DOI 10.1007/978-1-4302-6536-8_7

Table 7-1. *HTML5 <a> Tag Attributes Supported and Not Supported*

Global Parameter	Global Parameter Purpose
download	Specify if an element **content is editable or not**
media	Specify **context menu** for the HTML5 element (tag)
href	Specify **custom data attributes** for your document
hreflang	Specifies if an element is **draggable (or is not)**
rel	Specifies a **drop processing (copy, move or link)**
target	Specify **visibility (relevancy)** for each element
type	Specify **spelling and grammar check** for elements
charset	Specifies to execute scripts **after HTML Parsing**
coords	Specify a **keystroke shortcut to focus an element**
name	Allows **in-line CSS style declaration for element**
rev	Specifies the **tabbing order** for that element
shape	Specifies **extra information regarding an element**

Let's get into the seven HTML5 global parameters first.

Anchor Tag HTML5 Parameters: Hypertext's HREF

The most important parameter for using the anchor <a> tag in HTML5 is the **href**, or **hypertext reference**, parameter. It uses a URL, or Uniform Resource Locator, as the parameter value. The URL is a website address that begins with an **http://** Hypertext Transfer Protocol (HTTP) header and then the web address. For example, the Apress website is at **http://www.apress.com**.

The following is an example of a **hypertext link** using the <a> tag with the href parameter:

```
<a href="http://www.Apress.com">Click here to open the Apress website</a>
```

As the default, links not yet visited (clicked) are **blue**, visited links are **purple**, and active links are **red**. Links are also underlined by default, although, this can be changed using CSS3, if you want to style a link differently.

Without the href parameter, six of the twelve anchor tag parameters cannot be used. These include download, target, media, rel, type, and hreflang, which we'll cover next.

The HREFLANG Parameter: Hypertext Link Language Support

The **hreflang="language abbreviation"** parameter (or attribute) allows you to specify the **language** used by your hypertext link. We have looked at this before, so I will just reference a quick example, and then we can move on to the other anchor tag parameters. The following is an example of a language specified link using an <a> tag:

```
<a href="http://www.Apress.com" hreflang="fr">Bonjour! www.Apress.com</a>
```

Language codes are formally defined via **ISO 639**, which are found at the following websites:

- `http://www.iso.org/iso/home/standards/language_codes.htm` (ISO.org)

- `https://en.wikipedia.org/wiki/List_of_ISO_639-1_codes` (Wikipedia)

Next, let's look at the two tags that are only supported in HTML5: the **download** tag and the **media** tag.

The DOWNLOAD Parameter: Downloading Files Using the A Tag

When present, the **download** parameter (or attribute) tells the HTML5 parsing engine (browser or operating system) that the file referenced using the href parameter needs to be downloaded, rather than loaded and parsed as an HTML5 document or application.

To download a file, such as the animated MindTaffy logo found on `www.WallaceJackson.com`, you would specify the file name in the href parameter rather than an HTML website. You would also add the download parameter, which acts like a Boolean flag, so the download parameter present means download="true" and the download parameter absent means download="false". To accomplish this, you would modify your HTML5 tag markup to look like this example:

```
<a href="!http://WallaceJackson.com/MT240.gif" download>Download Logo!</a>
```

Next, let's take another brief look at a **media** parameter.

The MEDIA Parameter: What Media Device Does a Link Support?

The **media="media/device types"** parameter (or attribute) was covered in Chapter 4, so we do not need to cover it here, other than to show an example of its use with the <a> tag. The following is an example a link specifying a device type:

```
<a href=http://www.iTVset.com" media="screen">iTV Set - Display: Screen</a>
```

Next, let's take a look at how you can use the **target** parameter to tell the browser how and where to open your new hyperlinked document.

The TARGET Parameter: Where to Open a Hypertext Document

The **target="_constant"** parameter (or attribute) allows you to specify the location that your HTML5 application opens your URL link in. There are four value options for this parameter, **_blank**, **_self**, **_parent**, and **_top**. You can also use a frame name, although since framesets are seldom used anymore, this is quite rare, as are the _parent and _top options. Most developers use _blank to open a new tab in the browser, or _self (which is the default if there is no target parameter specified in the <a> tag), which replaces the current HTML5 content with that specified in the URL from using the href parameter.

To create a new tab for your linked document, you use the **target="_blank"** parameter inside your <a> tag, as shown in the following example:

```
<a href=http://www.iTVset.com" target="_blank">Open iTV Set in a new Tab</a>
```

To replace the currently displayed HTML content with the linked document, you should use the **target="_self"** parameter in your <a> tag, as shown in the following example:

```
<a href=http://iTVset.com" target="_self">Replace this site with iTV Set</a>
```

To replace the currently displayed HTML content in the parent frame with your linked document, you'd use the **target="_parent"** parameter in your <a> tag, as follows:

```
<a href=http://iTVset.com" target="_parent">Open iTV Set in Parent Frame</a>
```

To replace currently displayed HTML5 content at the top of your frameset (which fills an entire tab or window) with your linked document, you use the **target="_top"** parameter inside of your <a> tag, as follows:

```
<a href=http://iTVset.com" target="_top">Open iTV Set in the Full Window</a>
```

To replace currently displayed HTML content in any named frame within your frameset with your linked document, you would use the **target="frame-name"** parameter inside of the <a> tag, as shown in the following HTML5 markup example:

```
<a href=http://iTVset.com" target="framename">Open iTV Set in this Frame</a>
```

Next let's take a look at how to **define the relationship** between linked documents in HTML5 by using the rel parameter.

The REL Parameter: Define a Relationship to the Hypertext Link

The **rel="relationship type"** parameter (or attribute) allows you to define the type of relationship that exists between the current HTML5 document and the document specified in your href parameter by using the URL value. There are a dozen possible values that can be used in the <a> tag's rel attribute, including **alternate**, **author**, **bookmark**, **help**, **license**, **next**, **nofollow**, **noreferrer**, **prefetch**, **prev**, **search**, and **tag**. Some of these are the same as the rel parameter supported by the <link> tag; however, some of them are different parameters for the <a> tag. Table 7-2 lists these parameters along with their purpose.

Table 7-2. *HTML5 Anchor Tag rel Attributes*

REL Parameter	REL Parameter Purpose
alternate	Specifies an **alternate version of HTML5 document**
author	Specifies your **author profile** for HTML5 document
bookmark	Specifies **permanent URL** to bookmark the document
help	Specifies the URL (a link) to the **help document**
license	Specifies a URL (a link) to a **copyright document**
next	Specifies **next document** in a series of documents
nofollow	Specify **spelling and grammar check** for elements
noreferrer	Specifies to execute scripts **after HTML parsing**
prefetch	Specify a **keystroke shortcut to focus an element**
prev	Allows **in-line CSS style declaration for element**
search	Specifies the **tabbing order** for that element
tag	Specifies **extra information regarding an element**

To create an alternate version of a linked document, you use a **rel="alternate"** parameter inside the <a> tag, as shown in the following HTML5 markup:

```
<a href=http://www.iTVset.com" rel="alternate">Alternate iTV Version</a>
```

To reference your Author Profile version for your linked document, you would use this **rel="author"** parameter inside your <a> tag, as shown in the following HTML5 markup:

```
<a href=http://www.WallaceJackson.com" rel="author">Author Website</a>
```

To create a bookmark link version for a linked document, you use the **rel="bookmark"** parameter inside the <a> tag, as shown in the following HTML5 markup:

```
<a href=http://www.iTVset.com" rel="bookmark">Bookmark for iTV Set Site</a>
```

To create a help document version for a linked document, you use a **rel="help"** parameter inside the <a> tag, as shown in the following HTML5 markup:

```
<a href=http://www.iTVset.com" rel="help">iTV Set Website Help Document</a>
```

To create a licensing document for a linked document, you use the **rel="license"** parameter inside of an <a> tag, as shown in the following HTML5 markup:

```
<a href=http://www.iTVset.com" rel="license">Copyright License Document</a>
```

To designate the next version for your linked document series, you should use the **rel="next"** parameter, inside an <a> tag, as shown in the following example:

```
<a href=http://www.iTVset.com" rel="next">The Next Document in a Series</a>
```

To instruct search engine robots not to follow (or rank) a linked document, you should use the **rel="nofollow"** parameter, inside of your <a> tag, as shown in the following example:

```
<a href=http://www.iTVset.com" rel="nofollow">Do Not Follow (Rank) Link</a>
```

To hide the fact that links to another website came from your website, you would utilize the **rel="noreferrer"** parameter, inside of your <a> tag, as shown in the following example:

```
<a href=http://iTVset.com" rel="noreferrer">No Site Referrer Info Sent</a>
```

To instruct HTML5 rendering engines to "pre-load," or to **cache** a document before it is needed, that is, before your link is clicked by a user, you would use a **rel="prefetch"** parameter, inside of your <a> tag, as shown in the following example:

```
<a href=http://www.iTVset.com" rel="prefetch">Prefetch This Document</a>
```

To designate a previous version for your linked document series, you should use the **rel="prev"** parameter, inside the <a> tag, as shown in the following example:

```
<a href=http://www.iTVset.com" rel="prev">Previous Document in a Series</a>
```

If you create a search tool user interface (application) for the document you can link to this HTML5 search application, and then utilize the **rel="search"** parameter inside of your <a> tag, as shown in the following example:

```
<a href=http://www.iTVset.com" rel="search">Custom Search Utility Link</a>
```

To quote the W3C directly, regarding this parameter: "The search keyword indicates that the referenced document provides an interface specifically for searching the document and its related resources." Creating a custom search interface (user interface application) is no easy task, and is somewhat rare across smaller websites, but does exist on larger sites.

To instruct search engine robots that the text used in a <a> tag is a **relevant keyword** related to the current document's topic, you should use a **rel="tag"** parameter, inside of your <a> tag, as shown in the following example:

```
<a href=http://iTVset.com/itv-ebooks" rel="tag">Tag the ebooks keyword</a>
```

Next, let's take a brief review of your **type** parameter.

The TYPE Parameter: MIME Types, Media Types, and File Types

We covered the type parameter already, during Chapters 4 and 5, so let's just suffice it to say here that the anchor <a> tag supports the definition of a MIME (media or file) type with the **type="file type"** parameter. In case you are wondering, MIME stands for Multipurpose Internet Mail Extensions, as it was used originally for e-mail and expanded later to be used for servers, browsers, and applications. Usage of the type parameter in your <a> tag might look like the following HTML5 markup:

```
<a href=http://iTVset.com" type="text/html">iTV Set: An HTML Website!</a>
```

Next, let's cover non-HTML5 anchor tag parameters, so we have comprehensive coverage of hypertext during this chapter.

Anchor Tag Non-HTML5 Parameters: Legacy Code

Finally, let's take a quick look at the five anchor tag parameters that do not work in HTML5, but which do work for HTML4 and earlier, just in case you are doing some legacy code maintenance or supporting multiple browser revision numbers.

The CHARSET Parameter: Hypertext Link Character Set Support

We covered the charset parameter in Chapters 4 and 5, so I'll just reiterate here that your anchor <a> tag supports character set definition using the **charset="charset"** parameter. Most HTML documents or apps use the UTF-8 or ISO-8859-1 preset.

The following is an example of a character set specified link by using an **<a>** tag and charset parameter:

```
<a href=http://iTVset.com" charset="UTF-8">iTV Set: A UTF-8 Website!</a>
```

Next, let's take a closer look at the **coords** parameter.

The COORDS Parameter: Define Coordinates for Your Image Map

The **coords** parameter (or attribute) tells the HTML5 parsing engine the coordinates for the file referenced using the href parameter. It is used in conjunction with the shape parameter. It created image maps, which are no longer supported in HTML5.

HTML tag markup looks like this example:

```
<a href=http://iTVset.com" shape="rect" coords="0,0,240,320">Image Map</a>
```

Next, let's take brief look at the **name** parameter.

The NAME Parameter: Naming a Link (Supported Prior to HTML5)

Prior to HTML5, the **name** parameter (or attribute) specified the name of the anchor, but it was deprecated (support was discontinued) with the anchor (jump to different part of document) feature. Therefore, I do not need to cover it beyond showing an example of its use with the <a> tag. To simulate this in HTML5, use an **id** parameter. The following is an example of a named anchor in HTML4 and older versions:

```
<a href=http://www.iTVset.com" name="anchorname">iTV Set Anchor Name</a>
```

To create a named link in HTML5, you would use this HTML markup:

```
<a href=http://www.iTVset.com" id="linkname">iTV Set Link Name Using ID</a>
```

Next, let's take a look at the **rev** parameter.

The REV Parameter: Where to Open a Hypertext Document

The **rev** parameter (or attribute) is the opposite of the **rel** parameter. It is no longer supported in HTML5.

To create the reverse relationship for a linked document, you use the **rev="constant"** parameter inside your <a> tag, as follows:

```
<a href=http://www.iTVset.com" rev="alternate">An Opposite of an iTV Set</a>
```

Next, let's look at the **shape** parameter.

The SHAPE Parameter: Define the Shapes for Your Image Maps

The **shape** parameter (or attribute) tells the HTML5 parsing engine the shape (rect or circle) used for the file referenced using an href parameter. It is used in conjunction with the coords parameter. It created image maps, but it is not supported in HTML5.

HTML tag markup looks like this:

```
<a href="http://iTVset.com" shape="circle" coords="0,0,240,320">Image Map</a>
```

Now you are ready to move on to the remaining document content design, creation, and publishing tags supported in HTML5. We are making steady progress and we are about to have fun using multimedia design elements in our HTML5 applications!

Summary

This chapter covered hypertext in HTML5 by using the anchor or <a> tag and a dozen of its parameters. You learned about the href parameter and Hypertext Transfer Protocol (HTTP). You also looked at several parameters that work in HTML5, and some that do not.

The next chapter discusses the HTML5 tags that support the addition of new media elements, including imagery, audio, and video. These allow developers to add visual (and aural, with audio) pizazz to their HTML5 website, document, or application.

CHAPTER 8

■ ■ ■

HTML5 Multimedia: Utilizing New Media Assets

Before getting into the remaining child tags of the parent <body> tag, let's cover a few tags that allow you to implement **new media content elements** in your HTML5 designs. These elements are becoming more prolific in HTML5 documents and applications. This is happening due to the advent of different devices types, such as iTV Sets, smartwatches, smartphones, tablets, and e-book readers, just to name a few. And yes, there are HTML5 operating systems that drive popular products in each of these genres, challenging Android's market domination across consumer electronics devices. If you are interested in producing new media content in HTML5, check out **Appendix D** of this book, as well as my new media content production fundamentals book series at **www.apress.com**.

In this chapter, I go over the key tags to implement new media elements, such as digital images using the **<img>** tag, digital video using the **<video>** tag, digital illustration using the **<svg>** tag, and digital audio using the **<audio>** tag. We also cover advanced areas of new media that utilize APIs or a combination of new media features. This allows developers to achieve almost anything in HTML5 that a more advanced OOP programming language, such as C++ or Java, is able to. In fact, Java or JavaFX work inside HTML5, so the future is bright for HTML5 in multimedia!

HTML5 New Media Support: Nine Genres

This chapter covers the new media capabilities of HTML5. It discusses all of the new media genres and shows how developers can create content within these genres using tags, which are covered first, and then JavaScript and APIs. Table 8-1 lists the new media genres supported in HTML5, along with the file formats, and in some cases, the API that they utilize.

© Wallace Jackson 2016
W. Jackson, *HTML5 Quick Markup Reference*, DOI 10.1007/978-1-4302-6536-8_8

Table 8-1. *Nine HTML5 New Media Genres and Data Format Support*

New Media Asset	Supported Data Formats
Digital Imagery	JPEG, GIF, PNG8, PNG24, PNG32, WebP, BMP, PDF
Digital Audio	MP3, OGG Vorbis, WAVE, AIFF, MPEG-4, OPUS, FLAC
Digital Video	MPEG-4 AVC H.264, MPEG-H EVC H.265, WebM VP8/VP9
Digital Illustration	SVG (Scalable Vector Graphic)(also used via CSS)
Interactive 3D	WebGL or WebGL2 (<canvas> covered in Chapter 17)
Digital Painting	SVG, JPEG, GIF, PNG (8/24/32), WebP, WebM, MPEG
Visual FX (VFX)	Above Formats combined together using JavaScript
Speech Recognition	Recognizes Speech; Converts to Text (Web Speech)
Speech Synthesis	Synthesizes Speech, Using Text (Web Speech API)

The first section of Table 8-1 features new media assets that enjoy "native" or direct tag support in HTML5, including the <img>, <audio>, <video>, <svg>, and <canvas> tags.

The second section of Table 8-1 contains new media genres that require JavaScript and advanced APIs to create a more advanced new media asset, such as a digital painting, or a visual effects (VFX) pipeline, or an interactive user experience. If you're interested in new media for HTML5 I have a New Media Fundamentals series of books with Apress at Apress.com, just search for this Author's name.

The third section of Table 8-1 contains a speech synthesis and speech recognition entries, because there is now the Web Speech API for two of the popular browsers— Google Chrome and Apple Safari. It won't be long before other HTML5 platforms adopt the Web Speech API, especially as iTVs and smartphones with HTML5 operating systems are increasing in number. This means that the Web Speech API should exist in all popular browsers before 2017 rolls around.

Let's look at each of these new media areas in their own sections in the chapter, now that I have outlined the relevant file (data) formats that are supported. Next, let's look at the core tags and their parameters and related APIs, which allow HTML5 developers to implement multimedia applications that rival those created for Android, Windows, Linux, and iOS. This is an exciting chapter for HTML5 developers who wish to create never-before-seen (or heard) user experiences!

Digital Imagery: Using the <img> Tag

The most widely used new media element with HTML5 is the digital image, which uses the **<img>** tag. It was introduced in HTML 1.2 and standardized in HTML 2.0. Parameters include **src**, the **digital image asset file reference** parameter, as well as the **width** and **height** parameters and useful SEO parameters. Table 8-2 shows parameter support in HTML5.

Table 8-2. *Parameters Supported By <img> Tag*

IMG Tag Parameter	IMG Tag Parameter Purpose
src	A digital image asset source file name reference
alt	Alternate text description of image used for SEO
crossorigin	Cross-origin access control for third-party site
height	Height (in pixels) to display the image
width	Width (in pixels) to display the image
longdesc	URL for a detailed description of image
usemap	Specify image as a client-side image map
ismap	Specify image as a server-side image map
align	Specify the alignment of image to other elements
border	Specify the border width around image
hspace	Specify the whitespace width left/right of image
vspace	Specify the whitespace width top/bottom of image

The <img> tag has a dozen parameters, eight of which are supported in HTML5, and four of which have been deprecated due to the use of CSS to provide these functions. The 12 parameters are seen in Table 8-2; common usage parameters are in the first section and the less commonly used parameters are in the second section. The third section contains parameters supported in previous HTML versions, which you use CSS to implement in HTML5. You can use these parameters in legacy HTML4 or prior HTML versions such as HTML3.2, HTML 2.0, and XHTML 1.0 and 1.1.

If you want to master digital image compositing terms, principles, workflows, and fundamentals, check out *Digital Image Compositing Fundamentals* (Apress, 2015).

The following is an example of a **digital image asset** using the **<img>** tag with the **src** parameter:

```
<img src="imagename.jpg" />
```

To optimize a digital image asset for SEO purposes, you use the **alt** parameter, as shown in the following example HTML5 markup:

```
<img src="imagename.jpg" alt="Image Description Using Keywords for SEO" />
```

To scale a digital image asset, you use with the **width** and **height** parameters, as shown in following example:

```
<img src="imgname.jpg" width="400" height="300"/> <!-- Scale Down Image -->
```

Make sure to scale your image by a power of 2. Thus, your source image for the preceding markup should be 800 × 600, or 1600 × 1200 in physical pixel resolution. Always scale down not up!

To allow a **digital image asset** to be legally accessed from a third-party website, use the **crossorigin** parameter (as covered in Chapter 4), as shown in the following HTML5 markup:

```
<img src="imagename.jpg" crossorigin="use-credentials" />
```

To further optimize a **digital image asset** for SEO, using the **longdesc** parameter, you should utilize this following HTML5 markup, which provides the URL reference to a keyword-optimized description that you create using HTML5:

```
<img src="imgname.jpg" longdesc="http://www.serverlocation.com/desc.html"/>
```

To define a **client-side digital image map asset** with the **USEMAP** parameter, you would utilize the following HTML5 markup:

```
<img src="imagename.jpg" usemap="#mapname" width="640" height="480" />
    <map id="mapname">
        <area shape="rect" coords="10,10,640,240" href="URL" alt="SEO" />
        <area shape="circle" coords="320,360,120" href="URL" alt="SEO" />
    </map>
```

This provides the id reference to your **<map>** element definition, which contains **<area>** element definitions that define areas within your client-side image map.

To specify a **digital image asset** using **server-side** image mapping, use an **ismap** parameter, as shown in the following HTML5 markup:

```
<img src="imagename.jpg" alt="Image Description: SEO Keywords" ismap />
```

Next, let's look at digital audio assets and the HTML5 <audio> tag.

Digital Audio: Using the <audio> Tag

Your next most widely used new media element in HTML5 is digital audio, which uses the <audio> tag. This is new to HTML5 and it is not in previous versions of HTML. Parameters include the **src**, which references a **digital audio asset file name**, and **controls**, which adds the **audio transport user interface** feature. Table 8-3 shows the <audio> tag parameters supported in HTML5, with the two most important parameters in the top section, the most commonly used options in a middle section, with seldom used options in the bottom section of the table.

Table 8-3. *Parameters Supported By the <audio> Tag*

Audio Tag Parameter	Audio Tag Parameter's Purpose
src	Digital audio asset source file name reference
controls	Audio transport UI (user interface) controls
preload	Preloads the digital audio file asset
muted	Mutes the digital audio asset
loop	Loops the digital audio asset
autoplay	Automatically play audio on a page load event
autobuffer	Automatically buffer audio on page load event

This <audio> tag has seven parameters. These can be seen in Table 8-3 in the first section (common usage parameters) and in the second section (three less frequently used parameters). The third section of the table contains parameters that are supported but are not recommended for use unless absolutely needed. The reason for this is that autoplay bothers many users, and an autobuffer takes up system resources that may not even be used if the user chooses not to hit the transport play button.

If you want to master digital audio editing terminology, principles, workflows, data footprint optimization, compositing and fundamentals, you check out my *Digital Audio Editing Fundamentals* (Apress, 2015).

To create a digital audio asset, use the **<audio>** tag with the **controls** parameter, **<source>** child tags, and **noaudio** message (like noscript), using this following HTML5 markup structure:

```
<audio controls>
    <source src="preferred_audio_codec.ogg"    type="audio/ogg" />
    <source src="second_choice_audio_codec.mp3" type="audio/mp3" />
    ALERT! Your Browser Does Not Support Audio or the HTML5 Audio Tag!
</audio>
```

Using more than one <source> tag provides "fallback" file format support choices for the HTML5 platform that you are using, in case the first audio codec choice is not supported by the HTML5 browser (or HTML5 operating system).

To autoplay a **digital image asset** using the **autoplay** parameter, you would utilize the following HTML5 markup:

```
<audio controls autoplay>
    <source src="preferred_audio_codec.ogg"    type="audio/ogg" />
    <source src="second_choice_audio_codec.mp3" type="audio/mp3" />
    ALERT! Your Browser Does Not Support Audio or the HTML5 Audio Tag!
</audio>
```

To loop the **digital audio asset** using the **loop** parameter, you should utilize the following HTML5 markup:

```
<audio controls loop>
    <source src="preferred_audio_codec.ogg"    type="audio/ogg" />
    <source src="second_choice_audio_codec.mp3" type="audio/mp3" />
    ALERT! Your Browser Does Not Support Audio or the HTML5 Audio Tag!
</audio>
```

To preload a **digital** audio **asset, use a preload** parameter with the **auto** setting, utilizing this following HTML5 markup:

```
<audio controls preload="auto">
    <source src="preferred_audio_codec.ogg"    type="audio/ogg" />
    <source src="second_choice_audio_codec.mp3" type="audio/mp3" />
    ALERT! Your Browser Does Not Support Audio or the HTML5 Audio Tag!
</audio>
```

To preload only **digital audio metadata, use** the **preload** parameter with a **metadata** setting, using this HTML5 markup:

```
<audio controls preload="metadata">
    <source src="preferred_audio_codec.ogg"    type="audio/ogg" />
    <source src="second_choice_audio_codec.mp3" type="audio/mp3" />
ALERT! Your Browser Does Not Support Audio or the HTML5 Audio Tag! </audio>
```

To prevent any pre-loading of your digital audio **assets, use the** preload parameter with the **none** setting, utilizing this following HTML5 markup:

```
<audio controls preload="none">
    <source src="preferred_audio_codec.ogg"    type="audio/ogg" />
    <source src="second_choice_audio_codec.mp3" type="audio/mp3" />
ALERT! Your Browser Does Not Support Audio or the HTML5 Audio Tag! </audio>
```

Next, let's take a look at the digital video <video> tag.

Digital Video: Using the <video> Tag

Your next most widely used new media element in HTML5 is digital video, which uses the <video> tag. This is new to HTML5 and is not in previous versions of HTML. Parameters include the **src**, which references a **digital audio asset file name**, and **controls**, which adds the **video transport user interface** feature, and width and height, in case you wish to "downsample" or scale down your digital video asset (using a factor of 2 or 4). Table 8-4 shows the <video> tag parameters supported in HTML5 with the four most important parameters in the top section, the four most commonly used options in the middle section, and two less frequently used options listed in the bottom section.

Table 8-4. *Parameters Supported by the <video> Tag*

Video Tag Parameter	Video Tag Parameter's Purpose
src	Digital video asset source file name reference
width	Digital video asset width in pixels
height	Digital video asset height in pixels
controls	Video transport UI (user interface) controls
preload	Preload the digital video file asset
muted	Mutes the digital video asset
poster	Digital image to use as a poster while loading
loop	Loops the digital video asset
autoplay	Automatically plays a video on page load event
autobuffer	Automatically buffers video on page load event

The <video> tag has ten parameters. These are seen in Table 8-4 in the first section (common usage parameters) and in the second section (four less frequently utilized parameters).

If you want to master digital video editing terminology, principles, workflows, data footprint optimization, compositing, and fundamentals, check out the *Digital Video Editing Fundamentals* (Apress, 2015).

To create a **digital video asset**, use the **<video>** tag with the **controls** parameter, **width** and **height** parameters, three **<source>** child tags, and a **novideo** message (like a noscript), as shown in the following HTML5 markup structure:

```
<video width="400" height="300" controls>
    <source src="my_preferred_video_codec.mp4"  type="video/mp4" />
    <source src="second_choice_video_codec.ogg" type="video/ogg" />
    <source src="third_choice_audio_codec.webm" type="audio/webm"/>
    ALERT! Your Browser Does Not Support Video or the HTML5 Video Tag!
</video>
```

Using more than one <source> tag provides "fallback" file format support choices for the HTML5 platform that you are using, in case the first video codec choice is not supported by that particular HTML5 browser (or operating system).

To autoplay a **digital video asset**, you use the **autoplay** parameter, as shown in the following HTML5 markup:

```
<video width="400" height="300" controls autoplay>
    <source src="my_preferred_video_codec.mp4"  type="video/mp4" />
    <source src="second_choice_video_codec.ogg" type="video/ogg" />
    <source src="third_choice_audio_codec.webm" type="audio/webm"/>
    ALERT! Your Browser Does Not Support Video or the HTML5 Video Tag!
</video>
```

To loop a **digital video asset**, you use the **loop** parameter, as shown in the following HTML5 markup:

```
<video width="400" height="300" controls loop>
    <source src="my_preferred_video_codec.mp4"  type="video/mp4" />
    <source src="second_choice_video_codec.ogg" type="video/ogg" />
    <source src="third_choice_audio_codec.webm" type="audio/webm"/>
    ALERT! Your Browser Does Not Support Video or the HTML5 Video Tag!
</video>
```

To preload a **digital video asset, you** use the **preload** parameter with the **auto** setting, as shown in the following HTML5 markup:

```
<video width="400" height="300" controls preload="auto">
    <source src="my_preferred_video_codec.mp4"  type="video/mp4" />
    <source src="second_choice_video_codec.ogg" type="video/ogg" />
    <source src="third_choice_audio_codec.webm" type="audio/webm"/>
    ALERT! Your Browser Does Not Support Video or the HTML5 Video Tag!
</video>
```

As with the <audio> tag preload parameter, you can set a preload value to **none** or to only load the **metadata**.

In case you are wondering what **metadata** is, it includes information about the audio or video asset, such as the title, the name of the artist, and information about the music (or video) content.

To display an image during video buffering, use a **poster** parameter set to reference your **digital image asset's file name**, as shown in the following HTML5 markup:

```
<video width="400" height="300" controls poster="posterimagename.png">
    <source src="my_preferred_video_codec.mp4"  type="video/mp4" />
    <source src="second_choice_video_codec.ogg" type="video/ogg" />
    <source src="third_choice_audio_codec.webm" type="audio/webm"/>
    ALERT! Your Browser Does Not Support Video or the HTML5 Video Tag!
</video>
```

Next, let's look at the digital illustration <svg> tag and its child tags (which allow you to define illustration).

Digital Illustration: Using the <svg> Tag

Your next most widely used new media element in HTML5 is **digital illustration**, which uses the **<svg>** tag. It is also new in HTML5, meaning it was not included in previous versions of HTML. CSS is the most popular way to apply the power of **svg**, especially a plethora of special effects to apply to the vector element components of your HTML5 applications, including text, buttons, or vector illustrations. A number of new media software packages can generate SVG XML data, including Inkscape, GIMP, CorelDRAW, OpenOffice Draw, and Adobe Illustrator, to name just a few.

SVG tag parameters include **width** and **height** for your SVG digital illustration definition, as well as **child tags**, used to define SVG elements, which add features to **digital illustration assets**. SVG is based on **XML**, and SVG uses XML tags, which as you now know is compatible with HTML5 now that SVG support has been added. This is exciting for HTML5 developers, as vector support allows digital illustrators to create impressive **interactive 2D** artwork as well as visually exciting special effects for users.

Table 8-5 shows some of the SVG tag's child tag elements that are supported in HTML5. They also have their own parameters, such as **fill**, **stroke**, and **color**, and so forth, as you will see in some of the markup examples in this section. I cannot discuss SVG in detail in this book, because it is a topic in and unto itself. That said, the W3C's decision to add SVG support to HTML5 was easy due to shared SGML markup language origins.

Table 8-5. *Child Tags Supported By the <svg> Tag*

SVG Child Tag	Purpose of SVG Child Tag
circle	Draw a 2D circle element
rect	Draw a 2D circle element
ellipse	Draw a 2D circle element
polygon	Draw a polygon (n-sided shape element)
polyline	Draw a polyline
line	Draw a line
image	Digital image to use as a poster while loading
text	Loop video
font	Automatically play video on page load event
path	Loop video
filter	Automatically play video on page load event
animate	Automatically buffer video on page load event

The <svg> tag has many child tags and parameters, all of which are supported in HTML5 and are typically accessed using CSS to implement the digital illustration functions.

Some of the more often used SVG elements are seen in Table 8-5. The first section contains the basic shapes and the second section contains other useful vector design elements.

If you wanted to master digital illustration (SVG) terms as well as core SVG XML principles, SVG XML markup workflow, and SVG fundamentals, check out my *Digital Illustration Fundamentals* (Apress, 2015) title. In this book, I show readers how to create (and optimize) SVG assets using GIMP and Inkscape, so the book bridges digital imaging and digital illustration software with HTML5. The book also has chapters covering Android, Java and JavaFX code, HTML5 markup, XML, CSS, and cross-platform (cross-device) publishing.

To create a **digital illustration asset**, use the **<svg>** tag with the **width** and **height** parameters and with a child tag that defines an SVG circle shape, as shown in the following HTML5 markup:

```
<svg width="640" height="480">
    <circle cx="0" cy="0" r="25" fill="blue" stroke="red" stroke-width="4">
</svg>
```

To create an SVG **rounded rectangle**, utilize the following HTML5 markup, which includes parameters for rx (radius x) and ry (radius y):

```
<svg width="640" height="480">
    <rect x="20" y="20" rx="10" ry="10" width="200" height="200"
          style="fill:yellow; stroke:purple; stroke-width:6; opacity:0.5" />
</svg>
```

Notice the **style** parameter, which contains in-line CSS3 style information, which is more common for styling SVG illustrations.

Next, let's look at the other new media areas that can be simulated using features in HTML5.

Interactive 3D: Using a <canvas> Tag and WebGL

We are going to spend an entire chapter on advanced drawing for HTML5 using the **<canvas>** tag, which is how you implement interactive 3D, or i3D. This advanced new media area requires a special API called WebGL, which uses OpenGL. WebGL2 is due out in 2016. It brings the visual impact of OpenGL to HTML5. We'll go over all of this in Chapter 17. (I just wanted to put it in context in this chapter with the other new media genres.)

Digital Painting: Digital Painting using JavaScript

Digital painting is a combination of digital imaging, vector illustration, particle systems, and digital video. SVG is moving towards adding digital painting features, but you can use JavaScript and CSS3 with HTML5 to simulate digital painting now. This is an advanced area beyond the tag markup focus of this book, but if you want to learn more about digital painting, you should check out *Digital Painting Techniques* (Apress, 2016). In this book, I show readers how to create (and optimize) digital painting assets using Corel Painter 2016, GIMP, and Inkscape, which bridges digital imaging and digital illustration software with HTML5. This book has chapters covering data footprint optimization, Android, JavaScript, Java 8 and JavaFX coding, HTML5 markup, as well as cross-platform and cross-device new media content publishing.

Visual Effects: Creating VFX using JavaScript

Other advanced new media genres, such as visual effects, or VFX, can also be simulated using advanced JavaScript programming in conjunction with CSS3, WebGL2, and HTML5 tags. This is an advanced area beyond the tag markup focus of this book, but if you want to learn more about visual effects, you should check out *Visual Effects Fundamentals* (Apress, 2016). In this book, I show the readers how to create (and optimize) visual effects assets using BlackMagic Fusion and GIMP, so it bridges digital imaging, digital video, digital audio, and digital illustration software with HTML5. The book goes over data footprint optimization, Android, Java 8 and JavaFX coding, HTML5 markup, and cross-platform and cross-device publishing.

Web Speech: Speech Synthesis and Recognition

Finally, let's take a quick look at speech recognition and speech synthesis, which were recently added to HTML5 browsers Google Chrome and Apple Safari using the **Web Speech** API. Expect Firefox to add it as well since it is moving to support iTVs and smartphones. Opera is also doing the same. The future of new media is looking bright for HTML5-based platforms and browsers, which is especially exciting for multimedia producers. For an example of how speech recognition and speech synthesis work in Google Chrome, visit `https://www.google.com/intl/en/chrome/demos/speech.html`.

Summary

This chapter discussed new media support for HTML5 using the <img>, <audio>, <video>, and <svg> tags; their related child tags and parameter options; and other new media genre support in HTML5. In the next chapter, you learn about <header> tags, which support the organization of content into levels within your HTML5 document.

■ ■ ■

CHAPTER 9

HTML5 Organization: Document Content Hierarchy

Let's discuss tags which allow developers to implement **content hierarchy** into their HTML5 designs, such as different levels of document content, called **headings**, which use six different levels of "h" tags, and **DTP** (desktop publishing) tools such as **address** areas and **horizontal rules**, to divide the content visually. These allow you to organize your document content into **logical topical sections.** They're also utilized by search engines for **indexing** text-based content and for SEO **ranking** text-based content.

In this chapter, I go over the primary tags for implementing document content hierarchies, using **headings** with <**h1**> through <**h6**> tags that give developers six levels of content refinement. I also cover the <**address**> and <**hr**> tags (horizontal rule). The <hr> tag allows you to define sections for your documents. The <address> tag defines addresses for the physical and virtual (website and e-mail) address for your HTML document content. Even though these tags are legacy tags not new to HTML5, they need to be covered in this chapter.

HTML5 Content Organization Tags

This chapter covers text content organization capabilities for all versions of HTML spanning back to version 2. You look at the legacy text content hierarchy tags and see how developers define importance—to users and search engines—of text-based content with these tags.

Table 9-1 shows the text content heading or organization tags supported prior to HTML5 (the first seven tags) as well as two desktop publishing–related tags that are also supported in HTML5. These allow you to define a horizontal rule and the address area in HTML documents.

© Wallace Jackson 2016
W. Jackson, *HTML5 Quick Markup Reference*, DOI 10.1007/978-1-4302-6536-8_9

Table 9-1. *Eight HTML Content Organization Tags and Their Usage*

Organization Tags	Content Organization Tag Usage
h1	Top-level heading (most SEO important keywords)
h2	2nd-level heading (2nd SEO important keywords)
h3	3rd-level heading (most SEO important keywords)
h4	4th-level heading (most SEO important keywords)
h5	5th-level heading (most SEO important keywords)
h6	6th-level heading (most SEO important keywords)
hr	Horizontal rule content divider line
address	Address information for article/document

Let's take a look at these in logical sections, as delineated in this table, starting with the HTML "h" tags.

Heading Level Tags: Segmenting Content Logically

The heading level 1 **<h1>** through heading level 6 **<h6>** tags allow six levels of document headings, which can be used like section (paragraph or a collection of paragraphs) titles, or more accurately, cascading topical section headings. The search engine algorithms use headings to ascertain keywords and organize text content. This ranges from the most important keywords (broad stroke content) for the document defined using <h1> and <h2>, and the least important keywords (specific, or well-defined, content) defined in <h6>.

These should be used to logically stratify the content in a way that drills down into the organization of your text content so that the user can follow and assimilate its meaning effortlessly. The organization of the text content uses heading levels as a guide to how your content is refined. For instance, you might have a document that drills down to a discussion of the Ferrari models currently available in North America from a more general discussion of exotic cars.

An example looks like the following HTML markup, which is compatible with all versions of HTML. It contains a significant amount of textual content within each paragraph tag or contains a collection of paragraph <p> tags between each of the six HTML heading levels. It defines what is in the paragraph tags by using summary terms (which are keywords, as far as the search engine robots are concerned).

```
<!DOCTYPE html>
<html>
 <head>
  <title>Exotic Cars Example</title>
 </head>
 <body>
  <h1>Exotic Car Document</h1>
    <p>Top Level Keywords Relating to Exotic Cars from Every Nation</p>
  <h2>Exotic European Cars</h2>
```

```
    <p>Next Level Keywords Relating to Exotic Cars from European Union</p>
  <h3>Exotic European Sports Cars</h3>
    <p>Next Level Keywords Relating to Exotic European Sports Cars</p>
  <h4>Popular Exotic Italian Sports Cars (Ferrari and Lamborghini)</h4>
    <p>Next Level Keywords Relating to Exotic Italian Sports Cars</p>
  <h5>Currently Popular Ferrari Sports Cars</h5>
    <p>Next Level Keywords for Currently Popular Ferrari Sports Cars</p>
  <h6>Ferrari Sports Cars Available in North America (USA and Canada)</h6>
    <p>Next Level Keywords for Ferrari Sports Cars Available in America</p>
  </body>
</html>
```

For this markup example, I simply used some SEO keywords suggestions as the content for the <p> tag, which is covered in Chapter 11. Normally, this is the text-based content in a long paragraph format, but it would make the example too long!

Next, let's look at the **horizontal rule <hr>** tag and see how it allows you to draw a **visual divider line** between logical sections of a document in versions prior to HTML5, and to separate areas of the document semantically in HTML5 and later. Semantic HTML5 is discussed in Chapter 10.

Horizontal Rule Tag: Dividing Text Content Visually

Prior to HTML5, the horizontal rule or <hr> tag was used to **insert a line** between logical areas in a document. In HTML5, it is no longer used for visual demarcation, but instead as a logical or **semantic** demarcation of logical document sections. For this reason, the parameters seen in Table 9-2 are **no longer supported in HTML5**. HTML5 browsers may still draw this line for **presentation** purposes, which the <hr> tag was used for before HTML5, but the browser or operating system looks at it as a **semantic document sectional division**.

Table 9-2. *Parameters for the <hr> Tag, Used Prior to HTML5*

Organization Tags	Content Organization Tag Usage
align	Determine alignment (left, right, center values)
size	Specify line height using pixels (integer value)
width	Specify line width in pixels or as a percentage
noshade	Forces one solid color value to be used for line

This is a logical progression for document organization, as far as content/search (HTML5), styling (CSS3), and animation and interactivity (JavaScript) are concerned. It is also quite logical where the move toward the "semantic web" is concerned.

To create the **horizontal rule and semantic break** between your logical sections, use an **<hr>** tag after the last paragraph tag. This can be done for each of the six sections, using the following HTML5 markup and building on the previous example:

```
<!DOCTYPE html><html>
<head><title>Exotic Cars</title></head>
<body>
 <h1>Exotic Car Document</h1>
   <p>Top Level Keywords Relating to Exotic Cars from Every Nation</p>
      <hr>
 <h2>Exotic European Cars</h2>
   <p>Next Level Keywords Relating to Exotic Cars from European Union</p>
      <hr>
 <h3>Exotic European Sports Cars</h3>
   <p>Next Level Keywords Relating to Exotic European Sports Cars</p>
      <hr>
 <h4>Popular Exotic Italian Sports Cars (Ferrari and Lamborghini)</h4>
   <p>Next Level Keywords Relating to Exotic Italian Sports Cars</p>
      <hr>
 <h5>Currently Popular Ferrari Sports Cars</h5>
   <p>Next Level Keywords for Currently Popular Ferrari Sports Cars</p>
      <hr>
 <h6>Ferrari Sports Cars Available in North America (USA and Canada)</h6>
   <p>Next Level Keywords for Ferrari Sports Cars Available in America</p>
      <hr>
</body>
</html>
```

If you are developing legacy code for HTML4 and earlier, you should use the parameters shown in Table 9-2 to control the horizontal rule alignment, width, and height. Next, let's take a look at how to specify an address for your document or article.

The Address Tag: Specifying Address Information

The **<address>** tag defines the types of addresses in a document to provide **contact information** for the user. In versions prior to HTML5, the <address> tag was a child of the <body> tag and provided address information for the entire document. If you are using the <address> tag as a child tag in the new HTML5 **<article>** tag, which is covered in Chapter 10, the <address> tag defines the address (contact) information for semantically defined articles.

To create an **address information section** for a document, use the **<address>** tag with your **address**, **e-mail**, **websites**, and similar address-related information inside of it by using child tags. The following is an example of address HTML markup structure:

```
<body>
  <address>
    Document Created By: <a href="mailto:info@wallacejackson.com>Walls</a>
    <br><hr>
    Address: 12345 Streetname Road, Cityname, Statename, Zip Code, Country
    <br><hr>
    Website: <a href="http://www.wallacejackson.com>WallaceJackson.com</a>
  </address>
</body>
```

Notice that I used a **break**
 tag and a horizontal rule <hr> tag to define the different areas of the address with a semantic break (HTML5) and a horizontal line (rule) for HTML 4 and earlier. The break tag is covered in Chapter 11.

I saved the rest of the document organization tag topics for Chapter 10, which discusses semantic document definition, since HTML5 and later use special tags to define the **content areas** for the document (HTML5 browser) or the application (HTML5 operating system). This <address> tag is a great example of a semantic tag, and a good way to segue into the new HTML5 semantic tags.

Summary

This chapter discussed document headings and desktop publishing legacy support in HTML5 and all previous versions using the <h1> through <h6>, <hr>, and <address> tags and their related parameter options. The next chapter continues the document organization journey by using the new semantic tags added to HTML5 to support the organization of content in logical areas within a document. Defining text-based content through paragraphs, lists, forms, tables, and the like, is also covered.

CHAPTER 10

■ ■ ■

HTML5 Semantics: Defining Semantic Documents

Next, let's cover the new "semantic" tags in HTML5 that allow developers to more logically define the **content hierarchy** in their HTML5 designs. This is done with **headers, footers, sections, figures, captions, sidebars**, and **navigation panels**, to name a few. They allow you to organize document content into **logical sections**. Semantics is the study of a word's meaning, so what makes these tags **semantic** is that they define the content, so search engines can "see" the document design semantically (i.e., intelligently).

In this chapter, I go over **semantic tags**, which implement the new HTML5 semantic document organization paradigm. The tags have names that define the functional area of the HTML5 document they represent. Examples of semantic tags include <**header**> and <**footer**> tags, <**figure**> and <**figcaption**> tags, and the <**section**>, <**article**>, <**main**>, <**nav**>, <**aside**>, <**details**>, <**summary**>, <**mark**>, and <**time**> tags.

HTML5 Semantic Content Organization

This chapter covers **semantic content organization** capabilities in HTML5. Prior to HTML5, developers created their descriptive (semantic) names for document elements using the <div> tag, or other tags, and a **class** or **id** parameter, such as <div id="header"> for example. Since developers did not use standardized semantic labels, the W3C did it for them, so that search engine robots (algorithms) could start to implement **Web 3.0**, which is **semantic search**. According to the W3C: *The semantic Web allows data to be shared and reused across applications, enterprises, and communities.* Table 10-1 shows semantic content organization tags, which are all new in HTML5, categorized into primary document sections, functional document sections, multimedia capable figures, and detail-oriented document characteristics.

© Wallace Jackson 2016
W. Jackson. *HTML5 Quick Markup Reference*. DOI 10.1007/978-1-4302-6536-8_10

Table 10-1. *Thirteen HTML Semantic Organization Tags*

Organization Tags	Content Organization Tag Usage
header	Specifies the header information of the document
footer	Specifies the footer information of the document
section	Specifies the section information of the document
main	Specifies primary or main content of the document
nav	Navigation; usually a collection of anchor tags
article	Specifies the article information of the document
aside	Sidebar content related to the surrounding text
figure	Specifies figure and new media of the document
figcaption	Specifies the section information of the document
details	Specifies additional detail that users can show or hide
summary	Specifies the section information of the document
mark	Specifies figure and new media of the document
time	Specifies the figure caption of the figure media

It is interesting to note that there are some tags prior to HTML5 that just happened to be semantic, although they were not specifically designed to be so at the time. These include <form>, <table>, and abbreviated tags like <a> (anchor), <li> (list), and <p> (paragraph). The new media tags can also be considered semantic, because they describe <img> (imagery), <audio>, <video>, <svg> (scalable vector graphics or illustrations), and <canvas> (real-time 2D and 3D graphics) elements in the actual name of the tag, so a search engine knows the document's content.

Let's take a look at these semantic tags in logical sections, as delineated in Table 10-1, starting with the HTML5 <section>, <header>, and <footer> sectional tags. They define broad, high-level document areas used in desktop publishing to hold reference information and other ancillary information usually tied into these areas using superscript or subscript numbers in a primary (center or middle) document content area.

An example of a semantic document structure is seen in Figure 10-1, which shows some of the most important semantic tags.

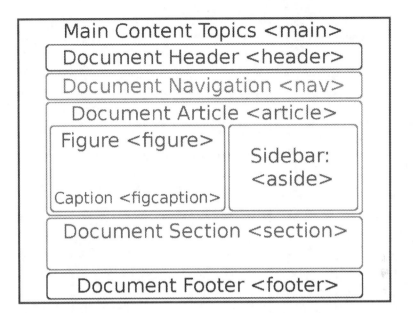

Figure 10-1. *An example of a semantic HTML5 document structure*

HTML5 Sectional Tags: Segment Content Logically

The sectional **<section>** tag and more specialized **<header>** and **<footer>** tags semantically define standard areas in a document, so that the search engine knows what you are doing with your document design. The <section> tag is for more general sectioning of a document. The <header> and <footer> are for specific introductory information and footnotes.

The SECTION Tag: Define Document Sections

A <section> tag is used to define any kind of section in a document, such as a chapter, for instance. If there were no <header> and <footer> semantic tags, <section> could be used to define headers and footers as well. The <section> tag is a child tag of the <body> and <article> tags. It is a parent tag to tags like <article>, <figure>, <p>, and the six heading tags, for instance.

There are no hierarchy rules, so <article> tags can have child <section> tags, and <section> tags can have child <article> tags. This makes the semantic content design far more flexible.

Let's use the <section> tag along with an id value in a content design with sections for both exotic and domestic cars. The following expands upon the heading tags example used in Chapter 9:

```
<!DOCTYPE html><html>
<head><title>Exotic and Domestic Cars</title></head>
<body>
 <section id="exotic">
  <h1>Exotic Car Document</h1>
   <p>Top Level Keywords Relating to Exotic Cars from Every Nation</p>
  <h2>Exotic European Cars</h2>
   <p>Next Level Keywords Relating to Exotic Cars from European Union</p>
  <h3>Exotic European Sports Cars</h3>
   <p>Next Level Keywords Relating to Exotic European Sports Cars</p>
 </section>
 <section id="domestic">
  <h1>Domestic Car Document</h1>
   <p>Top Level Keywords Relating to Domestic Cars from Every Nation</p>
  <h2>Domestic European Cars</h2>
   <p>Next Level Keywords Relating to Domestic Cars from European Union</p>
  <h3>Domestic European Sedans</h3>
   <p>Next Level Keywords Relating to Domestic European Sedans</p>
 </section>
</body>
</html>
```

Next, let's look at a special type of section tag called the <header> tag. This tag specifically provides information at the top or "header" of the document design.

The HEADER Tag: Define Introductory Content for the Document

The **<header>** tag defines the introductory content of the document. If there were no <nav> semantic tag, it could also be used to define navigation (user interface) elements. The <header> tag cannot be used as a child tag of <footer>, <address>, or another <header> tag. More than one <header> tag may be used in a single document, however. The <header> element (tag) usually contains a heading tag (<h1> for instance) and a paragraph <p> tag, and possibly an image, such as a logo, picture, or similar visual branding element.

Let's use a <header> tag to define the header for the car content design example. The example now uses sections for European and American cars underneath the <header> in an HTML5 content hierarchy. I changed the section id to reflect this new design change, as shown in the following HTML5 markup:

```
<!DOCTYPE html><html>
<head><title>Exotic and Domestic Cars</title></head>
<body>
```

```
<header>
 <h1>Exotic Cars Unleashed!</h1>
  <p>Top Level Keywords Relating to Exotic Cars from Every Nation</p>
</header>
<section id="european">
 <h2>Exotic European Cars</h2>
  <p>Next Level Keywords Relating to Exotic Cars from European Union</p>
 <h3>Exotic European Sports Cars</h3>
  <p>Next Level Keywords Relating to Exotic European Sports Cars</p>
</section>
<section id="american">
 <h2>Exotic American Cars</h2>
  <p>Next Level Keywords Relating to Domestic Cars from North America</p>
 <h3>Exotic American Sports Cars</h3>
  <p>Next Level Keywords Relating to Exotic North American Sports Cars</p>
</section>
</body>
</html>
```

Next, let's take a look at a special type of section tag called the <footer> tag. This tag provides information at the bottom or "foot" of your document design. It is usually **footnote** or other reference information that further defines or identifies the primary document content.

The FOOTER Tag: Footnote Information Referencing the Content

The <footer> tag defines footnote and similar reference content for the document. More than one <footer> tag may be used in a single document. The <footer> element usually contains copyrights, author contact information, or references to other documents used as resources.

Let's use a <footer> tag to define a footer for the car content design example. The footer references information that identifies the sources for the document content, as shown in the following HTML5 markup:

```
<!DOCTYPE html><html>
<head><title>Exotic and Domestic Cars</title></head>
<body>
 <header>
  <h1>Exotic Cars Unleashed!</h1>
   <p>Top Level Keywords Relating to Exotic Cars from Every Nation</p>
 </header>
 <section id="european">
  <h2>Exotic European Cars</h2>
   <p>Next Level Keywords Relating to Exotic Cars from European Union</p>
  <h3>Exotic European Sports Cars</h3>
   <p>Next Level Keywords Relating to Exotic European Sports Cars</p>
 </section>
```

77

```
<section id="american">
 <h2>Exotic American Cars</h2>
  <p>Next Level Keywords Relating to Domestic Cars from North America</p>
 <h3>Exotic American Sports Cars</h3>
  <p>Next Level Keywords Relating to Exotic North American Sports Cars</p>
</section>
<footer>
 <h4>Exotic Car Article Article, Contact and Sources:</h1>
  <p>Blog's Author: Wallace Jackson</p>
  <p>Author e-mail: <a href="mailto: wj@email.com">Wallace Jackson</a></p>
  <p>Blog's Source: Magazine or Book Resources and Links would go here</p>
 </footer>
</body>
</html>
```

Next, let's take a look at the HTML5 semantic tags, which allow you to define document "areas," such as the **main** document topic, **articles** within a document, informational **sidebars**, and **navigation** bars.

HTML5 Content Type Semantic Definition Tags

The next four tags in Table 10-1 define other document areas—articles, sidebars, navigation UI, and the top level (the main area) of your document—in semantic terms using tags named for the document areas, which is what the new HTML5 document semantics are all about! You need to use these tags properly and precisely to make your HTML5 document compatible with Web 3.0 (the Semantic Web). Search engines assimilate semantically optimized content, which is made possible by using the tags covered within this important HTML5 chapter.

The MAIN Tag: Defining the Top Level of the Document Content

The **<main>** tag defines the topmost level of the document. Only one <main> tag is used in a single document. This <main> tag can't be used as a child tag of <nav>, <header>, <footer>, <article>, or <aside> because it defines the top level of a document. The <main> element needs to contain unique information and design elements, which cannot be repeated across any other HTML documents.

Let's use this <main> tag to define the top level of the car content design example. The main tag has an opening tag for the top of the document (before the <header> tag) and a closing tag at the bottom of the document (after the <footer> tag), so that your entire document is contained (defined) inside of this <main> tag semantic structure. An example of this is shown in the following HTML5 markup:

```
<!DOCTYPE html><html>
<head><title>Exotic and Domestic Cars</title></head>
<body>
```

```
<main>
 <header>
  <h1>Exotic Cars Unleashed!</h1>
   <p>Top Level Keywords Relating to Exotic Cars from Every Nation</p>
 </header>
 <section id="european">
  <h2>Exotic European Cars</h2>
   <p>Next Level Keywords Relating to Exotic Cars from European Union</p>
  <h3>Exotic European Sports Cars</h3>
   <p>Next Level Keywords Relating to Exotic European Sports Cars</p>
 </section>
 <section id="american">
  <h2>Exotic American Cars</h2>
   <p>Next Level Keywords Relating to Domestic Cars from North America</p>
  <h3>Exotic American Sports Cars</h3>
   <p>Next Level Keywords Relating to Exotic North American Sports Cars</p>
 </section>
 <footer>
  <h4>Exotic Car Article Article, Contact and Sources:</h1>
   <p>Blog's Author: Wallace Jackson</p>
   <p>Author e-mail: <a href="mailto: wj@email.com">Wallace Jackson</a></p>
   <p>Blog's Source: Magazine or Book Resources and Links would go here</p>
 </footer>
</main>
</body>
</html>
```

Next, let's take a look at the <nav> tag, which contains the user interface design (document navigation HTML5 elements) for your HTML5 document or application. I also recommend using CSS to style the document navigation tags.

The NAV Tag: Defining the Navigation UI for Your Document

The **<nav>** tag defines the user interface of the document's navigation area, which is typically implemented using <a> tag anchor link styles. (CSS3 styling is not covered in this book, so make sure to get a good CSS3 book to go with this book.) Multiple <nav> tags may be used in a single document. The <nav> element (tag) must only contain links that are used for navigation.

Let's add the <nav> tag to our current example, as shown in the following HTML5 markup:

```
<!DOCTYPE html><html>
<head><title>Exotic and Domestic Cars</title></head>
<body>
 <main>
  <header>
   <h1>Exotic Cars Unleashed!</h1>
```

```
    <p>Top Level Keywords Relating to Exotic Cars from Every Nation</p>
  </header>
  <nav>
   <a http://www.web-address.com/car-info.html>CAR INFO</a>
   <a http://www.web-address.com/our-team.html>OUR TEAM</a>
   <a http://www.web-address.com/buy-cars.html>BUY CARS</a>
  </nav>
  <section id="european">
   <h2>Exotic European Cars</h2>
    <p>Next Level Keywords Relating to Exotic Cars from European Union</p>
   <h3>Exotic European Sports Cars</h3>
    <p>Next Level Keywords Relating to Exotic European Sports Cars</p>
  </section>
  <section id="american">
   <h2>Exotic American Cars</h2>
    <p>Next Level Keywords Relating to Domestic Cars from North America</p>
   <h3>Exotic American Sports Cars</h3>
    <p>Next Level Keywords Relating to Exotic North American Sports Cars</p>
  </section>
  <footer>
   <h4>Exotic Car Article Article, Contact and Sources:</h1>
    <p>Blog's Author: Wallace Jackson</p>
    <p>Author e-mail: <a href="mailto: wj@email.com">Wallace Jackson</a></p>
    <p>Blog's Source: Magazine or Book Resources and Links would go here</p>
  </footer>
 </main>
</body></html>
```

Next, let's take a look at the <article> tag, which creates topic-specific articles in the document.

The ARTICLE Tag: Defining Articles within an HTML5 Document

The <article> tag defines an article within your document. An article is unique, proprietary content that stands up independently to other document content. It is possible to use multiple <article> tags in one document.

Let's change the <section> tags to <article> tags in the car example, turning it into a magazine by using the following markup:

```
<!DOCTYPE html><html>
<head><title>Exotic and Domestic Cars Today</title></head>
<body>
 <main>
  <header>
   <h1>Exotic Cars Magazine: Current Exotic Car Articles</h1>
    <p>Top Level Keywords Relating to Exotic Cars from Every Nation</p>
  </header>
```

```
<nav>
 <a http://www.web-address.com/car-info.html>CAR INFO</a>
 <a http://www.web-address.com/our-team.html>OUR TEAM</a>
 <a http://www.web-address.com/buy-cars.html>BUY CARS</a>
</nav>
<article>
 <h2>Exotic European Cars: Maintaining a Lead Over US Manufacturers</h2>
  <p>Next Level Keywords Relating to Exotic Cars from European Union</p>
 <h3>Exotic European Sports Car Round-Up</h3>
  <p>Next Level Keywords Relating to Exotic European Sports Cars</p>
</article>
<article>
 <h2>Exotic American Cars: Gaining on the Domination of European Cars</h2>
  <p>Next Level Keywords Relating to Domestic Cars from North America</p>
 <h3>Exotic American Sports Car Round-Up</h3>
  <p>Next Level Keywords Relating to Exotic North American Sports Cars</p>
</article>
<footer>
 <h4>Exotic Car Article Article, Contact and Sources:</h1>
  <p>Blog's Author: Wallace Jackson</p>
  <p>Author e-mail: <a href="mailto: wj@email.com">Wallace Jackson</a></p>
  <p>Blog's Source: Magazine or Book Resources and Links would go here</p>
</footer>
</main>
</body>
</html>
```

Next, let's take a look at the <aside> tag, which creates informational sidebars in the document.

The ASIDE Tag: Defining Information Sidebars in Your Document

The **<aside>** tag defines an informational sidebar within your document. Sidebar content must be related to the content adjacent to it. It is possible to use multiple <aside> tags in one document.

Let's change the <section> tags to <article> tags in the car example, turning it into a magazine by using this markup:

```
<!DOCTYPE html><html>
<head><title>Exotic and Domestic Cars Today</title></head>
<body>
 <main>
  <header>
   <h1>Exotic Cars Magazine: Current Exotic Car Articles</h1>
    <p>Top Level Keywords Relating to Exotic Cars from Every Nation</p>
  </header>
```

```
<nav>
 <a http://www.web-address.com/car-info.html>CAR INFO</a>
 <a http://www.web-address.com/our-team.html>OUR TEAM</a>
 <a http://www.web-address.com/buy-cars.html>BUY CARS</a>
</nav>
<article>
 <h2>Exotic European Cars: Maintaining a Lead Over US Manufacturers</h2>
  <p>Next Level Keywords Relating to Exotic Cars from European Union</p>
 <h3>Exotic European Sports Car Round-Up</h3>
  <p>Next Level Keywords Relating to Exotic European Sports Cars</p>
  <aside>
   <h4>Sidebar: Top Selling European Sports Cars</h4>
    <p>Next Level Keywords Relating to Top Selling European Sports Cars</p>
  </aside>
</article>
<article>
 <h2>Exotic American Cars: Gaining on the Domination of European Cars</h2>
  <p>Next Level Keywords Relating to Domestic Cars from North America</p>
 <h3>Exotic American Sports Car Round-Up</h3>
  <p>Next Level Keywords Relating to Exotic North American Sports Cars</p>
</article>
<footer>
 <h5>Exotic Car Article Article, Contact and Sources:</h1>
  <p>Blog's Author: Wallace Jackson</p>
  <p>Author e-mail: <a href="mailto: wj@email.com">Wallace Jackson</a></p>
  <p>Blog's Source: Magazine or Book Resources and Links would go here</p>
</footer>
</main></body></html>
```

Next, let's take a look at how to use figures and figure captions in HTML5.

HTML5 Semantic New Media Figure Definition Tags

The next two tags shown in Table 10-1 allow you to define a new media element semantically, using a **figure** and a **figure caption**.

The FIGURE and FIGCAPTION Tags: Adding Captioned Imagery

A **<figure>** tag is used to define multimedia. A **<figcaption>** tag is nested to define the caption for the new media asset.

Let's use these two tags to define a captioned image for the sports car content, as shown in the following HTML5 markup:

```
<!DOCTYPE html><html>
<head><title>Exotic and Domestic Cars Today</title></head>
<body>
```

```
<main>
 <header>
  <h1>Exotic Cars Magazine: Current Exotic Car Articles</h1>
   <p>Top Level Keywords Relating to Exotic Cars from Every Nation</p>
 </header>
 <nav>
  <a http://www.web-address.com/car-info.html>CAR INFO</a>
  <a http://www.web-address.com/our-team.html>OUR TEAM</a>
  <a http://www.web-address.com/buy-cars.html>BUY CARS</a>
 </nav>
 <article>
  <h2>Exotic European Cars: Maintaining a Lead Over US Manufacturers</h2>
   <p>Next Level Keywords Relating to Exotic Cars from European Union</p>
  <h3>Exotic European Sports Car Round-Up</h3>
   <p>Next Level Keywords Relating to Exotic European Sports Cars</p>
   <aside>
    <h4>Sidebar: Top Selling European Sports Cars</h4>
     <p>Next Level Keywords Relating to Top Selling European Sports Cars</p>
   </aside>
 </article>
 <article>
  <h2>Exotic American Cars: Gaining on the Domination of European Cars</h2>
   <p>Next Level Keywords Relating to Domestic Cars from North America</p>
  <h3>Exotic American Sports Car Round-Up</h3>
   <p>Next Level Keywords Relating to Exotic North American Sports Cars</p>
  <figure>
   <img src="sport-car-image.png" alt="sports car image related keywords">
   <figcaption>Figure 1. Image of Popular American Sports Car</figcaption>
  </figure>
 </article>
 <footer>
  <h5>Exotic Car Article Article, Contact and Sources:</h1>
   <p>Blog's Author: Wallace Jackson</p>
   <p>Blog's Source: Magazine or Book Resources and Links would go here</p>
 </footer>
</main></body></html>
```

You can also place the <figcaption> child tag inside of the <figure> parent tag, before the <img> or <video> tag, if you want to have the figure text on top of your image or video, rather than underneath it. Having the caption underneath the new media element is the standard way to caption your image or video. You can also use a caption with your <audio> tag, but be sure to include the controls parameter so that there is something (the play-pause-rewind transport) there to caption!

Next, let's look at the final few semantic tags, which add various detail elements, including pop-up information, summaries, text marking, and system time.

HTML5 Semantic Document Detail Definition Tags

The last four tags in Table 10-1 allow you to define the **detail elements** of your semantic HTML5 documents. These include the <detail> tag that developers use to define interactive pop-up widgets that allow users to drill down into a document's semantic content. There is also a child <summary> tag that is used with the <detail> tag. Finally, the <mark> tag "marks up" text, and the <time> tag allows you to display the system date and time.

The DETAILS and SUMMARY Tags: Adding Pop-up Information

The **<details>** tag is used in conjunction with the **<summary>** tag to define **pop-up information** that allows users to "drill down" for more information. The information provided in the <summary> tag is clicked to toggle the show or hide functions in the <details> tag. The <details> tag has one parameter, called **open**, which signifies that open="true" and equates to the "show" state for the <details> element being the default state. If the open parameter is not present, this equates to open="false", and the **hide state** is the **default**; the user has to click the <summary> tag's text to "unhide" or open the <details> element.

Let's add a <details> tag and its <summary> child tag to the <header> section of the sports car content. Let's have it contain a pop-up widget labeled *Click Here for the List of Our Featured Articles!*. When the user clicks it, a list of the two <article> elements appear, as specified in the following HTML5 markup example:

```
<!DOCTYPE html><html>
<head><title>Exotic and Domestic Cars Today</title></head>
<body>
 <main>
  <header>
   <h1>Exotic Cars Magazine: Current Exotic Car Articles</h1>
    <p>Top Level Keywords Relating to Exotic Cars from Every Nation</p>
    <details>
     <summary>Click Here For the List of Our Featured Articles!</summary>
     <p>Exotic European Cars: Maintaining the Lead Over US Manufacturers</p>
     <p>Exotic American Cars: Gaining on the Domination of European Cars</p>
    </details>
  </header>
  <nav>
   <a http://www.web-address.com/car-info.html>CAR INFO</a>
   <a http://www.web-address.com/our-team.html>OUR TEAM</a>
   <a http://www.web-address.com/buy-cars.html>BUY CARS</a>
  </nav>
  <article>
   <h2>Exotic European Cars: Maintaining the Lead Over US Manufacturers</h2>
    <p>Next Level Keywords Relating to Exotic Cars from European Union</p>
   <h3>Exotic European Sports Car Round-Up</h3>
    <p>Next Level Keywords Relating to Exotic European Sports Cars</p>
```

```
 <aside>
  <h4>Sidebar: Top Selling European Sports Cars</h4>
   <p>Next Level Keywords Relating to Top Selling European Sports Cars</p>
 </aside>
</article>
<article>
 <h2>Exotic American Cars: Gaining on the Domination of European Cars</h2>
   <p>Next Level Keywords Relating to Domestic Cars from North America</p>
 <h3>Exotic American Sports Car Round-Up</h3>
   <p>Next Level Keywords Relating to Exotic North American Sports Cars</p>
<figure>
 <img src="sport-car-image.png" alt="sports car image related keywords">
 <figcaption>Figure 1. Image of Popular American Sports Car</figcaption>
</figure>
</article>
<footer>
 <h5>Exotic Car Article Article, Contact and Sources:</h1>
   <p>Blog's Author: Wallace Jackson</p>
   <p>Blog's Source: Magazine or Book Resources and Links would go here</p>
</footer>
 </main>
</body></html>
```

Next, let's take a look at the final two semantic tags, <mark> and <time>. If other legacy tags have been upgraded with new semantic features or functions, I'll cover those additions in future chapters.

The MARK and TIME Tags: Adding More Information

The **<mark>** tag highlights important text. The **<time>** tag defines human-readable time values. In Firefox the <mark> tag applies a **yellow tint** (Magic Marker effect) to the text enclosed inside the <mark> and </mark> tags. These tags could be used in our car example, as follows:

```
<!DOCTYPE html><html>
<head><title>Exotic and Domestic Cars Today</title></head>
<body>
 <main>
  <header>
   <h1>Exotic Cars Magazine: Current Exotic Car Articles</h1>
    <p>Top Level Keywords Related to <mark>Exotic Cars</mark> worldwide</p>
    <details>
     <summary>List of Our Articles Released at <time>10:00</time></summary>
     <p>Exotic European Cars: Maintaining the Lead Over US Manufacturers</p>
     <p>Exotic American Cars: Gaining on the Domination of European Cars</p>
    </details>
   </header>
   <nav>
```

85

```
    <a http://www.web-address.com/car-info.html>CAR INFO</a>
    <a http://www.web-address.com/our-team.html>OUR TEAM</a>
    <a http://www.web-address.com/buy-cars.html>BUY CARS</a>
   </nav>
   <article>
   <h2>Exotic European Cars: Maintaining the Lead Over US Manufacturers</h2>
    <p>Next Level Keywords Relating to Exotic Cars from European Union</p>
   <h3>Exotic European Sports Car Round-Up</h3>
    <p>Next Level Keywords Relating to Exotic European Sports Cars</p>
   <aside>
    <h4>Sidebar: Top Selling European Sports Cars</h4>
     <p>Next Level Keywords Relating to Top Selling European Sports Cars</p>
   </aside>
   </article>
   <article>
   <h2>Exotic American Cars: Gaining on the Domination of European Cars</h2>
    <p>Next Level Keywords Relating to Domestic Cars from North America</p>
   <h3>Exotic American Sports Car Round-Up</h3>
    <p>Next Level Keywords Relating to Exotic North American Sports Cars</p>
   <figure>
   <img src="sport-car-image.png" alt="sports car image related keywords">
   <figcaption>Figure 1. Image of Popular American Sports Car</figcaption>
   </figure>
   </article>
   <footer>
   <h5>Exotic Car Article Article, Contact and Sources:</h1>
    <p>Blog's Author: Wallace Jackson</p>
    <p>Blog's Source: Magazine or Book Resources and Links would go here</p>
   </footer>
  </main>
 </body>
</html>
```

At this point, you should go back and look at the diagram shown in Figure 10-1, which visualizes some of the semantic tags used in the examples in this chapter.

Summary

In this chapter, you learned about the new **semantic tag support** recently added to HTML5, including the <main>, <nav>, <header>, <footer>, <article>, <section>, <aside>, <figure>, <figcaption>, <details>, <summary>, <mark>, and <time> tags. In the next chapter, you look at the HTML5 tags that support publishing text-based content within your HTML5 documents and applications.

■ ■ ■

HTML5 Formatting: Publish Text-Based Content

Next, let's cover **text publishing** tags in HTML5, which allow developers to control text-based content with styling, superscript and subscript, line and word breaks, quotations, abbreviations, citations, and the like. These text-related tags allow you to define document content without having to use **stylesheets** for styling purposes.

In this chapter, I go over the key tags to implement text-based content in HTML. The paragraph <p> tag defines blocks (paragraphs) of text; it was already covered in the book. The other text-related tags in this chapter include those for **formatting** text, **styling** text, **breaking** (separating and spacing) text, **sizing** text, text **direction**, **quotations**, **citations**, and **special** types of text **circumstances**.

Create HTML5 Text Content for Publishing

This chapter covers the text-related tags in HTML5 used for creating text content for publishing in documents, websites, or applications. Most were supported in legacy versions of HTML. A couple of the tags are new in HTML5; I'll point these out.

These text tags are child tags of the semantic tags covered in Chapter 10. Your text-based content is encapsulated (wrapped) in standardized semantic containers, so that search engine robots (indexing and ranking algorithms) can optimally implement **Web 3.0** and the future of the Internet—**semantic search**.

Table 11-1 shows tags for creating, formatting, styling, and publishing text-based content. They are categorized into seven logical areas: text formatting, text styling, text breaking (separating, spacing), text sizing, text direction, text quotation, text captions (titles), and tags for special circumstances.

Table 11-1. *Twenty HTML and HTML5 Text Content Publishing Tags*

Text Content Tags	Text Content Tag Standard Usage
p	Specifies a **paragraph** of text content
pre	Specifies **pre-formatted** text content
abbr	Specifies an **abbreviation**
b	Specifies the **bold** style for the text content
i	Specifies the **italics** style for the text content
u	Specifies the **underline** style for the text content
br	Specifies a **line break** (new line, carriage return)
wbr	Specifies a **word break opportunity** for long words
small	Specifies a **small text** style for that text content
sub	Specifies **subscript** text style for text content
sup	Specifies **superscript** text style for text content
bdi	Specifies **bidirectional isolation** for text content
bdo	Specifies **bidirectional override** on text direction
q	Specifies a **short quotation** for the document
blockquote	Specifies a **long (block) quotation** for document
cite	Defines a **title (citation)** for a published work
data	Specifies **human-readable** and **machine-readable data**
s	Specifies text that is **no longer accurate/relevant**
del	Specifies text content which has been **deleted**
ins	Specifies text content which has been **inserted**

Let's go over each of these content publishing tags—one logical section at a time.

HTML5 Text Formatting: Paragraph, Pre, and Abbr

The first three tags tell the rendering engine how to **format** the text: as a block or paragraph of text; as a pre-spaced or specially formed arrangement of text; or as abbreviated text with an optional mouse-over definition. These tags are shown in the first section in Table 11-1.

Let's cover the paragraph <p> tag first because it's the most commonly used text-related tag in HTML5 document, website, and application design. Before HTML5, this tag had the **align** parameter, which supports **left**, **right**, **center**, and **justify**.

The align parameter was supported in pre-HTML5 versions, but it is not supported in HTML5. As I've mentioned, the trend in HTML5 and later versions is to use CSS3 to provide element (tags) styling, and for HTML5 tags to focus on the definition of the semantic content.

Let's start a new "publishing text content" example HTML document that uses the semantic and SEO tags you learned to define a header paragraph showing a text paragraph. This is done in the following HTML5 markup:

```
<!DOCTYPE html><html>
<head><title>Publishing Text Content in HTML5 Documents</title></head>
<body>
 <main>
  <header>
   <h1>Publishing Text: Using Text-Related Tags in HTML5</h1>
    <p>This is an example of a paragraph, containing text sentences. It is
       possible to have more than 1 sentence in a paragraph, of course!</p>
  </header>
 </main>
</body>
</html>
```

For legacy HTML markup, you can use an align parameter, as shown in the following HTML 4.01 (and previous versions) markup:

```
<p align="left">This is an example of a paragraph containing 2 sentences.
It is possible to have more than 1 sentence in a paragraph, of course!</p>
```

Let's cover the **preformatted <pre>** tag next, because it's the least commonly used text-related tag in an HTML document, website, and applications design. Before HTML5, this tag used the **width** parameter, which defines a **maximum width** for each line of preformatted text. This tag **maintains the character spacing**, so it doesn't "collapse" multiple space characters into one space.

The width parameter is not supported in HTML5.

Let's use a <pre> tag to create fun, text-based character art in the shape of a pine tree, often popular during the holiday season, as shown in the following HTML5 markup:

```
<!DOCTYPE html><html>
<head><title>Publishing Text Content in HTML5 Documents</title></head>
<body>
 <main>
  <header>
   <h1>Publishing Text: Using Text-Related Tags in HTML5</h1>
    <p>This is an example of a paragraph containing text sentences. It is
       possible to have more than a sentence in a paragraph, of course!</p>
  </header>
  <article>
   <h2>Pre-format Text: Maintaining Precise Character Spacing</h2>
    <p>You can use a PRE Element to implement character art, like this:</p>
    <pre>
```

```
                    88
                   8888
                   8888
                  888888
                 88888888
                8888888888
               888888888888
             8888888888888888
          888888888888888888888
               8888888888
              88888888888888
          888888888888888888888
        8888888888888888888888888888
               888888888888888
              88888888888888888
             888888888888888888888
           8888888888888888888888888
        88888888888888888888888888888888
               8888888888888888888
              8888888888888888888888
            88888888888888888888888888
           8888888888888888888888888888888
         88888888888888888888888888888888888
       8888888888   8888888   88888888888
                  88888
                  88888
                  88888
               88888888888
```
  </pre>
  </article>
 </main>
</body>
</html>

Next, let's take a look at the **abbreviation <abbr>** tag.

Let's use the <abbr> tag to create an abbreviation for the second <article> section in this example. Use the **title** parameter so that the abbreviation is defined in a mouse-over:

```
<!DOCTYPE html><html>
<head><title>Publishing Text Content in HTML5 Documents</title></head>
<body>
 <main>
  <header>
   <h1>Publishing Text: Using Text-Related Tags in HTML5</h1>
    <p>This is an example of a paragraph containing text sentences. It is
        possible to have more than a sentence in a paragraph, of course!</p>
  </header>
```

```
<article>
  <h2>Pre-format Text: Maintaining Precise Character Spacing</h2>
  <p>You can use a PRE Element to implement character art, like this:</p>
  <pre>
              88
             8888
             8888
            888888
           88888888
          8888888888
        8888888888888
      888888888888888888
    88888888888888888888888
          8888888888
        8888888888888
      8888888888888888888888
  88888888888888888888888888888
          88888888888888
        88888888888888888
      88888888888888888888888
    888888888888888888888888888
  888888888888888888888888888888888
          88888888888888888
        888888888888888888888
      888888888888888888888888888
    88888888888888888888888888888
  88888888888888888888888888888888888
  8888888888   8888888    88888888888
             88888
             88888
             88888
          88888888888
  </pre>
</article>
<article>
  <h3>Abbreviated Text: Using the ABBR Tag to Describe this Pine Tree</h3>
    <p>Christmas Tree is also <abbr title="Christmas">XMAS</abbr> Tree!</p>
</article>
</main>
</body></html>
```

Next, let's take a look at **text styling** elements (tags).

HTML5 Text Styling: Bold, Italics, and Underline

The next three tags tell the rendering engine how to **style** the text characters, either as a **bold** block of text, an **italicized** block of text, or as an **underlined** block of text. These HTML tags can also be used in combination with each other. They are shown in the second section of Table 11-1.

Let's cover the bold tag first because it's the most commonly used text-related tag in HTML document, website, or application design. Let's bold the word "paragraph" in the original example by surrounding that word with the **<b>** and **</b>** tags. This is shown in the following HTML markup example (it can also be used in HTML5):

```
<!DOCTYPE html><html>
<head><title>Publishing Text Content in HTML5 Documents</title></head>
<body>
 <main>
  <header>
   <h1>Publishing Text: Using Text-Related Tags in HTML5</h1>
    <p>This is an example of a <b>paragraph</b> containing text sentences.
       It's possible to have more than 1 sentence in a paragraph.</p>
  </header>
 </main>
</body>
</html>
```

To bold an entire block of text within the sentence, you include additional words inside your starting and ending tags:

```
<p align=left>An <b>example of a paragraph</b> containing text sentences.
              It's possible to have more than 1 sentence in a paragraph.</p>
```

▓ **Note**   From the W3C website (www.w3schools.com/tags/tag_b.asp): "According to the HTML 5 specification, this <b> tag should be used as a **last** resort, when no other tag is more appropriate. The HTML 5 specification states that headings should be denoted with the <h1> to <h6> tags, emphasized text should be denoted using the <em> tag, important text should be denoted with a <strong> tag, and marked/highlighted text should use a <mark> tag."

Now let's discuss the **italics <i>** tag and italicize the word "possible" in the original example by surrounding it with the **<i>** and **</i>** tags. This is shown in the following HTML5 markup (it can also be used in previous versions of HTML (2.0, 3.2, and 4.01)):

```
<!DOCTYPE html><html>
<head><title>Publishing Text Content in HTML5 Documents</title></head>
<body>
 <main>
```

```
<header>
 <h1>Publishing Text: Using Text-Related Tags in HTML5</h1>
  <p>This is an example of a <b>paragraph</b> containing text sentences.
   It's <i>possible</i> to have more than 1 sentence in a paragraph.</p>
 </header>
</main></body></html>
```

To italicize an entire block of text within a sentence, you should include more words inside of the starting and ending tags, as I have done here, around the "text sentences" text:

```
<p>An <b>example of a paragraph</b> containing <i>text sentences</i>.
  It's <i>possible</i> to have more than 1 sentence in a paragraph.</p>
```

Let's cover the **underline <u>** tag next, since it is the least commonly used text-related tag in HTML5 documents. The reason for this is because the anchor <a> tag (link) default is an underlined link, and therefore, using the <u> tag to underline text is likely to confuse users into thinking that that text represents a link. When a user clicks underlined text and nothing happens, it looks as if there is a coding (markup) error. Therefore, convention is not to use the underline tag unless it is absolutely necessary.

Let's underline the word "possible" in the original example by surrounding that word with the **<u>** and **</u>** tags. It looks like following HTML5 markup (it can also be used in previous versions of HTML):

```
<!DOCTYPE html><html>
<head><title>Publishing Text Content in HTML5 Documents</title></head>
<body>
 <main>
  <header>
   <h1>Publishing Text: Using Text-Related Tags in HTML5</h1>
    <p>An example of a <b>paragraph</b> containing <i>text sentences.</i>
     It's possible to have <u>more than 1 sentence</u> in a paragraph.</p>
   </header>
 </main></body></html>
```

Let's cover the **line break** and **word break** tags next.

HTML5 Break Tags: Line Break and Word Break

The next two tags tell the rendering engine how to **break** the text apart, either using a new-line and carriage return to create a **line break**, or by using a hyphen to break a long word across lines, which is called a **word break**. The line break uses the **
** tag, and the word break uses the **<wbr>** tag. These HTML tags can also be used in combination with each other. They are shown in the third section of Table 11-1.

Let's cover the word break tag first, as most developers do not know about it, and it is very simple to use and very useful for making sure that long words are broken across lines in a way that is completely controlled by a text content developer. Let's break the with <wbr>.

To do this, break up the longest word in the dictionary by using the **<wbr>** tag in the places that we want a rendering engine (browser and OS) to separate it across lines if it becomes necessary, as shown in the following HTML5 markup:

```
<!DOCTYPE html><html>
<head><title>Publishing Text Content in HTML5 Documents</title></head>
<body>
 <main>
  <header>
   <h1>Breaking Text Apart: Using Text-Related Tags in HTML5</h1>
    <p>This is an example of a word which is really long using word break:
    Pneumono<wbr>ultramicroscopic<wbr>silico<wbr>volcano<wbr>coniosis</p>
  </header>
 </main>
</body>
</html>
```

Now let's talk about the **line break
** tag next; it's one of the most commonly used text-related tags in HTML5 document, website, and application design. This tag is sometimes called the "break" tag because it uses <br> and not <lbr>.

Let's insert line breaks (new lines and line spacing) by using the **
** tag. The following HTML5 markup shows an example of this (it can also be used in previous versions of HTML):

```
<!DOCTYPE html><html>
<head><title>Publishing Text Content in HTML5 Documents</title></head>
<body>
 <main>
  <header>
   <h1>Breaking Text Apart: Using Text-Related Tags in HTML5</h1>
    <p>This is an example of using the line break tag to break apart<br>
    a paragraph containing text sentences<br>
    without using multiple paragraph tags.<br><br>
    It is possible to put line spacing between your sentences<br>
    and still use only one single paragraph.</p>
  </header>
 </main>
</body>
</html>
```

To add a carriage return and a new line, just as you can do with a manual typewriter, you would use a single <br> tag. To add a space between sentences (or paragraphs), add two <br> tags in succession, like this:

. This adds a space between your sentences shown. To widen this space, you can use three (or more) break tags, like this:

. The more break tags you add, the wider the space between sentences, paragraphs, or text blocks. Next, let's talk about **text sizing** elements (tags).

HTML5 Text Size: Small, Superscript, and Subscript

The next three tags tell the rendering engine how to **size** text characters: as a **small** character, a **superscript** raised small character, or a **subscript** lowered small character. These HTML tags are seen in the fourth section of Table 11-1.

Let's start with the **<small>** tag because it tells the HTML5 rendering engine to reduce the font size of your text. Let's reduce the size of the words "small text" in one of the sentences in the original example by surrounding those words with the **<small>** and **</small>** tags. This should look like this following HTML markup, which can also be used in HTML5:

```
<!DOCTYPE html><html>
<head><title>Publishing Text Content in HTML5 Documents</title></head>
<body>
 <main>
  <header>
   <h1>Publishing Small Text: Using Text-Related Tags in HTML5</h1>
   <p>An example of <small>small text</small> contained in a sentence.</p>
  </header>
 </main>
</body>
</html>
```

Let's cover the **superscript <sup>** tag next, since it is used for footnote references and math (power) representation. It is the second most commonly used size-related tag in HTML5.

Superscript text appears halfway above a normal line; it is usually rendered in the same font size used with the <small> tag.

Let's superscript the mathematical representation of ten squared, or ten to the second power. This is accomplished by surrounding the 2 with the **^{** and **}** tags. The following HTML5 markup shows an example of this (it can also be used in previous versions of HTML):

```
<!DOCTYPE html><html>
<head><title>Publishing Text Content in HTML5 Documents</title></head>
<body>
 <main>
  <header>
   <h1>Publishing Small Text: Using Text-Related Tags in HTML5</h1>
    <p>Here is an example of a subscript footer footnote representation:
    Ten Squared Equals One Hundred: 10<sup>2</sup> = 100</p>
  </header>
 </main>
</body>
</html>
```

Let's cover the **subscript <sub>** tag next since it is used for footnote references; it is the second-most commonly used size-related element (tag).

Subscript text appears halfway below the font baseline. It is usually rendered in the same font size used with the <small> tag.

Let's subscript the footnote reference for an article by adding a subscripted [1]. This is accomplished by surrounding the [1] reference with the **_{** and **}** tags. The following HTML5 markup is an example of this (it can also be used in all previous versions of HTML):

```
<!DOCTYPE html><html>
<head><title>Publishing Text Content in HTML5 Documents</title></head>
<body>
 <main>
  <article>
   <h1>Publishing Small Text: Using Text-Related Tags in HTML5</h1>
    <p>Here is the example of your subscript footnote referencing:
       Further Research Material<sub>[1]</sub> is in the Footer.</p>
  </article>
 </main>
</body>
</html>
```

Let's cover **text direction** tags next. Text direction was recently added to HTML 4 (and Android 4.2) to support languages that write from the right side of the screen toward the left side of the screen.

HTML5 Text Direction: The Bidirectional Text Tags

The next two tags tell the rendering engine which **direction** to render the text characters in by either using the **ltr** or **left-to-right** paradigm or the **rtl** or **right-to-left** paradigm. The Android OS added support for ltr vs. rtl rendering in version 4.2. Directional text HTML tags are listed in in the fifth section of Table 11-1; they include the **bidirectional isolation** **<bdi>** and the **bidirectional override <bdo>** tags.

Let's start with the **<bdi>** tag, which tells the HTML5 rendering engine to isolate (or to not apply the current text direction specified in your document) any text inside of the <bdi> and </bdi> tags.

Let's isolate the text direction for the words "isolated text" in a sentence in the original example by surrounding those words with **<bdi>** and **</bdi>** tags. An example of this is shown in the following HTML 4.01 markup (it can also be used in HTML5):

```
<!DOCTYPE html><html>
<head><title>Publishing Text Content in HTML5 Documents</title></head>
<body>
 <main>
  <header>
   <h1>Publishing Directional Text: Using Text-Related Tags in HTML5</h1>
    <p>An example of <bdi>isolated text</bdi> contained in a sentence.</p>
  </header>
 </main>
</body>
</html>
```

Let's cover the HTML 4 **bidirectional override <bdo>** tag next; it specifically defines the direction of a word, sentence, or block of text. It uses the required direction **dir** parameter, which takes either an **rtl** or an **ltr** data value.

Let's override the default left to right text direction and use the <bdo> tag to make some of the text go right to left by using the dir parameter. This is accomplished by surrounding the words "right to left" with the **<bdo>** and **</bdo>** tags in conjunction with the **dir="rtl"** parameter in the opening <bdo> tag. The following HTML5 markup shows an example of this (it can also be utilized in HTML 4.01):

```
<!DOCTYPE html><html>
<head><title>Publishing Text Content in HTML5 Documents</title></head>
<body>
 <main>
  <header>
   <h1>Publishing Directional Text: Using Text-Related Tags in HTML5</h1>
    <p>Here is the example of the default left to right text direction.</p>
    <p>Override this to create <bdo dir="rtl">right to left</bdo>text.</p>
  </header>
 </main>
</body>
</html>
```

Let's cover the **text quotation** tags supported in HTML5.

HTML5 Text Quotes: Quote and Block Quote Tags

The next two tags tell the rendering engine to render the text characters in a quotation format, using a **quote <q>** tag or a **block quote <blockquote>** tag. These HTML tags are seen in the sixth section of Table 11-1.

Let's start with the **<q>** tag, which tells the HTML5 rendering engine that your text is a quotation.

It is interesting to note that you **do not have to supply the quotation marks** when you utilize this tag. The following markup is an example of this (it can also be used in HTML5):

```
<!DOCTYPE html><html>
<head><title>Publishing Text Content in HTML5 Documents</title></head>
<body>
 <main>
  <header>
   <h1>Publishing Quoted Text: Using Text-Related Tags in HTML5</h1>
    <p>An example of a text quotation contained within a paragraph of text.
    <q>This is a quotation from the Author of HTML5 Quick Markup.</q></p>
  </header>
 </main>
</body>
</html>
```

97

There is also a **cite** parameter, if you want to reference the source of a quote using a **URL**. The following is an example of this:

```
<q cite="http://www.wallacejackson.com>
This is a sample quotation from the Author of HTML5 Quick Markup Reference.
</q>
```

Let's talk about the **block quote <blockquote>** tag next, since it is used for longer quotations, which are taken from and reference another source. In HTML5, the <blockquote> tag always specifies a section quoted from another source. HTML5 browsers usually **indent** a <blockquote> element.

This distinction does not exist in HTML 4.01 and earlier, where the <blockquote> simply signifies a quote as a block of text and does not have to represent something from an externally referenced work. This is shown in the following HTML5 markup (it can also be used in previous versions of HTML):

```
<!DOCTYPE html><html>
<head><title>Publishing Text Content in HTML5 Documents</title></head>
<body>
 <main>
  <article>
   <h1>Publishing Quoted Text: Using Text-Related Tags in HTML5</h1>
    <p>Here is an example of a block quote representation in a paragraph:
       <blockquote cite="http://www.apress.com/9781484218624">
       This compact quick scripting syntax reference on JSON covers
       syntax and parameters central to JSON object definitions, using
       the NetBeans 8.1 open source and Eclipse IDE software tool packages.
       </blockquote>
    </p>
  </article>
 </main>
</body>
</html>
```

Let's cover **text citation** tags supported in HTML5 next.

HTML5 Text Citations: The CITE Tag

The **cite** tag tells the rendering engine the **title** of the text. This HTML tag is in the sixth section of Table 11-1. The cite tag tells the HTML5 rendering engine to apply a title citation for an intellectual property work to any text inside the <cite> and </cite> tags. The IP owner's name is not the title of the work. Let's add a title citation to our HTML5 example by surrounding a title with a **<cite>** and **</cite>** tag structure. This is shown in the following HTML markup:

```
<!DOCTYPE html><html>
<head><title>Publishing Text Content in HTML5 Documents</title></head>
```

```
<body>
 <main>
  <header>
   <h1>Publishing Citation Text: Using Text-Related Tags in HTML5</h1>
   <p>I wrote <cite>JSON Quick Syntax Reference</cite> during 2016.</p>
  </header>
 </main>
</body>
</html>
```

Finally, let's discuss **text special circumstance** tags, which are supported by HTML5. These are seen in the seventh section of Table 11-1.

HTML5 Special Circumstances Text: Other Tags

The last four tags tell the rendering engine about **outdated**, **inaccurate**, **deleted**, or **inserted** text, and allow you to represent **data** using its native format.

Let's start with the **<data>** tag, which provides **machine-readable** data. It is useful in cases where data needs to be in a certain format to be processed using JavaScript, but it does not format well for human-readable applications; that is, it does not have that format that you prefer your users experience (read).

As a simple example, you prefer to present numbers to your users using text (i.e., one, two, three), but you also need to have JavaScript code that sorts the numbers to organize the data. JavaScript requires that the numbers be provided as numerals (1, 2, 3) to enable this sorting.

A <data> tag enables you to solve this problem by providing two different data representations. Text numbers are provided inside <data> and </data> tags; whereas integers for the JavaScript code are provided as a value parameter. The following HTML markup shows an example of this (it can also be used in HTML5):

```
<!DOCTYPE html><html>
<head><title>Publishing Text Content in HTML5 Documents</title></head>
<body>
 <main>
  <article>
   <h1>Publishing Special Circumstances Text: Using Text-Related Tags</h1>
   <p>An example of <data> tags contained in a paragraph. Numbers Include:
    <data value="1">One</data>
    <data value="2">Two</data>
    <data value="3">Three</data>
   </p>
  </article>
 </main>
</body></html>
```

Next, let's discuss the <s> tag, which was deprecated in HTML 4.01 and originally used to define **strike-through** text (in case you were wondering what the "s" stood for). As such, the default CSS3 definition for this element should look like this example:

```
s { text-decoration: line-through; }
```

Again, CSS3 is not the focus of this book, only HTML5 markup syntax. The <s> element is **redefined** in HTML5; it is now used to define text that is **no longer correct, accurate, or relevant**. This <s> tag should not be used to define replaced or deleted text, because the <del> tag defines replaced or deleted text. (I cover this tag next.) Here is the <s> tag used to update my Android apps book, using HTML5 markup:

```
<!DOCTYPE html><html>
<head><title>Publishing Text Content in HTML5 Documents</title></head>
<body>
 <main>
  <header>
  <h1>Publishing Deprecated Text: Using Text-Related Tags in HTML5</h1>
  <p>I wrote <s>Android Apps for Absolute Beginners 1st Ed.</s> in 2010.</p>
  <p>I wrote <b>Android Apps for Absolute Beginners 4th Ed.</b> in 2017.</p>
  </header>
 </main>
</body></html>
```

Next, let's look at the **delete <del>** tag used for text that has been deleted and replaced using the insert <ins> tag. Use <del> and <ins> for document updates or modifications.

HTML5 browsers normally draw a line through deleted text and underline inserted text. We cover the <ins> tag here because it's used with the delete tag and provides the exact opposite function. Here are the <del> and <ins> tags, which were used to update my *Android Apps for Absolute Beginners* (Apress, 2014) book:

```
<!DOCTYPE html><html>
<head><title>Publishing Text Content in HTML5 Documents</title></head>
<body>
 <main>
  <header>
  <h1>Publishing Deprecated Text: Using Text-Related Tags in HTML5</h1>
   <p>I wrote <del>Android Apps for Absolute Beginners 3rd Ed. (2014)</del>
            <ins>Android Apps for Absolute Beginners 4th Ed. (2017)</ins>
      for Apress, an imprint of International Publisher Springer.</p>
  </header>
 </main>
</body></html>
```

Let's save the phrase tags for the next chapter; after that, you'll be ready to get into lists, forms, and tables.

Summary

In this chapter, you looked at **20** text publishing tags supported in HTML5 and previous versions, including tags for **formatting** text, tags for **styling** text, tags for **breaking** (separating and spacing) text, tags for **sizing** text, tags for text **direction**, text for **quotations**, text for **citations** and tags for **special** types of text **circumstances**. In the next chapter, you look at the **phrase tags**, which support the publishing of non-standard text-based content inside of HTML5 documents, websites, and applications.

■ ■ ■

HTML5 Phrase Tags: Using Non-Standard Text

Now let's go over **phrase** tags in HTML5, which allow developers to actually control the browser's assimilation and classification of the text-based content by using styling, defining, hinting, formatting, Teletype and keyboard input, computer coding, variables, and the like. These more specialized text-related tags allow HTML5 developers to define their document content without having to resort to using **stylesheets** for styling purposes, or JavaScript, for coding-related activities.

In this chapter, you look at phrase tags for implementing non-standard text-based content in HTML5. These include the strong **<strong>** tag (like bold), the emphasis **<em>** tag (like italics), the code **<code>** tag, variable **<var>** tag and sample **<samp>** tag for **coding** related text, the definition **<dfn>** tag for **term definition**, a keyboard **<kbd>** tag for **keyboard data entry**, and the Teletype **<tt>** tag, for **Teletype data entry**.

HTML5 Phrase Tags: Special Text Content

This chapter covers the text-related "phrase tags" supported in HTML5. They are used to create non-standard types of text content for publishing in documents, websites, or applications. Most of them were supported in legacy versions of HTML. The <em> and <strong> tags have updated semantic definitions in HTML5; I point this out where applicable. These tags are also used as child tags of the semantic tags covered in Chapter 10 and the text publishing tags covered in Chapter 11. Phrase content is encapsulated (wrapped) in standardized semantic and text containers, so that the search engine robots (index and rank algorithms) can properly implement **Web 3.0 Semantic Search**.

© Wallace Jackson 2016
W. Jackson, *HTML5 Quick Markup Reference*, DOI 10.1007/978-1-4302-6536-8_12

Table 12-1 shows eight phrase tags that can be used for defining, styling, input, and coding.

Table 12-1. *Eight HTML Text Content Publishing "Phrase Tags"*

Text Phrase Tags	Text Phrase Tag Usage
dfn	Defines the **defining instance** for a term
strong	Defines an **important** term or statement
em	Defines an **emphasized** term or statement
kbd	Defines **keyboard** input
tt	Defines **Teletype** input (not supported in HTML5)
code	Defines a computer **code listing** or fragment
samp	Defines a computer **code sample** output
var	Defines a computer **code variable**

Let's take a look at the phrase tags in logical sections just like they are arranged in this table, starting with HTML5 phrase tags for styling <dfn>, <strong>, and <em>. These define important content, in one way or another, to the HTML rendering engine, and for that reason, should also be considered **semantic tags** as well. Each also has its own unique styling.

HTML5 Phrase Styling: Highlighting Important Text

The phrase-styling **<strong>** tag is used much like the bold <b> tag. The **<em>** tag is used much like the italics <i> tag. There is also a more specialized **<dfn>** tag used to semantically define important terms or abbreviations in your document, so that search engines understand the emphasis put on content elements.

The DFN Tag: Definition Terminology for the HTML5 Document

The definition <dfn> tag represents the "defining instance" of a term that you use in an HTML5 document, website, or application. This defining instance is the first usage of that particular term within a given document. The parent for this <dfn> tag needs to contain a definition or explanation of the term defined inside the child <dfn> tag. You can define a <dfn> element without using any parameters, as shown in the following HTML5 markup example:

```
<p>Did you know <dfn>JSON</dfn> stands for: JavaScript Object Notation?</p>
```

The <dfn> tag is also commonly used with the global **title** attribute or parameter, so that when you mouse-over the defined term, you see its definition. The following HTML5 markup shows an example of this:

```
<p>Did you know that <dfn title="JavaScript Object Notation">JSON</dfn>
    stands for: JavaScript Object Notation and can be used with HTML5?</p>
```

The <dfn> tag can also be used as the parent tag of the <abbr> tag, which you saw in Chapter 11, and which some consider to be a phrase tag as well.

In order for the mouse-over function to work properly, you need to make sure that the title attribute or parameter exists inside of the <abbr> tag, which is itself inside of the <dfn> element. This is done using the following HTML5 markup:

```
<p>HOT TIP: <dfn><abbr title="JavaScript Object Notation">JSON</abbr></dfn>
    stands for JavaScript Object Notation and can be utilized with HTML5?</p>
```

It is also possible to add a global **id** attribute to the <dfn> element, so that it could be referenced by using the **href** parameter, or in CSS3 stylesheets and via JavaScript code. This is shown in the following HTML5 markup:

```
<p>Do you know <dfn id="json" title="JavaScript Object Notation">JSON</dfn>
    stands for JavaScript Object Notation, and it can be used with HTML5?</p>
```

Your markup can refer back to the definition by using an <a> tag, if set up as follows whenever the JSON term is used:

```
<p>If you want to learn <a href="#json">JSON</a>, check out Wallace
    Jackson's Apress Title: <q>JSON Quick Syntax Reference (2016).</q></p>
```

Next, let's take a look at a special type of phrase tag called the <strong> tag. This tag is specifically utilized for highlighting important or key information in the document design.

The STRONG Tag: Defining Important Text and Terminology

The <strong> tag is the semantic search version of the bold <b> tag in as much that it not only bolds the text style, but also indicates a greater **importance** or "strength" for the term or phrase that is contained within the <strong> and </strong> tags. This tells a semantic search algorithm what is important, which allows it to do a better job at its attempt at semantic artificial intelligence.

Let's use a <strong> tag to increase my importance as an author. This example should enclose my name in the **<strong>** and **</strong>** tags, as shown in the following HTML5 markup:

```
<p>If you want to learn <a href="#json">JSON</a>, check out <strong>Wallace
    Jackson's</strong> Title: <q>JSON Quick Syntax Reference (2016).</q></p>
```

This should give my name a slight boost in search engine rank, at least versus using the <b> bold tag, because it tells the search engine algorithms that as the content developer, I am assigning an increased level of importance to myself. Some folks inform me that I do this way too much; then I simply cite SEO as my excuse to continue doing so.

The EM Tag: Emphasizing Important Text and Terminology

The <em> tag is the semantic search version of the italics <i> tag, in as much that it not only italicizes the text style, but also indicates a greater **focus** or "emphasis" for the term or phrase contained witihn the <em> and </em> tags. This tells a semantic search algorithm what is emphasized, which allows it to do a better job with the search engine's attempt to implement the semantic artificial intelligence.

Let's use an <em> tag to increase the emphasis on a book title in the previous example. This example encloses the book title in the **<em>** and **</em>** tags. This change from a quotation tag to an emphasis tag is shown in the following HTML5 markup:

```
<p>If you want to learn <a href="#json">JSON</a>, check out <strong>Wallace
    Jackson's</strong> Title: <em>JSON Quick Syntax Reference (2016).</em>
</p>
```

This change serves to change the styling from using quotation marks to delineate the book title to using italics, like this: *JSON Quick Syntax Reference.*

Next, let's look at the phrase tags that simulate keyboard and Teletype data input. The Teletype, or TTY, is an electro-mechanical typewriter that sends and receives typed messages, from point to point and from point to multipoint, over various types of communications channels. It is an early predecessor to the facsimile machine popular today.

HTML5 Phrase Input Tags: Keyboard and Teletype

The next two tags shown in Table 12-1 define phrase text styles, which make it appear as if custom input is being performed. These typically change the text font style in a browser to a font that connotes typing, such as **Courier** or a **monospace** font. It is important to note that these tags do not actually add an ability to take text from an external physical hardware device, but simply make the text used with those tags in your document make it **look** as though that is happening, so these tags are **input styling** rather than the previous **emphasis styling** tags. Let's go over the keyboard <kbd> tag first, because it is still supported in HTML5, and it is the tag you'll want to use to simulate keyboard input in documents.

The KBD Tag: Defining Keyboard Input

The **<kbd>** tag specifies keyboard input (or Teletype input for HTML5, which no longer supports the <tt> tag) in HTML5 documents, websites, and applications. More than one <kbd> tag may be used in a single document. This <kbd> tag uses the following style definition; if you like, you could change this to specify the **Courier** font in an external CSS stylesheet:

```
kbd { font-family: monospace; }
kbd { font-family: Courier; }       // This CSS3 will simulate a typewriter
kbd { font-family: 'Lucida Console'; } // This CSS3 will simulate Teletype
```

Let's use the <kbd> tag to change the book title style to look like a font that is used in coding. An example of this is shown in the following HTML5 markup:

```
<p>If you want to learn <a href="#json">JSON</a>, check out <strong>Wallace
    Jackson's</strong> Title: <kbd>JSON Quick Syntax Reference (2016).</kbd>
</p>
```

Next, let's take a look at the <tt> tag, which should be used in HTML versions earlier than HTML5 to simulate a Teletype machine in an HTML5 document or application.

The TT Tag: Defining Teletype Input

The **<tt>** tag specifies Teletype input for HTML versions prior to HTML5, which no longer supports the <tt> tag. More than one <tt> tag may be used in a single document. This <tt> tag uses the following style definition; if you like, you could change this to specify **Courier** font or a **monospace** font in an external CSS stylesheet:

```
tt { font-family: monospace; }     // This CSS3 will simulate a keyboard!
tt { font-family: Courier;   }     // This CSS3 will simulate a typewriter!
```

Let's use this <tt> tag to change the book title style to look like the font used in Teletypes. An example of this is shown in the following HTML5 markup:

```
<p>If you want to learn <a href="#json">JSON</a>, check out <strong>Wallace
    Jackson's</strong> Title: <tt>JSON Quick Syntax Reference (2016).</tt>
</p>
```

Next, let's look at phrase tags which simulate working with computer code.

HTML5 Phrase Coding Tags: Code and Variables

The final three phrase tags shown in Table 12-1 allow you to style text elements to look like they are computer coding–related content. This is done by using the **code fragment** **<code>**, **sample output <samp>**, and the **code variable <var>** tags.

107

The Code Tag: Code Sample Listings and Code Fragments

The <**code**> tag defines a "code fragment," which is a **snippet** or partial code listing. Usually, the entire code listing is too long, but it is possible to use this phrase tag to style an entire code listing. The CSS3 setting for a <code> tag defaults to using the **monospace** font to style the code text, as shown in the following CSS3 definition (with other coding-related, font-family styling options included):

```
code { font-family: monospace; }     // Default Style for the <code> element
code { font-family: Courier; }        // This CSS will simulate the typewriter
code { font-family: 'Lucida Console'; } // This CSS will simulate a Teletype
```

Let's use the tag to showcase a Java 9 code snippet from my *Pro Java 9 Games Development* (Apress, 2017) book, as shown in the following markup:

```
<p>If you want to learn <a href="#java">JAVA</a>, check out <strong>Wallace
    Jackson's</strong> Title <em>Pro Java 9 Game Development (2017).</em>
    Here is a sample snippet of Java 9 code from this upcoming Java 9 Game
    Development programming title:
    <code>
    legalButton.setOnAction(new EventHandler<ActionEvent>() {
        @Override
        public void handle(ActionEvent event) {
            infoOverlay.getChildren().clear();
            infoOverlay.getChildren().addAll(copyText, riteText);
            infoOverlay.setTranslateY(380);
            infoOverlay.setLineSpacing(-9);
            uiContainer.setBackground(uiBackground3);
            boardGameBackPlate.setImage(transparentlogo);
        }
    });
    </code>
</p>
```

Next, let's take a look at the sample output <samp> tag.

The SAMP Tag: Adding Sample Code Output

The <**samp**> tag is used to define code output, which is the result of running code. The CSS3 setting for a <samp> tag defaults to using the **monospace** font to style the code text, as shown in the following CSS3 definition:

```
samp { font-family: monospace; }     // Default Style for a <samp> element
samp { font-family: Courier; }        // This CSS will simulate a typewriter
samp { font-family: 'Lucida Console'; } // This CSS will simulate a Teletype
```

Let's use this tag to showcase a Hello World code sample, taken from my upcoming *Pro Java 9 Games Development* (Apress, 2017) book, as shown in the following HTML5 markup:

```
<p>If you want to learn <a href="#java">JAVA</a>, check out <strong>Wallace
   Jackson's</strong> Title <em>Pro Java 9 Games Development (2017).</em>
   Here is a sample snippet of Java 9 code output from Chapter 6 in the
   upcoming Pro Java 9 Games Development programming title:
   <samp>
           Hello World!
   </samp>
</p>
```

Next, let's take a look at the **code variable <var>** tag.

The VAR Tag: Adding Code Variables

The <var> tag defines **code variables**, which are the data values within your code. The CSS3 setting for the <var> tag defaults to using the italics to style the code text, as shown in the following CSS3 definition:

```
var { font-style: italic; }    // Default Style for the <var> tag is italic
var { font-style: italic; font-family: monospace; } // italic monospace font
```

The <var> tag is usually nested inside a <code> tag, as variables exist inside code. Let's use the tag to style variables in the <code> tag example in the following markup:

```
<code>legalButton.setOnAction(new EventHandler<ActionEvent>() {
     @Override
     public void handle(ActionEvent event) {
         infoOverlay.getChildren().clear();
         infoOverlay.getChildren().addAll(<var>copyText, riteText</var>);
         infoOverlay.setTranslateY(380);
         infoOverlay.setLineSpacing(-9);
         uiContainer.setBackground(uiBackground3);
         boardGameBackPlate.setImage(transparentlogo);
     }
  });</code>
```

Summary

In this chapter, you learned about the **phrase tag support** in HTML5 and previous versions, including the <dfn>, <em>, <strong>, <kbd>, <tt>, <code>, <var>, and <samp> tags. In the next chapter, you look at the HTML5 **list** tags.

CHAPTER 13

■ ■ ■

HTML5 Lists: Numbered, Bulleted, and Definition Lists

Let's discuss the six **list creation** tags for HTML5 next, which allow developers to create different types of list-based content using a **numbered** (or even a **lettered**) list, a **bulleted** list, or a **definition** list. These more specialized text-related tags allow HTML5 developers to define their document list content with a good deal of flexibility using only a half-dozen tags. These list tags are inherently semantic, as they clearly define lists and order, as well as list descriptions and terms.

In this chapter, you learn about list tags, which implement list-based content in HTML, as all of the tags are supported in HTML 4.01, and some in earlier versions of HTML.

These include a list **<li>** tag, an ordered list **<ol>** tag, the unordered list **<ul>** tag, and the description list **<dl>** tag, description term **<dt>** tag, and the description data **<dd>** tag.

HTML5 List Tags: Ordered Information

This chapter covers the six text-related "list tags" supported in HTML5. They create ordered collections of information, much like an array in JavaScript programming, but styled as a list or **data definition collection**, similar to what you experience with basic JSON definitions, such as the ones covered in *JSON Quick Syntax Reference* (Apress, 2016). All of these tags are supported in legacy versions of HTML; a few of the tags even go all the way back to HTML 2.0, which I'll point out, where applicable. These list tags are optimally used as child tags of the semantic tags covered back in Chapter 10, so that list-based content is encapsulated (wrapped) in standardized semantic containers, so that the search engine robots (the indexing and ranking algorithms) optimally implement **Web 3.0**, which is the future of the Internet: **Semantic Search**. Table 13-1 shows the six list tags supported in HTML5.

© Wallace Jackson 2016
W. Jackson, *HTML5 Quick Markup Reference*, DOI 10.1007/978-1-4302-6536-8_13

Table 13-1. *Six HTML Content Publishing Tags for Creating Lists*

HTML5 List Creation Tags	HTML5 List Creation Tag Usage
li	Defines a **list item**
ol	Defines an **ordered list**
ul	Defines an **unordered list**
dl	Defines a **definition list**
dt	Defines a **definition term**
dd	Defines the **definition data**

Let's take a look at these list creation tags in logical sections, in the same way that they are arranged in this table, starting with "core" HTML5 list tags <li>, <ul>, and <ol>. These define important **content lists** or **collections** to the HTML rendering engines. For this reason, these list tags should also be considered to be classified as **semantic search tags**.

HTML5 Stylized Lists: Ordered and Bulleted Lists

The list tags that go back the farthest in HTML support are the most often used: the list item **<li>** tag, which specifies each item in a list, and its parent **<ul>** or **<ol>** tags, which are used to specify unordered (bulleted) lists, or ordered (numbered/lettered/Roman Numeral) lists. These tags have enough parameters that you can create a wide array of professionally styled lists, without having to resort to any custom CSS3 stylesheet code.

The LI Tag: The Core List Tag Used to Define Each List Item

The **<li>** tag defines each "member" of the list with a starting **<li>** and an ending **</li>** tag around the word, sentence, or text block of the list member. The proper way to use the <li> tag is as a child element of a **<ul>** or **<ol>** parent container, however, browsers are very forgiving in how they render <li> elements, and render them without a parent <ol> or <ul> container. If you use an HTML "validator," to validate your markup, it won't be considered "valid" HTML markup, just so you know. Therefore, I am going to show you the correct way to use <li>.

Let's use a semantic <section> tag to create two section areas of bullets containing types of cars. We'll expand upon the semantic tags example in Chapter 10, and add bulleted lists (using the default unordered list <ul> parent tag). This is accomplished using the following HTML5 markup:

```
<!DOCTYPE html><html>
<head><title>Exotic and Domestic Cars</title></head>
<body>
 <section id="exotic car list">
   <h1>European Exotic Car Brand List</h1>
    <ul>
     <li>Ferrari</li>
```

```
    <li>Lamborghini</li>
    <li>Porsche</li>
    <li>Bugatti</li>
  </ul>
</section>
<section id="domestic car list">
 <h1>American Domestic Car Brand List</h1>
  <ul>
   <li>Cadillac</li>
   <li>Buick</li>
   <li>Jeep</li>
   <li>Lincoln</li>
  </ul>
</section></body></html>
```

Next, let's take a look at how the unordered list <ul> tag allows you to configure the child <li> members that it contains.

The UL Tag: Defining and Styling an Unordered List Container

The **<ul>** tag is used as a parent tag list container to define the list member content using symbols for what are commonly called "bullets." This tag has two parameters that are not supported in HTML5 due to the trend toward using CSS for styling and tag markup for content definition. I include them in Table 13-2 for those of you working on legacy HTML projects.

Table 13-2. *Two HTML Parameters for Creating Unordered Lists*

Unordered List Parameter	Unordered List Parameter Usage
type	Defines **bullet type (disc, circle, square)**
compact	Defines the list to be rendered: **smaller**

Let's look at how you configure the <ul> tag.

Let's use the **type** parameter to change a standard disc bullet to a **square bullet** for the first section's list, and the bullet to use the **hollow bullet** (called a **circle**) for the second section's list. This is accomplished in the following HTML markup (in HTML5 it is accomplished using CSS3):

```
<!DOCTYPE html><html>
<head><title>Exotic and Domestic Cars</title></head>
<body>
 <section id="exotic car list">
  <h1>European Exotic Car Brand List</h1>
   <ul type="square">
    <li>Ferrari</li>
```

```
   <li>Lamborghini</li>
   <li>Porsche</li>
   <li>Bugatti</li>
  </ul>
 </section>
 <section id="domestic car list">
  <h1>American Domestic Car Brand List</h1>
  <ul type="circle">
   <li>Cadillac</li>
   <li>Buick</li>
   <li>Jeep</li>
   <li>Lincoln</li>
  </ul>
 </section>
</body>
</html>
```

Note that most, if not all, of the HTML5 browsers should still respect the type parameter, implementing a correct bullet type even though the parameter is no longer supported in HTML5.

Next let's take a look at ordered list <ol> parent tags.

The OL Tag: Defining and Styling an Ordered List Container

The <ol> tag defines list-based content that is numbered, uses Roman Numerals, or uses alphabetic letter indicators to determine the order of the members in an ordered list. The <ol> tag has four parameters (one of which, **compact**, is no longer supported in HTML5 due to the trend toward using CSS3 for styling and using tag markup solely for content definition). The **type** parameter for the <ol> tag is supported in HTML5, as are the **reversed** and the **start** parameters, which are generally used with a **numeric** ordering type, set using a type parameter. I include these parameters in Table 13-3 for those of you working on legacy HTML markup projects.

Table 13-3. *Four HTML5 Parameters for Creating Ordered Lists*

Ordered List Parameter	Ordered List Parameter Usage
type	Defines **ordering type (1, A, a, I, or i)**
reversed	Defines **numbering direction (backward)**
start	Defines the **start number (for number type)**
compact	Defines the List to be rendered: **smaller**

Let's take a look at how we can configure this <ol> tag, substituting it for the <ul> tag used in a previous example.

To use numbered ordering starting with the number four and counting backward, you can specify the following parameters for the first section's list:

```
<!DOCTYPE html><html>
<head><title>Exotic and Domestic Cars</title></head>
<body>
 <section id="exotic car list">
  <h1>European Exotic Car Brand List</h1>
   <ol type="1" start="4" reversed>
    <li>Ferrari</li>
    <li>Lamborghini</li>
    <li>Porsche</li>
    <li>Bugatti</li>
   </ol>
 </section>
 <section id="domestic car list">
  <h1>American Domestic Car Brand List</h1>
   <ol type="A">
    <li>Cadillac</li>
    <li>Buick</li>
    <li>Jeep</li>
    <li>Lincoln</li>
   </ol>
 </section>
</body>
</html>
```

The second section uses capital letter alphabetic order, signified using the type="A" parameter. To use Roman numerals, use the type="I" parameter setting. It is usually not logical to count backward or starting with arbitrary letters or Roman numerals using these type settings, but it's possible to do so.

Next, let's take a look at HTML5 **description lists**. HTML versions prior to HTML5 defined the **<dl>** tag as a definition list (this was not as semantically relevant).

HTML5 Description Lists: Lists of Terms with Data

The last three tags in Table 13-1 allow you to define a description list. In HTML 4.01, a <dl> was called a "definition list." This list contained a group of terms and definitions. These terms and definitions represented a "many to many" interrelationship, as in one or more terms matched to one or more definitions. This HTML element was therefore misunderstood and subsequently misused, or not used at all. To make matters worse, this definition list was not usable for semantic search.

To fix all the issues with the <dl> tag, HTML5 redefines this tag as a **description list**. The <dl> element represents the associated (related) data list consisting of zero or more name-value pairs or name-value groups.

A **name-value pair** consists of the description term <dt> and its description data <dd> value, which is very similar to a JSON key-value pair. A **name-value group** consists of one or more description terms <dt> elements followed by one or more values in the form of description data <dd> elements.

Within a single description list <dl> element, there cannot be more than one single description term <dt> element for each description term name; that is, there can be no duplicate <dt> elements within a description list <dl> parent container.

Name-value pairs and name-value groups can be terms and definitions, metadata topics and values, questions and answers, or any other pairs or groupings of name-value data.

Those of you familiar with JSON may see the similarities between the key-value pairs used to define JSON data definition structures and object notation structures.

The DL Tag: Defining the Description List Parent Container

The **<dl>** tag defines the topmost level for the description list. The default CSS3 defined for the <dl> tag is shown here for reference purposes only. It keeps the data in the description list spaced very close together with minimal spacing around the description list block of data pairs/groups:

```
dl { display: block;
     margin-top: 1em;
     margin-bottom: 1em;
     margin-left: 0;
     margin-right: 0; }
```

Let's use the <dl> tag along with the <dt> and <dd> tags to define a data array for Italian exotic car brands and models in our content design example section. This example is shown in the following HTML5 markup:

```
<!DOCTYPE html><html>
<head>
 <title>Exotic and Domestic Cars</title>
</head>
<body>
 <section id="exotic car list">
  <h1>Italian Exotic Car Brand Description List</h1>
  <dl>
   <dt>Ferrari</dt><dd>LaFerrari</dd>
   <dt>Bugatti</dt><dd>Chiron</dd>
   <dt>Maserati</dt><dd>GranCabrio</dd>
   <dt>Lamborghini</dt><dd>Gallardo</dd>
  </dl>
 </section>
</body>
</html>
```

Next, let's take a look at the definition term <dt> tag.

The DT Tag: Defining Each Description Term Child Element

The **<dt>** tag defines the description term for each key-value data pair, as you saw in the previous section. Default CSS3 defined for this <dt> tag is shown here (for reference purposes only):

```
dt { display: block; }
```

Next, let's take a look at the definition data <dd> tag.

The DD Tag: Defining Each Description Data Child Element

The <dd> tag holds description data in a description list. Inside of a <dd> tag you can put paragraphs, line breaks, images, links, other lists, and similar text-based content. You can see how the tag is used in the preceding example. The default CSS for the <dd> tag is shown here for reference purposes only:

```
dd { display: block; margin-left: 40px; }
```

Next, let's look at another way to arrange data, in a tabular format, when we look at the HTML **table** tags in the next chapter.

Summary

This chapter described **list tag support** in HTML5 and prior versions, including the <li>, <ul>, <ol>, <dl>, <dt>, and <dd> tags. In the next chapter, you look at the HTML5 tags that support the publishing of table-based content within HTML5 documents and applications.

■ ■ ■

HTML5 Tables: Constructing Data in a Tabular Format

Let's talk about the ten **table creation** tags for HTML5. They allow developers to create different types of table-based content, using a **tabular** format in a **grid-based** layout. These more specialized table-related tags allow HTML5 developers to define their document tabular content with a significant amount of flexibility, using less than a dozen tags. The table tags are inherently **semantic** because they are clearly used to define tables of data collections and information grids.

The chapter explains table tags, which implement tabular content in HTML. All of the tags are supported in HTML5; and also are supported in earlier versions of HTML. They include the table **<table>**, table data **<td>**, table row **<tr>**, column **<col>**, table column group <colgroup>, caption **<caption>**, table body **<tbody>**, table header **<thead>**, table footer **<tfoot>** and table group header **<th>**.

HTML5 Table Tags: Tabular Information

This chapter covers the ten text-related table tags that are supported in HTML5. They create **tabular** collections of information, much like a **grid** in Android or Java programming, but styled as a table, which is like a 2D **data definition collection** (databases use tables as well) similar to what you experience with basic SQL definitions. All of these tags are supported in legacy versions of HTML; a few of the tags even go all the way back to HTML 2.0, and I'll point this out, where applicable. The table tags are optimally used as child tags of the semantic tags covered in Chapter 10, so that your table-based content is encapsulated (or wrapped) into standardized semantic containers. Table data is also semantic; it is assimilated by semantic search, as the table-related tag names describe what the data contained inside of the table tag name represents to the organization of your tabular content!

Because of the conformance to the new **Web 3.0** semantic thrust currently underway in HTML5, table tags have returned from the recent obscurity they were facing. For a while, developers were moving away from using tables and frames toward using other containers and CSS to achieve the same visual results. But used properly, table tags can create tables of interrelated data, much like a database. Table 14-1 shows the ten table tags that are supported in HTML5 as well as in earlier HTML versions.

© Wallace Jackson 2016
W. Jackson, *HTML5 Quick Markup Reference*, DOI 10.1007/978-1-4302-6536-8_14

Table 14-1. *Ten HTML Content Publishing Tags for Table Creation*

HTML Table Creation Tags	HTML Table Creation Tag Usage
table	Defines a **table**
caption	Defines a **table caption**
tr	Defines a **table row**
th	Defines a **table heading cell**
td	Defines a **table data cell**
thead	Defines a **table header**
tbody	Defines a **table body**
tfoot	Defines a **table footer**
col	Defines a **table column**
colgroup	Defines a **table column group**

Let's take a look at the table creation tags in logical sections, in the same way that they're arranged in this table, starting with your core HTML5 table tags <table>, <tbody>, and <caption>. These define important **table characteristics** to the HTML5 rendering engine. For this reason, these list tags could also be classified as semantic search tags, and so it is important that they be implemented correctly by HTML5 content developers.

Top Level HTML Table Creation: Table and Caption

The top-level table tags are used to define the table itself; these include the table **<table>** tag, which is used as the parent container for the table, and its child tags—**<tbody>** and **<caption>**, which are used to specify the primary table data, called **table body** and **table caption**, respectively.

The TABLE Tag: The Core Tag Used to Create the Table Element

A <table> tag defines the HTML table element. At a bare minimum, an HTML table must consist of the <table> element and one or more <tr>, <td>, and <th> elements.

Two <table> element parameters are still supported in HTML5: sortable and border. Eight parameters were replaced by CSS3, but are valid in prior HTML versions. They are all shown in Table 14-2.

Table 14-2. *Ten <table> Parameters Used for Table Configuration*

HTML Table Tag Parameters	HTML Table Tag Parameter Usage
sortable	Defines the **table as sortable**
border	Defines the table as having a **border**
align	Defines **alignment (left, right, center)**
bgcolor	Defines the table **background color**
cellpadding	Defines the **table cell padding value**
cellspacing	Defines the **table cell spacing value**
frame	Defines **outside borders** that are visible
rules	Defines **inside borders** that are visible
summary	Defines the **summary of the table content**
width	Defines the **table width**

As you see later on in this chapter, all of the other table tags are **child tags** of <table>. The <tr> element defines a table row, the <td> element defines each table cell, and the <th> element defines a table header labeling the table columns.

More complex tables would also include <caption>, <col>, <colgroup>, <thead>, <tfoot>, and <tbody> elements, all of which is covered in detail over the course of this chapter.

Let's use the <table> tag to create a table in a section containing popular brands and models of Italian sport cars, and use the two parameters supported in HTML5, border and sortable, to make this table have borders, and be able to be sorted. It's important to note that not all the browsers currently support a sortable parameter. This exotic car table is accomplished using the following HTML5 markup:

```
<!DOCTYPE html><html>
<head><title>Exotic Car Table</title></head>
<body>
 <section id="exotic car table">
  <table border="1" sortable>
   <tr>
    <th>Brand</th>
    <th>Model</th>
   </tr>
   <tr>
    <td>Ferrari</td>
    <td>LaFerrari</td>
   </tr>
   <tr>
    <td>Bugatti</td>
    <td>Chiron</td>
   </tr>
   <tr>
```

```
   <td>Maserati</td>
   <td>GranCabrio</td>
  </tr>
  <tr>
   <td>Lamborghini</td>
   <td>Gallardo</td>
  </tr>
 </table>
 </section>
</body></html>
```

Next, let's take a look at how the table caption <caption> tag allows you to add a caption to the parent Table <table> tag it is contained in.

The CAPTION Tag: Adding a Caption to Your Table

The <**caption**> tag is used as a child tag to define the caption for your table element. The <caption> tag needs to be inserted immediately after the <table> tag. This tag has one align parameter, which is not supported in HTML5 due to the trend toward using CSS for styling and tag markup for content definition.

Let's use the **caption** tag to add a caption to your table example. This is accomplished in the following HTML markup:

```
<!DOCTYPE html><html>
<head><title>Exotic Car Table with Caption</title></head>
<body>
 <section id="exotic car table">
  <table>
   <caption>Exotic Italian Car Manufacturers and Current Models</caption>
    <tr><th>Brand</th><th>Model</th></tr>
    <tr><td>Ferrari</td><td>LaFerrari</td></tr>
    <tr><td>Bugatti</td><td>Chiron</td></tr>
    <tr><td>Maserati</td><td>GranCabrio</td></tr>
    <tr><td>Lamborghini</td><td>Gallardo</td></tr>
  </table>
 </section>
</body></html>
```

Notice that I've also made the table markup more compact in the way I am spacing my tags, with table row constructs each occupying their own line of markup. As long as everything nests properly, spacing makes no difference to the HTML5 parsing engines.

Next, let's look at table content definition child tags.

HTML5 Table Content Definition: TR, TH, and TD

The next three tags in Table 14-1 allow you to define your table rows and their cells. There are five parameters for the <tr> tag, none of which is supported in HTML5. I include them in Table 14-3 for those of you working on legacy projects.

***Table 14-3.** Five Table Row <tr> Parameters Used Prior to HTML5*

HTML Table Tag Parameters	HTML Table Tag Parameter Usage
align	**Alignment (left, right, center, justify)**
bgcolor	Defines the table row **background color**
char	Aligns content to a **table row character**
charoff	Defines the **character alignment offset**
valign	**Vertical alignment (top, middle, bottom)**

A **table row** is kind of like a record in a database, with the table cells serving as data fields inside of a data record. In fact, with tables being sortable and semantic search relating more and more to data, the <table> tag and its children are very well positioned to be used in this fashion in Web 3.0.

As you've seen in the examples thus far, each <tr> element contains one or more <th> or <td> elements.

Since you have already seen how the <tr> element is used, I move on to cover table heading <th>, and table data <td> elements in this section, without using up any space for markup listings. To see these elements in action, simply refer back to the tags that I covered in the previous section.

The TH Tag: Defining the Table Heading Cells in the Table Row

The <**th**> tag defines the **table headings** in a table row. These headings are used to label subsequent rows of data by using headings for each column. An HTML table has two kinds of cells: heading cells, called **header cells**, which contain heading information, and **standard cells**, which contain table data. Standard cells are created by using the <td> element, which is covered in the next section.

The text content used inside these <th> elements are **bolded** and **centered** by default (automatically). The text in your <td> elements, on the other hand, would not be bolded, and should be left-aligned as a default, just like text in most tables and in spreadsheets, that is, data, and not heading text (labels, data field names, etc.).

This is seen in the default CSS3 stylesheet settings for the <th> element, which are shown here to reinforce this:

```
th { display: table-cell;
     vertical-align: inherit;
     font-weight: bold;
     text-align: center; }
```

123

Notice that CSS supports tables implicitly with a table-cell parameter and that the vertical alignment parameter is inherited, from the table row <tr> parent tag (see Table 14-3).

There are six parameters supported for the table heading <th> tag in HTML5, as seen in the top section of Table 14-4. There are nine other parameters that aren't supported in HTML5 but work in earlier versions of HTML. The **sorted** parameter allows you to define the **sort direction** (reversed, number, reversed number, or number reversed) and a **scope** parameter allows you to define your <th> tag's **scope of influence** (row, column, rowgroup, or colgroup).

Table 14-4. *Fifteen <th> Parameters Used for Table Headers*

HTML Table Tag Parameters	HTML Table Tag Parameter Usage
sorted	Defines a **sort direction for that column**
scope	Defines **header scope** (col, row or group)
abbr	Defines a **header abbreviation term**
headers	Defines **header cells** a header relates to
colspan	Defines a **number of columns header spans**
rowspan	Defines a **number of rows a header spans**
align	**Alignment (left, right, center, justify)**
axis	Defines **category names** for header cell
bgcolor	Defines the **header background color**
char	Aligns content to **table header character**
charoff	Defines the **character alignment offset**
height	Defines the **table height**
nowrap	Specify **no wrap flag** for header content
valign	**Vertical alignment (top, middle, bottom)**
width	Defines the **table width**

The **abbr** parameter defines the abbreviation for your header. The **headers** parameter defines the header cells that the <th> tag relates to. This allows you to have more than one level of header information. To use this headers parameter, assign an **id** to your top-level header, and reference it using a headers parameter. Here's an example of this using HTML markup:

```
<tr><th id="namedata" colspan="2">Enter Name Here:</th></tr>
<tr>
    <th headers="namedata">Proper Name:</th>
    <th headers="namedata">Family Name:</th>
</tr>
```

I also show a **colspan** parameter in the previous example, since your Enter Name Here needs to align over your Proper Name and Family Name headings, so it needs to span two columns using a **colspan="2"** parameter value. You can do this same thing using the **rowspan** parameter to have a heading span more than one row.

Next, let's look at complex tables that have different header, footer, and body sections.

Complex Table Definition: THEAD, TBODY, TFOOT

Similar to semantic tags, the <table> parent tag allows you to define a header and a footer for your table, as well as a main body of content. The <thead> element is used in conjunction with the <tbody> and <tfoot> elements, and each of these can specify the various component parts of your table definition; that is, a table header, or **<thead>**; a table body, or **<tbody>**; and a table footer, or **<tfoot>**. This more complex form of table definition uses the tags shown in the third section of Table 14-1.

The THEAD Tag: Defining Each Description Term Child Element

The <thead> tag groups header content in an HTML table. The <thead> element needs to be used in conjunction with the <tbody> and <tfoot> elements so that you are specifying each of the component semantic sections that are in your table. Browsers then leverage these semantic design elements for **asynchronous scrolling**, allowing a table body to independently move while the header and footer information remains locked in place. When printing a large table that spans multiple pages, defining these global table region elements enables a table header and a table footer to be printed at the top and bottom of each page, respectively.

This <thead> tag must always be a child tag of a <table> parent tag and needs to be declared after any <caption> as well as any <colgroup> elements. Additionally a <thead> must be used before the <tbody> or <tfoot> table section containers and used before any <tr> elements.

Default CSS3 defined for this <thead> tag is shown here, for reference purposes only, and, as you can see, the header is centered vertically, and its border color is inherited from its parent container, and it has its own table-header-group CSS3:

```
thead { display: table-header-group;
        vertical-align: middle;
        border-color: inherit;  }
```

None of the table header group parameters are supported in HTML5, but I list them in Table 14-5 for those of you working on legacy HTML markup projects. The parameters are all used for **alignment** and their usage is fairly self-explanatory.

Table 14-5. *Table Head <thead> Parameters Used Prior to HTML5*

HTML THEAD Tag Parameters	HTML THEAD Tag Parameter Usage
align	**Alignment (left, right, center, justify)**
char	Aligns content to a **table row character**
charoff	Defines the **character alignment offset**
valign	**Vertical alignment (top, middle, bottom)**

Next, let's take a look at the table body <tbody> tag.

The TBODY Tag: Defining Each Description Data Child Element

The <tbody> tag holds the main part of your table, and has the same considerations as discussed in the previous section covering thead. This <tbody> tag must always be a child tag of a <table> parent tag, and needs to be declared after any <caption> element, and after any <colgroup> elements and after the <thead> element. Additionally, a <tbody> must be used before the <tfoot> table footer section containers and used before any <tr> elements containing any <th> and <td> elements.

The default CSS for a <tbody> tag is seen as a grouping of table rows, and is middle (vertical center) aligned. This is shown here for reference purposes, because this book does not cover CSS3 quick syntax reference:

```
tbody { display: table-row-group;
        vertical-align: middle;
        border-color: inherit;  }
```

The <tbody> parameters are the same ones shown in Table 14-5, so I will not repeat them again here.

Next, let's morph the initial example in this chapter and use a more complex table version with <thead> and <tbody> to create the same results:

```
<!DOCTYPE html><html>
<head><title>Exotic Car Table with Caption</title></head>
<body>
 <section id="exotic car table">
  <table>
   <caption>Exotic Italian Car Manufacturers and Current Models</caption>
    <thead>
      <tr><th>Brand</th><th>Model</th></tr>
    </thead>
    <tbody>
      <tr><td>Ferrari</td><td>LaFerrari</td></tr>
      <tr><td>Bugatti</td><td>Chiron</td></tr>
```

```
      <tr><td>Maserati</td><td>GranCabrio</td></tr>
      <tr><td>Lamborghini</td><td>Gallardo</td></tr>
    </tbody>
  </table>
 </section>
</body></html>
```

Next, let's take a look at the table footer <tfoot> tag.

The TFOOT Tag: Defining Each Description Data Child Element

The <tfoot> tag holds the footer part of a table. It has the same considerations as discussed in the previous two sections. This <tfoot> tag must always be a child tag of a <table> parent tag, and needs to be declared after any <caption> element, and after any <colgroup> elements and after the <thead> element. Additionally, a <tfoot> must be used **before** the <tbody> table body section container, which is counter-intuitive to what you might assume. I would have assumed that the <tfoot> markup comes after the <tbody> markup. In fact, this is **not** the case, so remember this rule!

Default CSS for a <tfoot> tag looks like the following:

```
tfoot { display: table-footer-group;
        vertical-align: middle;
        border-color: inherit;  }
```

The <tfoot> parameters are the same ones shown in Table 14-5, so, I will not repeat them again here. Remember, they are not supported in HTML5, so only use them in legacy HTML projects and use CSS to implement these features. An HTML5 browser might render these deprecated parameters, so be sure to test your HTML markup across all popular browsers.

Next, let's morph the initial example in this chapter and use a more complex table version using <thead>, <tbody> and <tfoot>, to create an enhanced table result, which has a footer with references. This is done in the following HTML5 markup:

```
<!DOCTYPE html><html>
<head><title>Exotic Car Table with Caption</title></head>
<body>
 <section id="exotic car table">
  <table>
   <caption>Exotic Italian Car Manufacturers and Current Models</caption>
    <thead>
      <tr><th>Brand</th><th>Model</th></tr>
    </thead>
    <tfoot>
     <tr><th>References:</th></tr>
     <tr><td>Sports Car Brands and Models researched using Google</td></tr>
    </tfoot>
```

```
    <tbody>
      <tr><td>Ferrari</td><td>LaFerrari</td></tr>
      <tr><td>Bugatti</td><td>Chiron</td></tr>
      <tr><td>Maserati</td><td>GranCabrio</td></tr>
      <tr><td>Lamborghini</td><td>Gallardo</td></tr>
    </tbody>
  </table>
</section></body></html>
```

Next, let's take a look at **column-related** table tags.

Table Column Definition: COL and COLGROUP

Finally, let's look at a couple of the table tags that allow you to work with table columns. A <col> tag is generally used inside a <colgroup> tag to define column characteristics across an entire column, so that you don't have to do it inside every single <th> or <td> tag. None of the column parameters is supported in HTML5, but I list them in Table 14-6 for all of you working on legacy HTML markup projects.

Table 14-6. *Table Column Parameters Used Prior to HTML5*

HTML THEAD Tag Parameters	HTML THEAD Tag Parameter Usage
align	**Alignment (left, right, center, justify)**
char	Aligns content to a **table row character**
charoff	Defines the **character alignment offset**
width	Defines the **column width**
valign	**Vertical alignment (top, middle, bottom)**

Next, let's add a background color to each column in the example table. We'll use yellow for the car manufacturer column and orange for the car model column. This is accomplished by nesting these two <col> definitions in order and arranged from left to right inside the <colgroup> parent tag, as shown in the following HTML5 markup:

```
<!DOCTYPE html><html>
<head>
  <title>Exotic Car Table with Caption</title>
</head>
<body>
  <section id="bi-colored column exotic car manufacturer and model table">
    <table>
      <caption>Italian Car Manufacturer (Yellow) and Model (Orange)</caption>
      <colgroup>
        <col style="background-color:yellow" />
        <col style="background-color:orange" />
      </colgroup>
```

```
    <thead>
      <tr><th>Manufacturer</th><th>Model</th></tr>
    </thead>
    <tfoot>
     <tr><th>References:</th></tr>
     <tr><td>Sports Car Brands and Models researched using Google</td></tr>
    </tfoot>
    <tbody>
      <tr><td>Ferrari</td><td>LaFerrari</td></tr>
      <tr><td>Bugatti</td><td>Chiron</td></tr>
      <tr><td>Maserati</td><td>GranCabrio</td></tr>
      <tr><td>Lamborghini</td><td>Gallardo</td></tr>
    </tbody>
  </table>
 </section>
</body></html>
```

This puts yellow behind the car manufacturer column and orange behind the car model column. Note that the <colgroup> construct of the child <col> tag definition is after the <caption> tag, and before any <tr>, <thead>, <tfoot>, or <tbody> tags.

Summary

In this chapter, you learned about **table tag support** in HTML5 and earlier HTML versions, including the <table>, <tr>, <th>, <td>, <thead>, <tbody>, <tfoot>, <caption>, <colgroup>, and <col> tags. The next chapter looks at the HTML5 tags that support the publishing of form-based content within HTML5 documents and applications.

CHAPTER 15

■ ■ ■

HTML5 Forms: Creating Forms Using HTML5 Tags

Let's talk about the 13 **form creation** tags for HTML5 next; three are new to HTML5 and ten work in HTML5 and HTML legacy versions. They allow developers to create different types of form-based content, using a **form** container with **data entry (or data input) fields** along with advanced user interface controls in the form, such as buttons and drop-down lists that can make your forms **interactive**. These more specialized form-related tags allow HTML5 developers to define forms for their document with a significant amount of flexibility, using more than a dozen powerful tags. The form tags talk to the server-side processing component in most circumstances, so we are only going to cover the **client-side form design** HTML5 markup component in this process. For server-side processing, make sure to get a book on PHP, JSF, Drupal, Joomla, AJAJ, or AJAX at the Apress website (`www.apress.com`).

In this chapter, you look at forms tags related to implementing forms content in HTML, as all of these tags are supported in HTML5, and many in earlier versions of HTML. These tags include a form **<form>**, label **<label>**, input **<input>**, text area **<textarea>**, field set **<fieldset>**, legend **<legend>,** select **<select>,** options **<option>** and option group **<optgroup>**, button **<button>**, data list **<datalist>**, key generator **<keygen>**, and the output **<output>** tag that allows you to in-line calculations.

HTML5 Form Tags: Interactive Information

This chapter covers the 13 text-related form tags supported in HTML5, which create **interactive forms** to collect information. These are usually designed in a **grid** configuration, or even styled similar to a table. Ten of these tags are supported in legacy versions of HTML, and three of them are new to HTML5. These form tags would also optimally be utilized as child tags of the semantic tags covered in Chapter 10, so that the form-based content is encapsulated (or wrapped) into standardized semantic containers. Form data can also be **semantic**; it can be assimilated using semantic search, as the forms-related tag names describe what a form element defined by that tag does, and therefore what it represents to the content.

Table 15-1 shows 13 form tags supported in HTML5; ten of them are supported in legacy HTML versions.

© Wallace Jackson 2016

W. Jackson, *HTML5 Quick Markup Reference*, DOI 10.1007/978-1-4302-6536-8_15

Table 15-1. *Thirteen HTML Forms Design Content Publishing Tags*

HTML Form Creation Tag	HTML Form Creation Tag's Purpose or Usage
form	Defines a **form**
input	Defines an **input (data field)**
label	Defines an **input (field) label**
textarea	Defines **text area (multi-line input field)**
fieldset	Defines a **fieldset (group of input fields)**
legend	Defines a **legend (label) for a fieldset**
select	Defines a **drop-down list**
option	Defines an **option in drop-down list**
optgroup	Defines an **option group** in drop-down list
button	Defines a **button**
datalist (new in HTML5)	**Pre-defined option list** for input controls
keygen (new in HTML5)	Defines a **key-pair generator field** in form
output (new in HTML5)	Defines **output** (a result of a calculation)

Let's take a look at these form creation tags in logical sections, in the same way that they are arranged in this table, starting with core HTML5 form tags <form>, <label>, and <input>. These define important **form characteristics or components** to an HTML5 rendering engine. For this reason, these form tags should also be considered semantic search tags. As such, it is important these tags are **implemented correctly** for forms.

Basic HTML Form Creation: Form, Label, and Input

The top-level form tags define the form itself include the form **<form>** tag, which is utilized as the **parent container** for the form, and the **<label>** and **<input>** child tags, which specify form labels and data input fields.

The FORM Tag: The Core Tag Used to Create the Form Element

A **<form>** tag defines the HTML form construct, which is used for obtaining **user data input**. An HTML form, at a bare minimum, must consist of this <form> element, as well as one or more of the elements seen in Table 15-1.

Two <form> element parameters were introduced in HTML5, **autocomplete** and **novalidate**, and six HTML parameters are still supported. One is no longer supported, as shown in Table 15-2.

Table 15-2. *Nine <form> Parameters Used for Form Configuration*

HTML5 Form Tag Parameter	HTML5 Form Tag Parameter's Usage
accept (no HTML5 support)	Specifies a **comma-separated list** of **file types** that a server accepts, which is submitted through a file upload process
autocomplete (New in HTML5)	Specifies **autocomplete on or off for form**
novalidate (New in HTML5)	Specifies a form should **not be validated**
accept-charset	Specifies **character encodings** that are specified for use for a form submission
action	Specifies **where to submit the form data**
enctype	Specifies how form data should be **encoded**
method	Specifies **HTTP method** to use (**get** or **post**)
name	Allows you to specify the **form name**
target	Specifies **where to display** the response is received after submitting the form (**_blank**, **_parent**, **_self**, **_top**)

As you see in this chapter, all the other form tags are **child tags** of <form>. The following HTML creates an empty form:

```
<!DOCTYPE html><html>
<head>
 <title>Empty Exotic Car Preference Form</title>
</head>
<body>
 <section id="exotic car preference form">
  <form action="myForm.asp" method="get" autocomplete="on" novalidate>
   <!-- Your Form Design and Child Tags will be nested in here -->
  </form>
  <p>Form data will be sent to a page on the server called "myForm.asp"</p>
 </section>
</body>
</html>
```

This <form> tag defines the **myForm.asp** for the form data submission, defines an **HTTP** "get" method for the server to read the data from the client form, sets the **autocomplete** feature to "on" and sets the **novalidate** feature to "true" by including the novalidate parameter itself inside of the opening <form> tag.

Next, let's take a look at how to use the input <**input**> tag, to get data input from the person filling out your form.

The INPUT Tag: Adding Data Input Fields to the Form

The **<input>** tag is used as a child tag to define DATA input areas for users to enter text. These are commonly called **fields** in forms and in databases. This tag has so many parameters that I am going to include two tables: one has the parameters that are **new to HTML5** and the other has parameters that are not supported in HTML5. There are also those parameters that work in **both HTML5 and legacy HTML** versions. We'll get to parameters after a short example of using two <input> child tags in a parent <form> tag.

Let's use **<input>** tags to ask our users to enter the car manufacturer and model they prefer, as shown in the following markup:

```
<!DOCTYPE html><html>
<head>
  <title>My Exotic Car Preference Form with Two Input Fields</title>
</head>
<body>
 <section id="exotic car preference form">
  <form action="myForm.asp" method="get" autocomplete="on" novalidate>
  Manufacturer: <input type="text" name="manufacturer" value="Ferrari"><br>
  A Model Name: <input type="text" name="model-name" value="LaFerrari"><br>
  </form>
  <p>Please enter favorite exotic car manufacturer and model name above!</p>
 </section>
</body>
</html>
```

Parameters specify **text** input, field **name**, and a **default value**. The autocomplete="on" parameter tells the browser that it is allowed to predict or guess the data value that the user is typing in currently. When a user starts to type in a field, the browser should display options to fill in the field, based on earlier typed values, or on pre-defined input. You see how this pre-defined input is defined a bit later on in the chapter when we cover the **<datalist>** tag, which is used to define a list of data elements. It is used with the **autocomplete** parameter (and function) to greatly enhance the user experience of your form design by giving the appearance of an "artificial intelligence" on the part of the form, which give the users feedback as to what the field in a form is looking for from them.

Table 15-3 lists the 19 new HTML5 <input> tag parameters.

Table 15-3. *HTML5 <input> Parameters Used in Form Configuration*

HTML5 Input Tag Parameter	HTML5 Input Tag Parameter's Usage
autocomplete	Specifies **autocomplete on or off for input**
autofocus	Specifies **autofocus for input on page load**
dirname	Specifies **respect text direction** for input
form	Specifies a **form that the input belongs to**
formaction	Specifies **URL that the form is processed at**
formenctype	Specifies **encoding** (for **submit** or **image**)
formmethod	Specifies **HTTP method** to use (**get** or **post**)
formnovalidate	Specifies input should **not be validated**
formtarget	Specifies **where to display** the response
height	Specifies the **height for the input element**
list	Specifies **datalist containing input options**
max	Specifies a **maximum value for input element**
min	Specifies a **minimum value for input element**
multiple	Specifies **more than one value for an input**
pattern	Specifies the "regular expression" that an <input> element **value is checked against**
placeholder	Specifies a **short hint**, describing expected value to be entered in an <input> element
required	Specifies an **input field as being required**
step	Specifies **legal number intervals for input**
width	Specifies the **width for the input element**

Table 15-4 lists 11 legacy HTML <input> tag parameters.

Table 15-4. *HTML <input> Parameters Used in Form Configuration*

HTML Input Tag Parameter	HTML Input Tag Parameter's Usage
align (Not in HTML5)	Specifies the **alignment of an image** input; only for type="image" (**left, right, top, middle, bottom**)
accept	Specifies the **types of files** that a server accepts; only for type="file" (audio/type, video/type, image/type)
alt	Specifies **alternate text** for images; this is only for type="image"
checked	Specifies **input element pre-selected** after the pageload; this is for type="checkbox" or for type="radio" (radio buttons)
disabled	Specifies <input> element should be **disabled**
maxlength	Specifies **maximum characters in input field**
name	Specifies the **input field (element) name**
readonly	Specifies that **input field is read-only**
size	Specifies **input field width in characters**
src	Specifies a **URL** for an image to use as a submit button; only used for **type="image"**
type	Specifies a **type of input element** to display
value	Specifies the **input element default value**

The **align** parameter isn't supported in HTML5 because it is done with CSS3. These other 11 parameters are supported in both HTML5 and in earlier (legacy) versions of HTML.

Let's add a limit to the number of characters that your user is allowed to use to designate a car brand and model name:

```
<form action="myForm.asp" method="get" autocomplete="on" novalidate>
Manufacturer:
<input type="text" name="manufacturer" value="Ferrari" maxlength="16"><br>
A Model Name:
<input type="text" name="model-name" value="LaFerrari" maxlength="24"><br>
</form>
```

This **maxlength** parameter allows you to control the width for text data fields, so that you can have a compact form design, and limit a user to a reasonable character data length.

Let's add **autofocus** to the first data entry field so the user has their cursor in the correct data field, ready to type:

```
<form action="myForm.asp" method="get" autocomplete="on" novalidate>
  Manufacturer:
  <input type="text" name="manufacturer" value="Ferrari"
         maxlength="16" autofocus><br>
  A Model Name:
  <input type="text" name="model-name" value="LaFerrari" maxlength="24"><br>
</form>
```

Now let's "wire" the input fields to the form they're in by using the **name** attribute inside the <form> tag, and the **form** attribute in the <input> tag, referencing the same characters:

```
<form name="carpreferenceform" action="myForm.asp" method="get"
      autocomplete="on" novalidate>
  Manufacturer:
  <input type="text" name="manufacturer" value="Ferrari"
         maxlength="16" form="carpreferenceform" autofocus><br>
  A Model Name:
  <input type="text" name="model-name" value="LaFerrari"
         maxlength="24" form="carpreferenceform"><br>
</form>
```

Notice that since I have a **method="get"** inside of my <form> tag, that I don't have to use formmethod="get" inside of each <input> tag. For design purposes, I can also define **width** and **height** in pixels for these data fields as well:

```
<form name="carpreferenceform" action="myForm.asp" method="get"
      autocomplete="on" novalidate>
  Manufacturer:
  <input type="text" name="manufacturer" value="Ferrari"   height="24"
         maxlength="16" form="carpreferenceform" autofocus width="128"><br>
  A Model Name:
  <input type="text" name="model-name" value="LaFerrari" height="24"
         maxlength="24" form="carpreferenceform"          width="128"><br>
</form>
```

I'm not going to cover 30 parameters for the <input> element in detail here, because some of these are self-explanatory, some are seldom used, and others are used in conjunction with the server side of the form processing, which is likely a different team member that is specifying what parameters to use!

Next, let's take a look at the **<label>** tag. This allows you to label the <input> elements, especially those that use a **type** parameter, to designate something other than a data field, such as a radio button, GUI button, or check box, for instance.

The LABEL Tag: Fixed Text Label Definitions for Input Elements

Whereas an <input> tag is an **empty tag** and contains no content, only parameters, a <label> tag can contain a **descriptive label**, in between the <label> and </label> opening and closing tags. The <label> tag is specifically used to define a label for a related <input> element. This <label> tag does not render as anything special for the user other than a text label. However, it does provide a **user experience improvement** for touchscreen and mouse users, because if the user touches or clicks text specified using this <label> element, it toggles the input (control) element specified by the **<input type="control-name">**.

There are only two parameters for this <label> tag; the **form** parameter, which you have seen with the <input> tag, which "wires" the <label> to a <form>, and the **for** parameter, which wires the <label> to the <input> itself, using an **id** parameter.

The **for** parameter for the <label> tag should be equal to the id attribute for the related <input> element, to **bind** them together. This is shown in the following HTML5 markup example:

```
<!DOCTYPE html><html>
<head>
  <title>My Exotic Car Preference Form using Six Radio Buttons</title>
</head>
<body>
 <section id="exotic car preference form">
  <form name="carform" action="myForm.asp" method="get" novalidate>
   <label for="ferrari">Ferrari</label>
   <input type="radio" name="cartype" form="carform" id="ferrari"
          value="Ferrari Brand Selected" /><br>
   <label for="maserati">Maserati</label>
   <input type="radio" name="cartype" form="carform" id="maserati"
          value="Maserati Brand Selected" /><br>
   <label for="bugatti">Bugatti</label>
   <input type="radio" name=cartype form="carform" id="bugatti"
          value="Bugatti Brand Selected" /><br>
   <label for="laferrari">Ferrari</label>
   <input type="radio" name="carmodel" form="carform" id="laferrari"
          value="Ferrari La Ferrari Model Selected" /><br>
   <label for="grancabrio">GranCabrio</label>
   <input type="radio" name="carmodel" form="carform" id="grancabrio"
          value="Maserati GranCabrio Model Selected" /><br>
   <label for="chiron">Chiron</label>
   <input type="radio" name=carmodel form="carform" id="chiron"
          value="Bugatti Chiron Model Selected" /><br>
   <input type="submit" value="Please Submit My Choices" form="carform" />
  </form>
  <p>Please select your favorite exotic car manufacturer and model name</p>
 </section>
</body></html>
```

This time we are using **radio buttons** to designate a user selection of their favorite car manufacturer, and favorite car. The radio buttons are grouped by **name**, so that you can't select more than one, and are wired to the form and input described earlier using **form** and **for** parameters respectively. The **value** you provide is what is sent to the server (or e-mail address) when the form is submitted using the **<input type="submit">** tag, which is used for a simple **Submit** button. Complex buttons are covered later in this chapter. Next, let's take a look at larger areas of form data entry such as **text areas** or paragraph text entry and **groups of fields** or field sets.

HTML Form Content Groups: TextArea or FieldSet

The next three tags in Table 15-1 allow you to define large data entry areas for text and collections of data input fields. There are over a dozen parameters for these tags, all of which are supported in HTML5. I include them in Tables 15-5 and 15-6, and try to cover all the key parameters in the examples.

The TEXTAREA Tag: Define a Block or Paragraph of Text Input

The <textarea> tag allows you to define multi-line text input controls. These text area controls can hold an unlimited number of characters, although this is not advised, and text renders using a fixed-width font such as monospace or Courier). The size of the text area should be specified using the **cols** and **rows** parameters, as I have done in the following example markup, where I ask the users for a written description of their favorite car brand and model. I am also using just about every <textarea> tag parameter possible within the example, including autofocus, required, name, form, placeholder, and maxlength.

```
<!DOCTYPE html><html>
<head>
 <title>Exotic Car Preference Written Description Form</title>
</head>
<body>
 <section id="exotic car preference paragraph form">
  <form name="cardescription" action="myForm.asp" method="get" novalidate>
   <textarea rows="5" cols="250" maxlength="1250" required
             name="myfavoritecar" form="cardescription" autofocus
             placeholder="Write a short paragraph on your favorite car">
    Please write a short paragraph on your favorite car and brand in here!
   </textarea>
  </form>
  <p>Please write a short paragraph on your favorite car and brand above</p>
 </section>
</body></html>
```

The dozen parameters for this <textarea> tag is listed in Table 15-5, with the five legacy parameters listed in the first section, and the seven new HTML5 parameters listed in the second section.

Table 15-5. *Twelve HTML5 Parameters for Text Area Configuration*

TextArea Tag Parameter	TextArea Tag Parameter's Usage
cols	Specifies text area **columns (characters)**
rows	Specifies text area **rows (lines)**
name	Specifies the **text area (element) name**
disabled	Specifies text area should be **disabled**
readonly	Specifies that **text area is read-only**
autofocus	Specifies text area **autofocus on page load**
dirname	Specifies please respect **text area direction**
form	Specifies the **form text area belongs to**
maxlength	Specifies **text area maximum character count**
placeholder	Specifies **description of what text is needed**
required	Specifies that text area **completion required**
wrap	Specifies how text area needs to be **wrapped** (options are **hard** or **soft**)

Next, let's look at how to logically group fields and data entry controls together, using the <fieldset> element.

The FIELDSET Tag: Grouping Data Fields and Input Controls

The <fieldset> tag is used to group related form data field and control elements together within a complex form. The <fieldset> tag **draws a box** around related elements to group them visually.

Let's use the radio button control example, and put the car brand selection and car model selection radio buttons into their own logical sections, by using this <fieldset> element.

This should look like the following HTML5 markup:

```
<!DOCTYPE html><html>
<head>
 <title>Exotic Car Preference Form: 6 Radio Buttons in 2 Field Sets</title>
</head><body>
 <section id="exotic car preference form">
  <form name="carform" action="myForm.asp" method="get" novalidate>
   <fieldset name="carbrands" form="carform">
    <label for="ferrari">Ferrari</label>
```

```
<input type="radio" name="cartype" form="carform" id="ferrari"
        value="Ferrari Brand Selected" /><br>
<label for="maserati">Maserati</label>
<input type="radio" name="cartype" form="carform" id="maserati"
        value="Maserati Brand Selected" /><br>
<label for="bugatti">Bugatti</label>
<input type="radio" name=cartype" form="carform" id="bugatti"
        value="Bugatti Brand Selected" /><br>
</fieldset>
<fieldset name="carmodels" form="carform">
<label for="laferrari">Ferrari</label>
<input type="radio" name="carmodel" form="carform" id="laferrari"
        value="Ferrari La Ferrari Model Selected" /><br>
<label for="grancabrio">GranCabrio</label>
<input type="radio" name="carmodel" form="carform" id="grancabrio"
        value="Maserati GranCabrio Model Selected" /><br>
<label for="chiron">Chiron</label>
<input type="radio" name=carmodel" form="carform" id="chiron"
        value="Bugatti Chiron Model Selected" /><br>
</fieldset>
<input type="submit" value="Please Submit My Choices" form="carform" />
</form>
<p>Please select favorite exotic car manufacturer and model name above</p>
</section>
</body></html>
```

Notice that I have wired everything together using the form and name parameters, as well as naming the logical fieldsets. Three HTML5 <fieldset> parameters are listed in Table 15-6.

Table 15-6. *Three <fieldset> Parameters Used Prior to HTML5*

HTML FieldSet Tag Parameter	HTML FieldSet Tag Parameter's Usage
disabled	Specifies text area should be **disabled**
form	Specifies the **form text area belongs to**
name	Specifies the **text area (element) name**

Next, let's take a look at the complex form's **<legend>** element.

The LEGEND Tag: Adding a Legend to the Field Set Groupings

The **<legend>** tag defines a caption for the <fieldset> element. It has one **align** parameter (see Table 15-4) that is no longer supported in HTML5, as you now need to use CSS for this alignment function (although the parameter may still work in some browsers attempting to provide backward compatibility). Align parameter values include **top**, **bottom**, **left**, and **right**.

```
<form name="carform" action="myForm.asp" method="get" novalidate>
 <fieldset name="carbrands" form="carform">
  <legend>Choose Your Favorite Exotic Sports Car Brand:</legend>
   <label for="ferrari">Ferrari</label>
    <input type="radio" name="cartype" form="carform" id="ferrari"
           value="Ferrari Brand Selected" /><br>
   <label for="maserati">Maserati</label>
    <input type="radio" name="cartype" form="carform" id="maserati"
           value="Maserati Brand Selected" /><br>
   <label for="bugatti">Bugatti</label>
    <input type="radio" name=cartype form="carform" id="bugatti"
           value="Bugatti Brand Selected" /><br>
 </fieldset>
 <fieldset name="carmodels" form="carform">
  <legend>Choose Your Favorite Exotic Sports Car Model:</legend>
   <label for="laferrari">Ferrari</label>
    <input type="radio" name="carmodel" form="carform" id="laferrari"
           value="Ferrari La Ferrari Model Selected" /><br>
   <label for="grancabrio">GranCabrio</label>
    <input type="radio" name="carmodel" form="carform" id="grancabrio"
           value="Maserati GranCabrio Model Selected" /><br>
   <label for="chiron">Chiron</label>
    <input type="radio" name=carmodel form="carform" id="chiron"
           value="Bugatti Chiron Model Selected" /><br>
 </fieldset>
    <input type="submit" value="Please Submit My Choices" form="carform" />
</form>
```

Next, let's look at the **option selection** tags for complex forms.

HTML Form Option Selection: Select and Option

HTML5 forms have some fairly complex options for selecting options and option grouping, much like the menus in the application software packages, which makes form design one of the most advanced area in HTML5 publishing, along with new media and interactivity, as you see later on in this book. The third section of Table 15-1 shows tags used to create these **selection sets**, called **drop-down lists**, in HTML5 form design.

The SELECT and OPTION Tags: Defining Drop-Down Lists

The **<select>** element creates **drop-down lists**. The **<option>** tag is used inside of the <select> element to define any **options** you want to make available using this list. These are similar to radio buttons, in that you can only select one member of the list. If you want to select more than one, use a group of check boxes, where multiple data items can be selected.

There are seven parameters supported for a <select> tag, three of these are new in HTML5 and are seen in the top section of Table 15-7. Another four parameters are supported for legacy HTML versions, and are seen in the bottom section of the table.

Table 15-7. *Seven <select> Parameters Used for Selection Lists*

HTML5 Select Tag Parameter	HTML5 Select Tag Parameter's Usage
autofocus	Specifies selector **autofocus on page load**
form	Specifies the **form selector belongs to**
required	Specifies that a **selection is required**
disabled	Specifies the selector should be **disabled**
multiple	Specifies **more than one value for selector**
name	Specifies the **selector name**
size	Defines the **number of selection options**

Let's create a manufacturer and model selection example, that uses the <select> and <option> tags inside of a <fieldset> tag, inside of a <form> tag inside of a semantic <section> tag, instead of using radio buttons to provide a user with a single selection option.

You wire the <select> tag into the <form> tag, using the **name** parameter inside of the <form> tag, and using the **form** parameter inside of each of the <select> tags.

You use the **required** parameter in <select> tags and the **size="4"** parameter to specify the number of options. You should set the **autofocus** parameter in the first <select> so that it is pre-selected for use, and finally use a **name** parameter to give each <select> element a unique identity.

Here's an example of this using HTML5 markup:

```
<!DOCTYPE html><html>
<head>
 <title>Exotic Car Selection Form: 8 List Selections in 2 Field Sets</title>
</head>
<body>
 <section id="exotic car preference form">
  <form name="carform" action="myForm.asp" method="get" novalidate>
   <fieldset name="carbrands" form="carform">
    <select form="carform" required name="brandlist" autofocus size="4">
     <option value="ferrari" label="Ferrari">Enzo Ferrari</option>
     <option value="maserati" label="Maserati">Alfieri Maserati</option>
     <option value="bugatti" label="Bugatti">Ettore Isidoro Bugatti</option>
     <option value="lmbo" label="Lamborghini">Ferruccio Lamborghini</option>
    </select>
   </fieldset>
   <fieldset name="carmodels" form="carform">
    <select form="carform" required name="modellist" size="4">
     <option value="laferrari">LaFerrari</option>
```

143

```
      <option value="grancabrio">GranCabrio</option>
      <option value="chiron">Chiron</option>
      <option value="gallardo">Gallardo</option>
     </select>
   </fieldset>
   <input type="submit" value="Please Submit My Selection" form="carform"/>
   </form>
   <p>Please select favorite exotic car manufacturer and model name above</p>
 </section>
</body></html>
```

Also notice that I am using a **label** attribute to specify a shorter version of an option text value. This shorter version is displayed in the drop-down list. Also note that this is not yet fully implemented in all of the browsers across all of the HTML5 platforms, but it is only a matter of time before it is fully supported as its implementation is quite logical.

Next, let's look at the **option group** or **<optgroup>** tag.

The OPTGROUP Tags: Grouping the Drop-Down List Options

The **<optgroup>** tag **groups related options** in drop-down lists. If you have long lists full of options, then a grouping of related options is easier to digest for your end users. Let's group the car manufacturer list options into a more expensive and less expensive list grouping to see how this <optgroup> tag is used. The HTML5 markup looks like this:

```
<select form="carform" required name="brandlist" autofocus size="4">
 <optgroup label="More Affordable Exotic Cars">
  <option value="ferrari" label="Ferrari">Enzo Ferrari</option>
  <option value="maserati" label="Maserati">Alfieri Maserati</option>
 </optgroup>
 <optgroup label="Less Affordable Exotic Cars">
  <option value="bugatti" label="Bugatti">Ettore Isidoro Bugatti</option>
  <option value="lambo" label="Lamborghini">Ferruccio Lamborghini</option>
 </optgroup>
</select>
```

Next, let's take a look at the **<button>** form design tag.

The BUTTON Tag: Creating User Interface Buttons

The **<button>** tag defines **clickable buttons** for submitting or resetting a form, or for custom purposes. You may place content, such as text or imagery, inside of the <button> elements. This is the primary difference between the <button> element and submit buttons created earlier in the chapter using the <input type="submit"> element.

Be sure to always specify a **type** parameter, using either the **submit, reset,** or **button** value with the <button> elements. It is important to note that different HTML5 browsers use different default types for this <button> element, so you need to "force the issue" by specifying what you want the button to do, and not rely on default values to be set correctly for you!

Eight HTML5 <button> parameters are listed in Table 15-8, along with three legacy HTML parameters.

Table 15-8. *HTML5 <button> Parameters for Button Configuration*

HTML5 Button Tag Parameter	HTML5 Button Tag Parameter's Usage
autofocus	Specifies **autofocus for button on page load**
form	Specifies a **form that the button belongs to**
formaction	Specifies **URL the form is processed at**
formenctype	Specifies **encoding** (for **submit** or **image**)
formmethod	Specifies **HTTP method** to use (**get** or **post**)
formnovalidate	Specifies button should **not be validated**
formtarget	Specifies **where to display** the response
name	Specifies the **button element name**
disabled	Specifies that a **button is disabled** for use
type	Selects **button type (button, reset, submit)**
value	Specifies a **text value for the button label**

Let's replace that <input type="submit"> in the example with **<button type="submit">** and **<button type="reset">** markup:

```
<!DOCTYPE html><html>
<head>
 <title>Exotic Car Selection Form: 8 List Selections in 2 Field Sets</title>
</head><body>
 <section id="exotic car preference form">
  <form name="carform" action="myForm.asp" method="get" novalidate>
   <fieldset name="carbrands" form="carform">
    <select form="carform" required name="brandlist" autofocus size="4">
     <option value="ferrari" label="Ferrari">Enzo Ferrari</option>
     <option value="maserati" label="Maserati">Alfieri Maserati</option>
     <option value="bugatti" label="Bugatti">Ettore Isidoro Bugatti</option>
     <option value="lmbo" label="Lamborghini">Ferruccio Lamborghini</option>
    </select>
   </fieldset>
   <fieldset name="carmodels" form="carform">
    <select form="carform" required name="modellist" size="4">
     <option value="laferrari">LaFerrari</option>
```

```
  <option value="grancabrio">GranCabrio</option>
  <option value="chiron">Chiron</option>
  <option value="gallardo">Gallardo</option>
</select>
</fieldset>
<button type="submit" value="Submit Choices" form="carform" name="B1" />
<button type="reset" value="Reset Choices" form="carform" name="B2" />
</form>
<p>Please select favorite exotic car manufacturer and model name above</p>
</section></body></html>
```

Note that I am using the two pre-defined type values to create two functional buttons, as well as button label values, button names, and a recommended tie-in to the form name using the form parameter. Next, let's take a look at the **new HTML5 form tags**.

New HTML5 Form Tags: DataList, KeyGen, Output

There are three new tags in HTML5 for form design. They allow you to define data lists for auto-complete, generate keys for data security, and output the results of calculations on data.

The DATALIST Tag: Defining Each Description Term Child Elem

The <**datalist**> tag specifies a list of pre-defined options for an <input> element to use via the **list** parameter shown in Table 15-3. The <datalist> tag is for use in providing the auto-complete feature on <input> elements. When a <datalist> is provided, users see a drop-down list of pre-defined options appear once they start to input data. To **bind** the <input> element list parameter together with a <datalist> element, use the **id** parameter in a <datalist> tag, as shown in the following HTML5 markup:

```
<input list="italiancars">
 <datalist id="italiancars">
  <option value="Ferrari">
  <option value="Maserati">
  <option value="Bugatti">
  <option value="Lamborghini">
</datalist>
```

Next, let's take a look at a **Key Generator** <keygen> tag.

The KEYGEN Tag: Defining Each Description Data Child Element

The <**keygen**> tag allows you to specify a **security key-pair generator field**, used for securing form data. When the form is submitted, a private key is stored locally, and a public key is sent to the server.

Here is a sample form and username input that uses this <keygen> tag and a <button> tag to submit the **secure key** to the server, as shown in the following HTML5 markup:

```
<form action="private_keygen.asp" method="get" name="keyform">
 Username: <input type="text" name="user_name">
 Encryption: <keygen name="security_key">
 <button type="submit" value="Submit Secure Key" form="keyform" name="K1"/>
</form>
```

Table 15-9 shows the six HTML5 parameters supported by the <keygen> tag.

Table 15-9. *Six <keygen> Parameters for Secure Key Generation*

HTML5 KeyGen Tag Parameter	HTML5 KeyGen Tag Parameter's Usage
autofocus	Specifies **KeyGen autofocus on page load**
form	Specifies **form that the KeyGen belongs to**
disabled	Specifies **KeyGen element will be disabled**
keytype	Specifies a **security algorithm** for the key
name	Defines the **KeyGen element name**
challenge	Specifies that the value of the <keygen> element is **challenged on submission**

Next, let's take a look at the output <output> tag.

The OUTPUT Tag: Defining Each Description Data Child Element

The **<output>** tag represents the result of a calculation, such as one performed using <input> data fields, as done in the example, or from a more complex JavaScript calculation. Table 15-10 shows the three parameters supported in HTML5 for the new <output> tag (element).

Table 15-10. *Three <output> Parameters for Output Generation*

HTML5 Output Tag Parameter	HTML5 Output Tag Parameter's Usage
for	Specifies the **relationship** between the result of the calculation and elements that were used in that calculation
form	Specify **form that the output belongs to**
name	Defines the **output element name**

Let's create a <form> construct that adds two numbers, using the <input> fields to collect the data, an oninput event in the <form> tag to do a simple output=inputA+inputB calculation, and an <output> tag to hold the output. The <form> and <output> constructs are wired together using the o.value (form oninput), and the name="o" (output tag parameter).

The HTML5 markup for this looks like the following:

```
<form name="add2numbers" onsubmit="return false"
    oninput="o.value = parseInt(a.value) + parseInt(b.value)">
    <input name="a" type="number" step="any"> +
    <input name="b" type="number" step="any"> =
    <output name="o"></output>
</form>
```

Next, we're going to get into defining areas with HTML5.

Summary

This chapter discussed forms tag support in HTML5 and previous versions, including the <form>, <input>, <label>, <textarea>, <fieldset>, <legend>, <select>, <option>, <optgroup>, <button>, <datalist>, <keygen>, and <output> tags. In the next chapter, you learn about HTML5 tags support the **positioning** of content within HTML5 documents and applications as well as defining areas in HTML5 using pixels or percentages, so that your HTML design is precise!

▨ ▨ ▨

HTML5 Position: Document Layout and Text Spanning

Let's talk about the tags in HTML5 that allow developers to **group elements** and control the content's **position**. Let's also discuss tags that allow the grouped elements to be **styled** as if they were one single functional unit. These tags include the division **<div>** tag and the span **<span>** tag. These tags do nothing in and of themselves; they must be styled.

This chapter looks at the powerful tags in HTML5 that implement advanced content design techniques. We start with the <span> tag because it affects only text elements, and then we progress to the more complex and powerful <div> tag. The <span> and <div> tags have no HTML5 parameters, because they are styled using CSS3. The chapter features no tables, only HTML5 markup examples.

Defining Text Spans: Using the SPAN Tag

The **<span>** tag is utilized to group in-line elements within your HTML5 document. The <span> tag provides no visual result in and of itself, it must be styled using CSS3 or manipulated using JavaScript. Therefore, the <span> tag provides developers with a way to add external access to be able to hook onto a section of text content, image or document portion encapsulated using the starting **<span>** tag along with an ending **</span>** tag.

The following HTML5 markup example uses a <span> tag and the global HTML5 **style** parameter to color part of the sentence:

```
<p>Ferrari's come in a <span style="color:red">Ferrari Red</span> color</p>
```

The primary difference between a <span> tag and a <div> tag is that the <span> tag is used **in-line** (inside of other tags), whereas the <div> tag creates **block constructs** or deeply nested HTML5 markup constructs (that look like blocks of HTML5 markup, and hence the name "block level construct").

There are no local or native parameters for a <span> tag in HTML5; however, there are certain global HTML5 parameters that are commonly used with the <span> tag. These include an **id** or a **class** parameter, used to access the <span>, using external CSS3 definitions, and the **title** tag to allow mouse-over pop-ups to be attached to spanned

© Wallace Jackson 2016
W. Jackson, *HTML5 Quick Markup Reference*, DOI 10.1007/978-1-4302-6536-8_16

text elements. Here is an example of these parameters using HTML5 markup from the previous example:

```
<p>The Ferrari La Ferrari Model will usually come painted in the
  <span id="myspan" title="This text will pop-up when you mouse-over span">
  Ferrari Red color
  </span>, unless you order it in some custom (other than red) color.</p>

span#myspan { color:red; } /* Externalized CSS3 linked via a .CSS file */
```

A span can also be used with imagery! This is especially useful when using event handler parameters. Surround the <img> tag with a <span> tag configured to use **onMouseDown**, **onMouseOut**, and **onDblClick**, to allow your user to single click an image and turn a Ferrari image blue, double-click an image to turn the Ferrari image yellow, and remove the mouse from over the image, to restore the default red Ferrari image. This is done in the following HTML5 markup:

```
<p>Click image to see a Blue Ferrari, Double-Click for a Yellow Ferrari:</p>
  <span onMouseDown="document.ferrarigif.src='blueferrari.gif'"
      onMouseOut="document.ferrarigif.src='redferrari.gif'"
      onDblClick="document.ferrarigif.src='yellowferrari.gif'">
  <img src="redferrari.gif" height="240" width="480" name="ferrarigif">
  </span>
```

It is also useful to use the language related parameters of **dir** (text direction) and **lang** (language definition) with the <span> tag, because <span> is primarily utilized to affect text elements, which are affected by languages and text direction.

You can change the text direction within the <span> by using the dir parameter via the following HTML5 markup:

```
<p>Ferrari comes in a standard <span dir="ltr">Ferrari Red</span> color</p>
```

You can also define the language used in a span of text by using the <span lang="language"> configuration. Let's say a Ferrari is very sexy in Italy as shown in the following HTML5 markup:

```
<p>Ferrari's are considered <span lang="it">Molto Sexy</span> in Italy</p>
```

Next, let's take a look at the <div> tag and how you can use this tag to build complex HTML5 document designs, enclosing HTML5 constructs in <div> tags which have been assigned the id, or class, parameter. First, let's take a look at the difference between using the id parameter and the class parameter for CSS3 applications, which the <div> tag leverages extensively.

Use of id, vs. Name, vs. Class

There has generally been some confusion as HTML5 has evolved in regards to three different parameters that are used to identify design elements (tags). These are the **id**, **name**, and **class**. I try to clarify what each of these is best suited for in this section of the chapter, since <div> and <span> rely heavily on these to identify them for external processing, since these two tags do not do anything, in and of themselves.

Identifiers: Use an id for JavaScript and Fragments

The **id** parameter is short for **identifier**; more precisely, it is short for **fragment identifier**. It allows you to go to a specific section of your document, using a URL plus a **hash sign** (or pound sign) "#" fragment designation. This is done with the # character between the URL and the value which was used in the id="fragment-id-value" parameter. This is an example of fragment URLs:

```
http://www.website-name-here.com/webpage-name.html#fragment-id-value
```

It is created in your HTML5 markup using the <p> tag:

```
<p id=fragment-id-value>This is a paragraph of text you want to jump to</p>
```

Within the same document that you are currently in, this is referenced using only the **fragment-id-value**, inside of the <a> tag using the href parameter and the # sign, like this:

```
<a href="#fragment-id-value">Click here to go to this fragment/section</a>
```

It is important to note that you can only use an id name once for any XHTML, HTML, or HTML5 document. A duplicate id tag causes your page to fail validation and can have a negative effect when you are using ids with JavaScript. Besides defining document fragment navigation, the id parameter is important in defining the document elements that you process using JavaScript. Using ids for non-standard applications such as CSS can potentially interfere with this, so use the **class** parameter for CSS3 selector definitions.

CSS3 can select ids to apply individual styles to them by using the hash sign (#), but JavaScript relies on id as well due to its use of the **getElementById()** function utilized in .js externalized JavaScript.

For this reason, I'll recommend segregating the usage of these three different assignment parameters to the use they are most often used for: **id** for JavaScript and fragment navigation; **class** for CSS3 selector designation; and **name** for forms, server, and database usage (remote data server access). This way, you never get mixed up regarding what you're using a parameter for!

151

Classes: Use CLASS to Classify CSS3 Selectors

Just as is used with CSS3, similarly, **class** can be used in JavaScript programming. The class parameter is quite different from the id parameter, because class can be **used multiple times** within the same HTML document. The separation of content (elements, tags, markup) from presentation (CSS styles) is what makes HTML5 powered by CSS so very powerful. Developers do not understand the full extent to which they can use classes because many have become used to using (the much simpler) ids.

It's important to note that not only can classes be used more than once, but more than one class designation can be used in an HTML5 element (tag), using the **same class parameter**! Here's an example of this using HTML markup and CSS definition:

```
<p>Ferrari automobile's are considered to be:
  <span lang="it" class="left2right asexycolor">Molto Sexy</span>
  in most parts of Italy!
</p>
-------------------------CSS3 Selector Definition Below----------------
.left2right { direction: ltr; }
.asexycolor { color:    red; }
```

The first piece of code is valid HTML; it shows a <span> using two separate classes in a single class parameter, using a space to separate the two classnames. This technique can reduce your CSS3 stylesheet data footprint (size) considerably if used effectively. It is important to note that you can use both ids and classes on the same HTML5 element, to reference JavaScript (id) and CSS3 stylesheets (class), optimally.

Names: Naming Forms, Controls and UI Elements

The **name** attribute is most often used when sending data in a form submission, and for wiring different form components together with the form, as you just observed extensively in Chapter 15. Due to slightly different parameter conventions, different controls respond to these similar (name and id) parameters differently.

You can have several radio buttons that all have different id attributes, but need to use the same name parameter value to properly define their **grouping** so that users can only select one option.

At the end of the day, whether you use name, id, or class is entirely up to you so long as you implement classes and ids properly, and the HTML5 works identically across all of the different browsers, when you test it! It's really just a matter of personal choice regarding how and when to leverage these parameters.

Define Document Areas: Using a DIV Tag

The division **<div>** tag is used much like the span <span> tag, except that the area defines is a square area, called a **block**, rather than a line (or in-line) area, as is common to define with text. I frequently use <div> tags to "stitch" together images and animations to create a seamless user experience. Unlike the semantic tags, the <div> (and <span>) tags are invisible to the search engines and only relate to positioning and styling the content around them, and do not affect the content itself. You should use these design (positioning, styling, and aligning) tags in conjunction with semantic tags to achieve a HTML5 result that is both visually stunning as well as semantically accurate.

The DISPLAY Property: Block, In-Line, and None

As I mentioned earlier, the <span> in an **in-line** tag and the <div> is a **block** tag. These happen to describe the CSS3 **display** property, which can also be set to **none**, which hides that tag (element) from the HTML5 rendering engine altogether. This is different from the **hidden** property, which renders the space that the element would take up in the design, but makes it invisible (transparent). The none display property actually removes that element from the design altogether, so to make sure your semantic tags did not affect your visual design, you could set their display property to none!

There are also custom display types related to lists and tables, and some hybrid types such as **flex** and **run-in** that bridge the gap between block and in-line for advanced styling.

Examples of elements besides the division <div> that use this **block** display property include the paragraph <p> tag, the header <header> tag, footer <footer> tag, and section <section> tag, the heading 1-6 <h1> through <h6> tags, and the form <form> tag.

Examples of elements (besides <span>) that use an **in-line** display property include the anchor <a> tag and the image <img> tag. You might be thinking, "Images are square. Why are these not a block display type?" The reason imagery is in-line is because a text element **wraps** around it for desktop publishing effects, making the image in-line with that text, in essence.

Examples of some elements that default to a **none** display property include the script <script> tag, which is covered in Chapter 17, the style <style> tag, which is covered in Chapter 18, the title <title> tag, the head <head> tag, the link <link> tag, the meta <meta> tag, and the base <base> tag.

The Division or DIV Tag: Core Properties

The <div> tag defines some division in or section of an HTML5 document. This is done by using the <div> tag to group elements at the block-level, and then formatting these elements inside of the <div> container by using CSS3 style definitions. In fact, the <div> element is most frequently used as a generic container for HTML5 visual design, where CSS3 aligns, positions, z-orders, shows/hides, fades, assigns effects to, and styles all HTML5 content contained inside of that division.

Let's use the <div> tag to add a background color to the previous example, as seen in the following HTML5 markup:

```
<div style="background-color:yellow">
 <p>Click image to see Blue Ferrari, Double-Click for Yellow Ferrari:</p>
  <span onMouseDown="document.ferrarigif.src='blueferrari.gif'"
        onMouseOut="document.ferrarigif.src='redferrari.gif'"
        onDblClick="document.ferrarigif.src='yellowferrari.gif'">
   <img src="redferrari.gif" height="240" width="480" name="ferrarigif">
  </span>
 <p>Everything in this document division will have yellow behind it!</p>
</div>
```

This places yellow highlighting behind all of the paragraph text above and below the interactive image and the image itself. As you can see, you have put a global style on all of these contained document elements by using the <div> tag as a division container.

The more common way for a <div> element to be styled is to assign it a classname using the **class** parameter, like this:

```
<div class="example">
 <p>Click image to see Blue Ferrari, Double-Click for Yellow Ferrari:</p>
  <span onMouseDown="document.ferrarigif.src='blueferrari.gif'"
        onMouseOut="document.ferrarigif.src='redferrari.gif'"
        onDblClick="document.ferrarigif.src='yellowferrari.gif'">
   <img src="redferrari.gif" height="240" width="480" name="ferrarigif">
  </span>
 <p>Everything in this document division will have yellow behind it!</p>
</div>
------------
div.example { background-color :yellow; position: absolute;
              top: 108px; left: 120px; width: 500px; height: 500px;
              z-index: -1; opacity: 0.5; border: solid 1px #000000; }
.example    { background-color: yellow; }
```

The preceding code adds a background color, positions the <div>, sets a 50% translucency, sets a z-index to be in the background, and draws a one-pixel solid black border around the division. I also showed an example of how any element with class="example" is background-colored yellow to show the power of classes.

Although this is not a CSS3 book, I show you some CSS3 in this chapter and in Chapter 18, because it is necessary to show you this material bridge between CSS3 and HTML5 markup, and to show you how certain tags, such as <div>, <style>, <link>, and <span> can work together with CSS3.

It is important to note that the default behavior of the <div> tag when rendered in a browser (or OS) is to place a line break before, as well as after, the <div> element. This can be, and frequently is, changed by the developer using CSS3. In fact, the next thing to look at is how I seamlessly stitch <img> tag assets together using <div> tags and CSS3 for my multimedia-related HTML5 content production pipeline.

Seamless Image Stitching: Using DIVs with CSS3

Now that we have looked at some less advanced <div> examples, I should show you a more advanced example. Let's look at how DIVs are used to assemble the various image and animation components for the iTVset.com site, as well as overlaying JavaScript clock elements, all done using <div> tags. JavaScript is covered in Chapter 17 and CSS3 is covered in Chapter 18. Figure 16-1 shows the result of the HTML5 markup we're going to look at next. This is styled using a CSS3 stylesheet, which we explore after that.

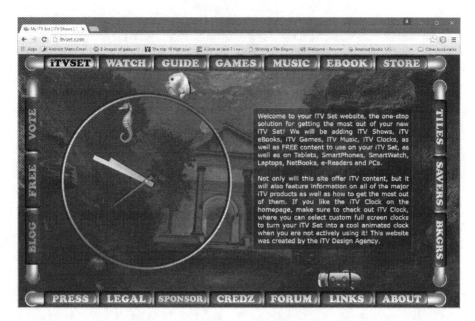

Figure 16-1. *HTML5 Design stitched together using DIVs and CSS3*

As you can see in the following HTML5 markup, I am using <div> tags that contain <img> tags, using the **class** property to address these, and the **id** property to reference the JavaScript. The <canvas> tag (id="clock") is covered in Chapter 19.

```
<div class="c">
  <img src="bk2.png" class="c2" />
  <img src="bk3.gif" class="c3" />
  <img src="bk4.png" class="c4" />
</div>
<div class="d">
  <img src="bk5.png" class="c5" />
  <img src="bk6.png" class="c6" />\
</div>
<div class="h"></div>
<div class="tx"></div>
<div class="p"><p>TEXT CONTENT FOR THE HTML5 DOCUMENT IS IN HERE</p></div>
<div class="j"></div>
<div class="s"></div>
<div class="bu"></div>
<div class="t">
  <img src="tl.png" class="tp1" />
    <!-- TOP UI LINKS ANCHOR TAG MARKUP -->
</div>
```

```
<div class="l">
  <img src="lt.png" class="lt1" />
    <!-- LEFT UI LINKS ANCHOR TAG MARKUP -->
  <img src="lb.png" class="lt2" />
</div>
<div class="r">
  <img src="rt.png" class="rt1"/>
    <!-- RIGHT UI LINKS ANCHOR TAG MARKUP -->
  <img src="rb.png" class="rt2"/>
</div>
<div class="b">
  <img src="bl.png" class="bt1"/>
    <!-- BOTTOM UI LINKS ANCHOR TAGS MARKUP -->
  <img src="b.png" class="bt2" />
</div>
<div class="time">
  <canvas id="clock" width="500" height="500"></canvas>
</div>
```

To create what you see in Figure 16-1, I'm using CSS3 to define a **background-image**
property for the <div> tags that do not contain <img> tags. I use **absolute positioning**
and I define **precise pixel locations** by using the **top**, **left**, **width**, or **height** properties.
I control image tiles using the **fixed** and **no-repeat** properties, and **opacity**, **background-
color**, and **border** using the CSS3 properties that bear those names. You can look at the
DIV classname to see what CSS3 positions and loads each image area.

```
div.time  {position:absolute;top:108px;left:120px;width:500px;height:500px;}
div.p     {position:absolute;top:-216px;left:694px;width:446px;height:400px;}
div.tx    { position:absolute; top:150px; left:680px; width:460px;
            height:400px; background-color:#000; opacity:0.35;
            border:solid 1px #ccc; }
div.c     { position:absolute;top:48px;left:0px;width:1280px;height:624px; }
div.c img.c2 {position:absolute;left:0px;width:270px;height:80px;top:0px; }
div.c img.c3 {position:absolute;left:270px;width:640px;height:80px;top:0px;}
div.c img.c4 {position:absolute;left:910px;width:370px;height:80px;top:0px;}
div.d     { position:absolute;top:128px;left:0px;width:1280px;height:544px; }
div.d img.c5 {position:absolute;left:0px;width:1280px;height:480px;top:0px;}
div.d img.c6 { position:absolute; left: 0px; width: 1280px; height: 64px;
               top:480px; }
div.s     {position:absolute; left:0px; width:1280px; height:56px; top:608px;
            background: no-repeat; background-image: url(s.png); }
div.h     {position:absolute; left:0px width:1280px; height:128px; top:128px;
            background: fixed no-repeat; background-image: url(sy.gif); }
div.j     { position:absolute; left:176px; width:96px; height:720px; top:0px;
            background: fixed no-repeat; opacity: 0.6;
            background-image: url(jy.gif); }
div.bu    { position:absolute; left:525px; width:44px; height:720px; top:0px;
            background: fixed no-repeat; opacity: 0.4;
            background-image: url(bu.gif); }
```

```
div.t    { position:absolute; top:0px; left:0px; width:1280px; height:48px;
           background-image: url(bk1.png); }
div.t img.tp1 { position:absolute;left:18px;width:56px;height:45px;top:2px;}
div.t img.tp2 { position: absolute; left: 1187px; width: 56px; height: 45px;
               top:2px; }
div.l    { position: absolute; top: 0px; left: 0px; width: 64px;
           height: 652px; background-image: url(bkg7.jpg); }
div.l img.lt1 { position: absolute; left: 18px;width: 45px; height: 56px;
               top: 64px;}
div.l img.lt2 { position: absolute; left: 18px; width: 45px;
               height: 56px; top: 594px; }
div.b    { position: absolute; top: 664px; left: 0px; width: 1280px;
           height: 48px; background-image: url(bk7.png); }
div.b img.bt1 { position: absolute; left: 18px; width: 56px;
               height: 45px;top: 3px; }
div.b img.bt2 { position: absolute; left: 1187px; width: 56px;
               height: 45px; top: 3px; }
```

Next, let's look at the JavaScript **<script>** tag. I reference the **<canvas id="clock">** tag in my clock JavaScript.

Summary

This chapter covered tags that define areas in HTML5 and earlier versions, including the <div> and <span> tags. The next chapter looks at the HTML5 **JavaScript** <script> tag.

CHAPTER 17

■ ■ ■

HTML5 Scripting: Using JavaScript and <script> Tag

Now let's discuss the **<script>** tag in HTML5. It allows you to use the JavaScript programming language with your HTML5 content creation pipeline (markup, design, programming, and publishing). The JavaScript language is based on ECMAScript 262. It connects the inner-workings of a browser and now the HTML5 OS powering your smartphone, smartwatch, tablet, notebook, and iTV Set with HTML5 markup content definition and CSS3 stylesheet design.

In this chapter, you look at the <script> tag in HTML5, which implements advanced JavaScript content that can take your HTML5 and CSS3 content to the next level. I did this with the iTVset.com website by adding a seamless clock to the HTML5 and CSS3 in the previous chapter. I am not going to go into minute details regarding the JavaScript programming languages, because this book focuses on HTML5 markup, but we'll look at how to bridge JavaScript and HTML5. I suggest that you visit Apress (`www.apress.com`) and check out some JavaScript titles so that you can master this area.

Using JavaScript: The HTML5 SCRIPT Tag

The **<script>** tag defines client-side JavaScript assets. The <script> element (tag) contains script statements, also known as JavaScript code, or references an external JS script file. This is done with the src parameter in the <script> tag or with the <link> tag. If the src attribute is present in the <script> opening tag, then the <script> element itself is empty. Common JavaScript usage includes adding interactivity, new media asset manipulation, form validation, user interface design, and similar dynamic and advanced real-time changes of your HTML5 application content. The <script> tag parameters used in HTML5 are listed in Table 17-1.

© Wallace Jackson 2016
W. Jackson, *HTML5 Quick Markup Reference*, DOI 10.1007/978-1-4302-6536-8_17

Table 17-1. Six HTML5 <script> Tag Parameters

Script Tag Parameter	Script Tag Parameter's Usage
async (New in HTML5)	Specifies that a JavaScript is to be executed **asynchronously**; this is for external scripts
charset	Specifies the **character set encoding** used in the external JavaScript file
defer	Specifies that a JavaScript is to be executed when the page has **finished parsing**; this is only for external JavaScript files
src	Defines the **source file** for the JavaScript
type	Defines the **JavaScript Media (MIME) type**
xml:space (No HTML5)	Determines preservation of whitespace (XHTML)

It's important to include the <noscript> element for the users who have disabled JavaScript in their browser, or have a browser, or operating system, which does not support client-side Java scripting.

JavaScript Execution: Parsing Synchronization

There are several ways that external JavaScript can be executed; **before** rendering your HTML5 markup and CSS3 style, **after** rendering the HTML5 markup and CSS3 style, and **during** the rendering of your HTML5 markup and CSS3 styles. **Synchronization** of JavaScript execution with HTML5 and CSS3 markup parsing is controlled using the parameters in Table 17-1.

If neither the async nor the defer parameter is present, then JavaScript is the first asset fetched and executed before the browser continues parsing your markup. This "first" parameter is not shown in Table 17-1. It is simply set by not setting any parameter in the <script> tag, and so it is the default way that a JavaScript is processed (first). This is because there are often things that JavaScript does to set up an HTML5 rendering environment and document structure; therefore, JavaScript needs to be executed into memory before any other elements are rendered into system memory. This is quite logical, if you think about it from a programming standpoint, because JavaScript is processed prior to HTML5 markup, which is processed before styling!

If the new in HTML5 **async** parameter is present inside of the <script> tag, then a script is executed **asynchronously** with the rest of the page. This means that a script is executed **while** the page in the process of parsing the HTML5 tags and applying the CSS3 styles to those tags.

If an async parameter is not present in the <script> tag and the **defer** parameter is instead present, then the script can only be executed when the page has **finished parsing**; that is, the script is paused or held back from executing until the CSS and HTML5 markup are fully applied to your document (browser) or application (operating system).

JavaScript Formats: MIME Type and Character Set

The other parameters in Table 17-1 handle data formats, which define the JavaScript code itself. The JavaScript MIME Type (now called a Media Type) should be one of these following combinations: **text/jscript**, **text/javascript**, or **text/ecmascript**. Any of these types will work across all of the popular browsers and OSes that are widely used today (Mozilla Firefox, Google Chrome, Apple Safari, and Opera). The most often utilized of these three is the text/javascript MIME type, as it most clearly and simply defines the contents of the .JS file.

If you are creating an application, you would substitute the word text with the word application. If you are interested in seeing the complete list of media types, visit this URL:

```
http://www.iana.org/assignments/media-types/media-types.xhtml
```

These following three are valid commonly used MIME Types as well: application/x-javascript, application/ecmascript, and, application/javascript.

In HTML5, the character set is typically designated **UTF-8**, unless you are in a country that uses a custom character set, in which case you use UFT-16 that supports non-Roman characters, such as Asian characters.

In-Line JavaScript Code: Using the SCRIPT Tag

Since I already showed you how to externalize a JavaScript code asset in Chapter 4, let's look at how to use a <script> tag to add the JavaScript logic to run the clock that is referenced in the <canvas id="clock"> HTML5 markup in Chapter 16. In this way, you use CSS3 with the class parameter and you use the id parameter to reference JavaScript with the **document.getElementById('clock');** call. The JavaScript code is inside the <script> tag, as seen in the following HTML5 markup example:

```
<script type="text/javascript" charset="UTF-8">
var hour_hand=null, minute_hand=null, second_hand=null, ctx=null,
    degrees=0, clock_face=null, clock_face=null, HEIGHT=500, WIDTH=500;
function init_itv() {
var canvas = document.getElementById('clock');
  if(canvas.getContext('2d') )          {
    ctx = canvas.getContext('2d');
    hour_hand = new Image();
    hour_hand.src = 'hour_hand.png';
    minute_hand = new Image();
    minute_hand.src = 'minute_hand.png';
    second_hand = new Image();
    second_hand.src = 'second_hand.png';
    clock_face = new Image();
    clock_face.src = 'clock_face.png';
    clock_face.onload = imgLoaded;      }
  else                                  {
    alert("Canvas not supported!"); }
}
```

161

```
function clearCanvas() { ctx.clearRect(0, 0, HEIGHT, WIDTH); }
function imgLoaded()   { setInterval(draw, 500);              }
function getRequiredMinuteAngle(currentTime) {
  return Math.floor(((360/60) * currentTime.getMinutes()),0); }
function getRequiredHourAngle(currentTime)   {
  return Math.floor(((360/12) * currentTime.getHours()),0);   }
function getRequiredSecondAngle(currentTime) {
  return Math.floor(((360/60) * currentTime.getSeconds()),0); }
function draw()  {
  var currentTime = new Date();
  clearCanvas();
  ctx.drawImage(clock_face, 0, 0);
  ctx.save();
  ctx.translate(HEIGHT/2, WIDTH/2);
  rotateAndDraw(minute_hand, getRequiredMinuteAngle(currentTime));
  rotateAndDraw(hour_hand, getRequiredHourAngle(currentTime));
  rotateAndDraw(second_hand, getRequiredSecondAngle(currentTime));
  ctx.restore();
}
function rotateAndDraw(image, angle)  {
  ctx.rotate(angle * (Math.PI / 180));
  ctx.drawImage(image, 0-HEIGHT/2, 0-WIDTH/2);
  ctx.rotate(-angle * (Math.PI / 180));
}
</script>
```

Global variables accessed by all of the functions in the <script> tag are declared first at the top, and local variables are declared at the top (inside) of each function. If you want to learn JavaScript, be sure to get a good JavaScript title from Apress because this book focuses on HTML5 markup only and doesn't cover JavaScript or CSS3 in any significant detail.

Figure 17-1 shows the clock JavaScript running inside a <canvas> tag (covered in Chapter 19) and referenced using the id parameter inside a canvas tag like the <canvas id="clock">.

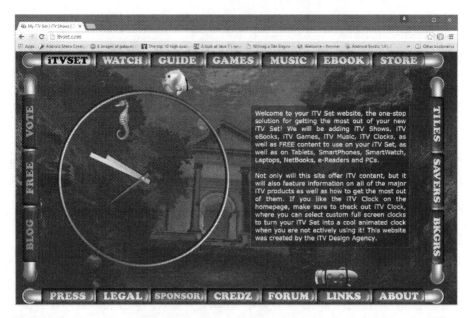

Figure 17-1. *JavaScript document.getElementById('clock'); wired to <canvas id="clock">
HTML5 element to create iTVset.com clock*

As you can see in the <script> HTML5 markup, this time I am not using the "hide JS
from non-supporting parsing engines" convention that I mentioned earlier in the book.
Let's discuss why that is next, as browsers and operating systems become more advanced
and 100% HTML5 and HTML 5.1 this becomes less and less necessary to do, and in some
cases, less and less desirable.

Hiding JavaScript: To Do or Not to Do?

When HTML browsers first became available, not all of them supported JavaScript, just
as not all of them support WebGL2 (see Chapter 19) now. There used to be a convention
of hiding the JavaScript inside of the <script> tag with HTML comments, so the JavaScript
(external or in-line) element appeared to be empty to parsing engines that did not
understand that element. HTML engines that did understand JavaScript would ignore
these comments and process compile and execute) the JavaScript code correctly. Markup
is parsed, whereas code is compiled and executed (or processed, to use a single term).

HTML Comments: Use <!-- and --> to Hide JS Code

The convention that has been in place for well over a decade is to hide JavaScript code in HTML comments, like this:

```
<script>
        <!--
                JAVASCRIPT CODE
        -->
</script>
```

There is now discussion in the HTML5 community that this is no longer necessary or even desirable, due to the acceptance of JavaScript as HTML's defacto standard language and because there are so many different versions of XHTML and HTML that would parse and potentially misinterpret comments and the symbols. The current consensus seems to be to vacate this practice and not use any comments in the script.

XHTML Comments: Use <!-- and --> to Hide JS Code

Some discussion of this convention suggests that to support XHTML correctly, you should use a different form of commenting that involves the [CDATA [code-here]] code encapsulation approach inside a different (XML-centric) type of commenting convention. This looks like the following:

```
<script>
        //<![CDATA[
                    JAVASCRIPT CODE
        //]]>
</script>
```

My take on all of this is that if you are developing for HTML5 (which is now legacy code, as you'll see in Chapter 23) or HTML 5.1, you should not worry about XHTML 1.x or HTML 2/3/4 parsing engines. They are too ancient to worry about supporting due to a widespread proliferation of affordable HTML5 devices.

Summary

This chapter discussed the <script> tag, which allows you to use JavaScript code with your HTML5 and CSS3 markup. The next chapter looks at the HTML5 **cascading style sheet** <style> tag.

■ ■ ■

HTML5 Styling: Using the \<style\> Tag to Access CSS3

Now let's cover the **\<style\>** tag in HTML5, which allows you to use CSS3 cascading style sheet syntax with your HTML5 content creation pipeline (design, markup, style, program, and publish). The CSS3 syntax is loosely based on SGML. It extracts the UI design and HTML5 content styling into its own encapsulated language. You looked at how to externalize CSS3 in Chapter 4. This chapter provides an overview of CSS3 and explains how to access CSS3 style sheets "in-line" by using the \<style\> tag. You can also use the \<style\> tag to **override** the externalized CSS3 master style sheet for HTML5 content, allowing you to tweak the master style sheet on a document-by-document basis, without adding any data footprint to your external CSS3 site-wide or application-wide style sheet definition.

In this chapter, you look at the \<style\> tag in HTML5. It implements advanced style sheet content that allows you to design, configure, and customize your HTML5 document, as I did with the iTVset.com website design, using \<div\> and \<img\> tags with class parameters in the previous chapter.

Cascading Style Sheets: A History of CSS

The style sheet has been utilized to style markup since the very beginning when SGML (Standard Generalized Markup Language) was conceived in the 1980s. One requirement of the HTML style sheet language was that style sheets be able to originate from different resources across the World Wide Web. For this reason, existing style sheet languages, such as DSSSL and FOSI, were not suitable. **CSS**, on the other hand, allows your document's styling to be influenced by multiple disparate style sheets. This is done by "cascading" through style sheet definitions. CSS, or cascading style sheets, were subsequently developed to provide style sheets for use with HTML and XHTML. I cover the history and future of CSS in this first section.

CSS was first proposed by Opera's CTO, Håkon Wium Lie, on October 10, 1994. Håkon Wium Lie worked with Tim Berners-Lee at CERN, where a number of other style sheet languages for the World Wide Web were being tested around the same time. The initial World Wide Web Consortium (W3C) **CSS1** proposal was released in 1996. Bert Bos was also involved in this proposal. He is co-author of CSS1. He and Håkon Wium Lie are regarded as the co-creators of CSS.

© Wallace Jackson 2016
W. Jackson, *HTML5 Quick Markup Reference*, DOI 10.1007/978-1-4302-6536-8_18

CSS2 was proposed on November 4, 1997 and published as a W3C recommendation on May 12, 1998. CSS3 was proposed in 1998; it is still under development today.

CSS2 includes core capabilities, like absolute, relative, and fixed positioning of elements, z-index (3D), media types, bidirectional text, font properties, shadows, and support for aural (audio) style sheets, which were replaced by CSS3 speech modules.

CSS3 is divided into several separate documents, called **modules**. Each module adds new capabilities or extends features defined in CSS2. CSS3 is also backward compatible with CSS2. The earliest CSS3 proposal was published in June 1999. CSS3 is currently being worked on as a specification.

CSS4 should be implemented after CSS3 is completed. There is no unified **CSS4** specification, because CSS3 and CSS4 are split into separate modules. There are Level 4 modules instead of a unified specification proposal. Level 4 module specifications can collectively be referred to as CSS4.

Using CSS3 with HTML5: The STYLE Tag

The <**style**> tag defines style information for an HTML document that is not defined externally using a CSS file asset. It also overrides styles defined in an external master CSS3 definition in a local document; this departs from the styling norm for some reason. Inside a <style> element, you use CSS3 syntax to specify how HTML5 elements should be rendered in your browser, operating system, iTV Set, or smartphone. It is permissible for each HTML document to contain multiple <style> tags. As you learned in Chapter 4, use the <link> tag to link to an externally defined style sheet.

These <style> tags should exist in the <**head**> section of your HTML5 document unless the **scoped** parameter is present. The scoped attribute is new to HTML5. It allows you to define styles specifically for a (hopefully semantic) section of your document. If the scoped attribute is present, the styles only apply to that style element's parent and child elements; that is, elements **nested** inside a <style> tag.

The <style> tag parameters used in legacy HTML or HTML5 are listed in Table 18-1. The new HTML5 parameter is listed first; the legacy HTML parameters are listed afterward.

Table 18-1. HTML5 <style> Tag Parameters

Style Tag Parameter	Style Tag Parameter's Usage
scoped (New in HTML5)	Specifies style only applies to element's parent and element's child elements
media	Specifies media or device media resource is optimized for
type	Defines the **CSS3 Media (MIME) Type**

The **media** parameter allows you to specify the media device that the CSS3 style is optimized for. Styles are certainly customized to match devices types, such as printers, iTV Sets, or smartphone screens, so this is an important parameter for HTML5 <style> tags (elements).

The value string (inside the quotation marks) can accept several values, including Boolean operators such as AND, NOT, and OR (OR uses a comma, not a keyword).

The supported device keyword values for the media parameter include **aural** for speech synthesizers; **braille** for Braille feedback devices; **handheld** for handheld devices (small screen, limited bandwidth devices, such as phones, PDA, or mini-tablets); **projection** for DLP, LCD, or LED projectors; **print** for printers, print preview mode, or printed page; **screen** for computer screen; **tty** for Teletypes and media using a fixed-pitch character grid; and **tv** for iTV Sets and similar television set–related devices that feature large screens, HD and UHD resolution, and limited scrolling capabilities.

Pixel data values can also be specified to specify the width or height of the targeted display area or the device, including **min-width**, **max-width**, **min-height**, **max-height**, **device-width**, and **device-height**. You can also specify the orientation (portrait, landscape), aspect ratio, device aspect ratio, monochrome, resolution, grid or scan, color, and color index. A max and min value range can also be specified for any of these parameters, if needed.

CSS3 Formats: MIME or Media Type Designation

The type parameter (see Table 18-1) handles your data format, which defines the MIME type for the CSS3 code. The CSS MIME type (now called the media type) should be designated as **text/css**. This type designation works across all widely used browsers and operating systems (Mozilla Firefox, Google Chrome, Apple Safari, and Opera).

If you are interested in seeing the complete definition for the text/css media (MIME) type, visit the following website:

```
https://www.iana.org/assignments/media-types/text/css
```

In HTML5, the character set is generally designated UTF-8. You can also use the US-ASCII or ISO-8859-X character set designations with CSS3 files if you decide to specify a charset parameter (using the <link> tag, of course).

The SCOPED Parameter: Tag-Local HTML5 Styling

With the new **scoped** parameter, there are now three levels of CSS3 localization. Global CSS3 styles can be externalized, or defined globally across any document that imports (links to) those CSS files. Using the <style> tag in the <head> section to define "document local" styles has always been possible. If you use the scoped parameter with the <style> tag, you can use <style> tags inside the **<body>** section, for "element local" styling! Let's scope out (no pun intended) this cool new capability!

Here's an example of a scoped style that is declared down in the <body> section of the HTML5 document:

```
<!DOCTYPE html><html>
<head>
 <title>Locally Scoped CSS3 Targeting DIV in Semantic Section</title>
</head>
```

```
<body>
 <section id="DIV Tag Locally Scoped Style Definition">
  <div>
   <style scoped>
     h1 {color:green;}
     p  {color:brown;}
   </style>
   <h1>This is a heading which has been locally styled green.</h1>
   <p>This is a paragraph which has been locally styled brown.</p>
  </div>
 </section>
</body>
</html>
```

In-Line CSS3 Code: Using the STYLE Parameter

Whereas the <style scoped> tag and parameter essentially allow what amounts to "block level" styling, remember that you can also apply CSS3 style definitions inside a tag using the style parameter for in-line styling. This gives you a full range of ways to apply styles, from global application-wide external CSS style sheets using the <link> tag, to <head><style></head> document-level styling, to <body><style scoped></body> block-level styling, to the global HTML5–style parameter's in-line element styling. Here's how the block-level scoped <style> approach is replaced by the in-line style parameter approach:

```
<!DOCTYPE html><html>
<head>
 <title>Locally Scoped CSS3 Targeting DIV in Semantic Section</title>
</head>
<body>
 <section id="DIV Tag Locally Scoped Style Definition">
  <h1 style="color:green">Heading which has been in-line styled green</h1>
  <p style="color:brown">Paragraph which has been in-line styled brown</p>
 </section>
</body></html>
```

I've tried to give you an idea of how CSS and JavaScript work with HTML5 without getting off track, as these topics are extremely complex and deserve their own books to be able to master their complexity. I only have a few hundred pages to cover more than 120 HTML 5 and 5.1 tags, so I have to concentrate on these tags, and their parameters.

That said, I continue to suggest that you purchase books on specialized topics, such as CSS3, JavaScript, WebGL, Web Speech API, Web RTC, and new media content production fundamentals. I have a *New Media Content Production Fundamentals* series at Apress (www.apress.com). If you're interested, search for my name for on the site.

Summary

In this chapter, you learned a little of the history of CSS. You also learned about the HTML <style> tag that allows you to use CSS3 style sheet syntax with HTML5 markup and all of the ways that you can style HTML5 elements.

In the next chapter, you look at HTML5 **Canvas**, **WebGL**, and **WebGL 2**, which are accessed using the <canvas> tag.

■ ■ ■

HTML5 Real-Time Rendering: Using the <canvas> Tag

Now let's discuss the **<canvas>** tag in HTML5, which allows you to use the **canvas**, an advanced real-time rendering surface that you can access directly in real-time using JavaScript code. Since the <canvas> tag specifies (creates in memory) a real-time drawing surface, it is covered it in this book to show you what it can do for your HTML5 applications and documents. The HTML5 content creation pipeline just got a little bit more complex (design, markup, style, program, real-time render, and publish). Other operating systems, such as Android, also have a Canvas feature. A canvas is needed for i2D and i3D applications and games, because it is engineered to be fast enough to develop gaming applications or OpenGL interactive 3D.

Using the CANVAS Tag: New for HTML5

The HTML5 **<canvas>** element provides a **drawing surface**—like a color, digital 2D or 3D Etch A Sketch—to draw graphics, such as animated graphics or interactive graphics, by using a scripting language. In HTML5, the canvas uses JavaScript as the programming language; in Android OS, Java is the programming language. The <canvas> element or tag is a specialized container for high-speed graphics, much like a graphics engine of sorts. You must use JavaScript to actually draw and interact with the real-time graphics surface.

HTML5 Canvas has methods for drawing boxes, circles, paths, text, lines, points, polygons, splines, and images. These canvas elements can be colored and animated. They can graph data to create presentation aids such as line graphs and bar charts.

Canvas objects can move realistically; anything is possible—from realistic bouncing balls with gravity and friction causing bounce decay, to complex interactive games.

Canvas objects respond interactively with JavaScript events, or any user actions: key press, mouse clicks, button clicks, touchscreen finger movement, and similar event-processing logic, just as HTML5 tags use via the onMouseDown event parameter.

Canvas offers many possibilities for HTML5 gaming applications. In fact, more than one HTML5 <canvas> element can be used at the same time, if you write your code carefully enough to conserve processing power.

The two <canvas> tag parameters used in HTML5 are shown in Table 19-1. They are relatively simple. They define the width and height of the canvas. You also use the global HTML id parameter to assign your name to the Canvas element so that it can be referenced from your JavaScript. You saw this in action with the Chapter 17 clock.

Table 19-1. HTML5 <canvas> Tag Parameters

Canvas Tag Parameter	Canvas Tag Parameter's Usage
width	Specify the **canvas width** value, using pixels
height	Specify the **canvas height** value, using pixels

Next, let's see how to declare a <canvas> tag or element in your HTML5 documents and applications.

Declaring an HTML5 Canvas: Using Parameters

The <canvas> element needs some parameters to be defined correctly; otherwise, it cannot be used as a drawing surface. It needs to have two spatial dimensions— width and height. Also, it must have an id attribute so that it can be referenced using JavaScript.

By default, the <canvas> element has no border and no content; it's simply an empty surface. Let's use a global **style** parameter to add a border so that you're able to better visualize where this canvas is located on your screen. Since the default canvas color is black, we'll use a red border color that is a thick three pixels in width. (Of course, if the document's background color were white, you would be able to see the canvas anyway!) The HTML5 markup to code this looks like the following:

```
<!DOCTYPE html><html>
<head>
 <title>Declaring an SD Resolution Canvas for Use in GamePlay</title>
</head>
<body>
 <section id="A Game Play HTML5 Canvas Declaration Example">
  <canvas id="gamePlayCanvasSample" width="720" height="480"
        style="border: 3px solid #FF0000; top: 0; left: 0;">
     If you are seeing this message, then your HTML5 Browser,
     or operating system, doesn't support the Canvas Element!
  </canvas>
 </section>
</body>
</html>
```

Notice I am positioning the <canvas> at 0,0 in the style parameter. This positions, sizes and names the canvas container and gives it a nice border, but it is still an empty canvas, as they say in the art world. Remember the <canvas> element has no drawing capabilities of its own just like a real canvas needs a brush and paint. Canvas is only a container for graphic design; you must use JavaScript to actually draw graphics in real-time.

JavaScript has a **getContext()** method to return an object that provides methods and properties for drawing on the canvas. These methods (functions) and properties (variables) represent the current state of the Canvas surface at any time, which is logically referred to as the **context** of the object, hence, the getContext() method name. For instance, there's a **save()** to save the current context, as well as a **restore()** to restore it.

The properties and methods of this **getContext("2d")** object, which are used to draw text, lines, boxes, circles, paths, polygons, ellipses, and such on a canvas, are covered in the next section. Afterward, you look at using 3D with the <canvas> using WebGL and WebGL 2.

Drawing on a Canvas: 2D Methods and Properties

Let's take a look at some of the method groupings, and then some of the properties that allow you to draw 2D graphics on the HTML5 <canvas> element. If you wanted to see an example of 2D content, being drawn in real-time using this <canvas> tag and JavaScript, refer to the clock JavaScript, in Chapter 17.

The first table containing JavaScript methods, shown in Figure 19-2 contains two methods used in image compositing.

If you wanted to learn about digital image compositing, check out my *Digital Image Compositing Fundamentals* (Apress, 2015). Compositing involves the layering of imagery, which uses alpha channels to create one perceived image from several (even hundreds) of image layers. The two methods (see Table 19-2) allow you to control canvas **transparency** using **globalAlpha()**, and **compositing**, using **globalCompositeOperation()** to composite layers.

Table 19-2. HTML5 <canvas> Tag Methods for Compositing

Canvas Drawing Method	Canvas Drawing Method's Usage
globalCompositeOperation	Sets or returns how the new image is drawn on top of (or under) existing image
globalAlpha	Sets or returns a current alpha channel, or transparency values, for the draw operation

There are four rectangle methods (see Table 19-3) that allow you to create, fill, stroke, and erase portions of a basic 2D rectangular (and thus square) drawing objects.

Table 19-3. Four HTML5 <canvas> Methods for Drawing Rectangles

Canvas Drawing Method	Canvas Drawing Method's Usage
rect	**Creates a 2D rectangle** object on the canvas
fillRect	**Fills** a 2D rectangle object on the canvas
strokeRect	**Strokes** a 2D rectangle object on the canvas
clearRect	**Clears an area** in the 2D rectangle object

There are four line styling methods (see Table 19-4) that allow you to style line objects, which are drawn using Path commands. You can control line caps, the way that lines join, line width, and miter length.

Table 19-4. Four HTML5 <canvas> Methods Used for Styling Lines

Canvas Drawing Method	Canvas Drawing Method's Usage
lineCap	Sets or returns the type of line cap used
lineJoin	Sets or returns the type of line corner created where two lines meet
LineWidth	Sets or returns the current line width used
miterLimit	Sets or returns a maximum line miter length

There are four methods for filling (and stroking) shapes using patterns and gradients (see Table 19-5). They allow you to create **patterns**, **linear** and **radial** gradients, and gradient **stops**, which control where gradient colors start and stop.

Table 19-5. Four HTML5 <canvas> Methods for Filling 2D Shapes

Canvas Drawing Method	Canvas Drawing Method's Usage
createPattern	Repeats a specified element in the specified direction to create a pattern fill or stroke
createLinearGradient	Creates a linear gradient to use on canvas
createRadialGradient	Creates a radial gradient to use on canvas
addColorStop	Specify color and stop positions in gradient

There are six **properties** that control the application of the stroke, fill, and shadows characteristics (see Table 19-6). These allow you to set up **strokes**, **fills**, **shadow color**, and **shadow blur**, which controls the shadow edge softness and the x and y shadow distance (**offset value**) from the text or shape.

Table 19-6. Six HTML Canvas Methods for Fill, Stroke, and Shadow

Canvas Draw Property	Canvas Draw Property's Usage
fillStyle	Sets or returns the color, gradient, or pattern used to **fill** the drawing object
strokeStyle	Sets or returns the color, gradient, or pattern used to **stroke** the drawing object
shadowColor	Sets or returns the **color** to use for shadows
shadowBlur	Sets or returns the blur value for shadows
shadowOffsetX	Sets or returns the **horizontal distance** of the shadow from the shape or text shadowed
shadowOffsetY	Sets or returns the **vertical distance** of the shadow from the shape or text shadowed

There are five methods for transforming 2D shape objects in 2D space, such as move (translate), rotate, or scale (see Table 19-7). These allow you to change, or animate, the 2D shapes, lines, paths, new media, or even other canvas objects using timelines (animation) or interactively.

Table 19-7. Five HTML5 Canvas Methods for 2D Transformations

Canvas Drawing Method	Canvas Drawing Method's Usage
scale()	**Scales** the current canvas drawing surface
rotate()	**Rotates** the current canvas drawing surface
translate()	**Remaps** the (0,0) position for your canvas
transform()	**Replaces** the current transformation matrix
setTransform()	**Resets** the current transform to the identity matrix and then calls the transform() method

There are six methods for using text or fonts (see Table 19-8). They define the text object font, text alignment, baseline, filled text, stroked (outlined) text, and text width. A text object is a line object that uses a font to show the canvas how to draw the lines, so it's really a type of polygon.

Table 19-8. Six HTML Canvas Methods for Text and Font Usage

Canvas Drawing Method	Canvas Drawing Method's Usage
font	Sets or returns the current font properties
textAlign	Sets or returns the current text alignment
textBaseline	Sets or returns the current text baseline
fillText()	Draws filled text on the canvas
strokeText()	Draws text on the canvas (no fill)
measureText()	Returns an object that contains text width

There are seven methods allowing you to work with visual new media assets such as digital images, digital video, or even another canvas object instance, as shown in Table 19-9. These allow you to draw an image or video asset on the canvas in real-time using the **drawImage()** method, as well as extract pixel data from the image and determine its dimensions (height, width). You can also create an empty ImageData object using the **createImageDate()** method and copy current canvas data into an ImageData object, using the **getImageData()** method. You can also put ImageData onto the canvas, using the **putImageData()** method.

Table 19-9. Seven HTML Canvas Methods for Digital New Media

Canvas Drawing Method	Canvas Drawing Method's Usage
drawImage()	Draws an image, canvas, or video onto canvas
width	Returns the width of an ImageData object
height	Returns the height of an ImageData object
data	Returns an object that contains image data of a specified ImageData object
createImageData()	Creates a new, blank ImageData object
getImageData()	Returns an ImageData object that copies the pixel data for a specified area on a canvas
putImageData()	Puts the image data (from a specified ImageData object) back onto the canvas

Finally, there are a dozen methods that deal with 2D Path objects (see Table 19-10). They allow you to fill and stroke paths, and create straight lines, arcs, cubic Bézier and quadratic Bézier curves, clip areas, and path-related utilities such as beginPath, closePath, and isPointInPath. They let you create 2D scalable vector graphics (SVG) type illustrations and similar artwork, which can be combined with image, text, and styling methods to create powerful 2D graphic imagery using the HTML5 <canvas> element as a drawing surface. It's important to note that you can also use the HTML5 <canvas> element for 3D and i3D graphics with WebGL and WebGL 2, which you see in the next section. I wanted to show you some of these powerful 2D JavaScript methods first.

Table 19-10. Twelve HTML Canvas Methods for Lines and Paths

Canvas Drawing Method	Canvas Drawing Method's Usage
fill()	Fills the current Path object
stroke()	Strokes the current Path object
beginPath()	Begins a Path object or Resets a Path object
moveTo()	Moves the Path object to a specified point in the canvas, without creating any lines
closePath()	Creates a Path object from the current point back to the starting point to close the Path
lineTo()	Adds a new point and creates a line to that point from the last specified point in the canvas
clip()	Clips a region of any shape and size from the original canvas
quadraticCurveTo()	Creates a quadratic Bézier curve
bezierCurveTo()	Creates a cubic Bézier curve
arc()	Creates an arc/curve (used to create circles, or parts of circles)
arcTo()	Creates an arc/curve between two tangents
isPointInPath()	Returns true if the specified point is in the current path, otherwise false

If you are an object-oriented programming (OOP) expert, you already know how to use these method calls and parameters. If you are not an OOP expert and you want to create the HTML5 new media applications that stand apart from the crowd, go to the Apress website (`www.apress.com`) to purchase a JavaScript title or two!

Next, let's take a look at one of the most powerful and underused APIs available for HTML5, called WebGL. This month, a WebGL 2 version was released that takes 3D and i3D to an all new level, and it is already supported in Firefox and Chrome, so by the time you read this, the <canvas> element support WebGL or WebGL 2 in most of the major browsers and HTML5 operating systems.

Interactive 3D: WebGL or WebGL 2 3D Rendering

We've covered a lot of cool things so far in this book, such as i2D, speech synthesis, semantic web, new media support, and the like, but i3D is one of the coolest things that HTML5 supports. It allows user experiences similar to *Halo 4* and *Madden NFL* to be done in HTML5 browsers and operating systems. It will probably be in place via WebGL 2.0 by the time that you read this book. What's even cooler is that few developers are even leveraging these new i3D technologies, leaving HTML5 wide open for conquering.

I've been doing i3D since Acrobat 3D came out, so I'm especially excited for real-time i3D rendering to come to HTML5. With iTV Sets having quad-core and octa-core CPUs with GPU support, as with smartphones, tablets, and laptops, there are literally billions of potential i3D HTML5 players accumulating out there, waiting for this type of content to be produced. This is why I am exposing you to this technology before this chapter on the HTML5 <canvas> element comes to an end, so that you know all about it if you want to push the leading-edge of what can be done using the HTML5 canvas real-time drawing and rendering engine.

The History of WebGL: Mozilla in 2006 and Opera in 2007

The WebGL API has been evolving for the past decade. It started with i3D experiments using the HTML <canvas> undertaken by Mozilla's engineering director, Vladimir Vukićević, in 2006. By the end of 2007, Opera had made its own separate WebGL implementation. By early 2009, non-profit technology consortium The Khronos Group had created the WebGL Working Group, which had initial participation from Apple (Safari), Google (Chrome), Mozilla (Firefox), Opera, and others. Version 1.0 of the WebGL specification was released in March of 2011. The Working Group is chaired by Ken Russell.

Development of the WebGL 2 specification started in 2013 and finished three years later. The WebGL 2 specification is based on OpenGL ES 3, whereas WebGL is based on OpenGL ES 2. This WebGL, or Web Graphics Library, is the JavaScript API for rendering interactive 3D, or i3D, computer graphics, as well as i2D graphics, on any compatible web browser and without the use of any plug-in! WebGL allows GPU-accelerated physics simulations, real-time image processing, and special effects as part of the HTML5 canvas element.

WebGL elements can be seamlessly combined with your HTML content by using the <canvas> element and alpha channels, so that other HTML5 elements are composited with interactive 3D content. CSS3 allows all elements to take advantage of z-index, opacity, alpha channels (masked transparency), SVG filters, and Porter-Duff modes, essentially turning HTML5 into a compositing engine. It does most of what Photoshop or GIMP can do for you.

The WebGL API has i3D scene graph asset management. It controls code written in JavaScript. It also controls code for rendering and shaders executed on the computer graphics processing unit (GPU). If WebGL or WebGL 2 is not working on an HTML5 device, you need to make sure that the 3D hardware support is present. AMD has a CPU series called **APU**, which includes 3D GPU. You can learn more at the following website:

`http://www.pricewatch.com/cpu/`

If you are interested in seeing the complete definition for the WebGL 2 specification, please visit the following website:

`https://www.khronos.org/registry/`**`webgl`**`/specs/latest/`**`2.0`**`/`

The complexities of i3D programming in WebGL 2 go far beyond the scope of this book. If you are interested in this area, I suggest that you buy a book or two on WebGL and WebGL 2 from the Apress website.

Summary

This chapter discussed the HTML5 <canvas> tag, which allows you to render 2D, 3D, i2D, and i3D graphics in real-time on an advanced drawing surface inside your HTML5 document, website, or application.

The next chapter looks at the object, embed, and applet HTML5 elements.

■ ■ ■

HTML5 Plug-ins: Using the <object>, <embed>, <applet>, and <param> Tags

Now let's talk about the tags in HTML5 that allow developers to plug in non-JavaScript content that does not use the <canvas> tag to render to the screen. This includes older technologies such as Shockwave Flash or newer technologies such as JavaFX, which is now integrated with Java. Java is used for the Android OS and all desktop operating systems; it also works in browsers.

This chapter looks at three powerful tags in HTML5 that allow you to seamlessly plug in external content to your HTML5 content. These include the embed **<embed>** tag, the Java applet **<applet>** tag, and the object **<object>** tag. You'll learn when to use each of the tags and what they allow you to add to your content production, publishing, and delivery work process. The related **<param>** tag is also covered.

Plug-in Applications: The EMBED Tag

The <embed> tag defines an area that serves as a container for any external application or interactive content that you want to seamlessly integrate with your HTML5 markup and HTML design. Sometimes this is referred to as a **plug-in**, or a **Java applet**. The <embed> tag is "technically" a new tag (element) in HTML5, although most of the popular web browsers have supported this <embed> tag across several legacy HTML versions. Interestingly, the <embed> tag was not a part of the HTML 4.01 specification. This means that the <embed> tag is new to HTML5, as far as markup validation is concerned, and therefore, <embed> now validates inside your HTML5 pages. However, if you use <embed> in your legacy HTML 4.01 pages, those pages will not validate!

© Wallace Jackson 2016
W. Jackson, *HTML5 Quick Markup Reference*, DOI 10.1007/978-1-4302-6536-8_20

Table 20-1 describes the four parameters supported by the <embed> tag.

Table 20-1. *Four HTML5 <embed> Tag Parameters*

Embed Tag Parameter	Embed Tag Parameter's Usage
height	Defines the **height** of the embedded application
src	Defines the **source** of the embedded application
type	Defines embedded application **Media (MIME) type**
width	Defines the **width** of the embedded application

Here's an example of how you should embed Shockwave Flash content into your HTML5 markup:

```
<!DOCTYPE html><html>
<head><title>Exotic and Domestic Cars</title></head>
<body>
 <section id="x-shockwave-flash-example">
  <h1>Embedded Shockwave Flash Application</h1>
   <embed src="shockwave-flash-example.swf"
          type="application/x-shockwave-flash"
          width="480" height="320"
          id="javaScriptID" class="cssStyleClassName" />
 </section>
</body>
</html>
```

Let's spend the rest of this chapter looking at a couple alternatives to using the <embed> tag, including when you want to use these alternatives for plugging external content into your HTML5 content creations.

Next, let's discuss the **<applet>** tag, which is **not supported in HTML5**. But many developers **still use** it to embed Java applets. This is because it has more cross-browser support and because HTML5 browsers utilize HTML4 elements, even if they have been deprecated in HTML5.

Java or JavaFX Applets: The APPLET Tag

The **<applet>** tag was originally designed to embed Java applets in HTML4 web pages. Browsers have always supported Java applets and probably will continue to do so. Table 20-2 shows 11 parameters supported by the <applet> tag.

Table 20-2. *Eleven HTML4 <applet> Parameters Deprecated in HTML5*

Parameter	Parameter Data Value	Applet Tag Parameter's Usage
code	**URL**	Specify Java applet **class file name**
object	**name**	Specify reference to a **serialized** representation for the applet
alt	**text**	Specify **alternate text** for applet
align	**left, right, top, bottom, middle, or baseline**	Specify an **alignment** for an applet
archive	**URL**	Specify **remote JAR archive location**
codebase	**URL**	Specify the **relative base URL** for the applet specified in your **code** attribute (use if class isn't local)
height	**pixels**	Specify the **height** for the applet
hspace	**pixels**	Define the **horizontal spacing** around the applet
name	**name**	Define the **name** for the applet (used in JavaScript, or other referencing)
vspace	**pixels**	Define the **vertical spacing** around the applet
width	**pixels**	Specify the **width** for the applet

The applet element was deprecated in HTML4 when the more generalized object element was introduced. I cover objects in the next section. Interestingly, since those browsers or operating systems that moved to support object introduced bugs related to embedding Java applications, the <applet> tag currently is more stable, and a more reliable method for Java applet embedding for "legacy" applications. Going out, for HTML5 and 5.1, applet support is being deprecated, and discontinued in favor of HTML5 internal programming language JavaScript. Use Java for Android!

The <applet> **code** parameter specifies the name of the Java **.class** file that contains a **compiled** applet. This value is relative to your URI, specified using a **codebase** attribute. For installations that have an applet .class file in a server root, a codebase attribute need not be specified as a path; and "base URI" is not necessary for referencing the location of an asset.

The **width** and **height** attributes are needed to define the dimensions for your Java applet. These values should be specified using pixels (picture elements), or a percentage of your parent element that contains the <applet> child tag's width or height. Let's take a look at some sample HTML5 markup for this <applet> tag.

You can define a basic <applet> element using a **code** and **archive** parameter to reference your **.class** and **.jar** files that contain a Java (or JavaFX) applet. You can also use a **name** parameter to reference an <applet> element and the dimensions for your applet's canvas, which are defined by using the width and height parameters. This is shown in the following HTML5 markup example:

```
<!DOCTYPE html><html>
<head>
 <title>Basic Java Applet Element Insertion Example</title>
</head>
<body>
 <section id="Java or JavaFX Applet Object Example">
  <h1>Java or JavaFX Applet HTML Markup Example</h1>
   <applet code="javaAppletName" archive="javaAppletName.jar"
           width="1024" height="600"
           alt="Your HTML5 Browser, or OS, does not support Java!"
           codebase="https://www.YourRemoteServerURLgoesHere.net"
           name="appletTagsName" align="middle">
    <param name="permissions" value="sandbox" />
           ALERT: Your HTML5 Browser, or OS, does not support Java!
   </applet>
 </section>
</body></html>
```

As you can see, the **alt** parameter provides alternate text for HTML5 platforms that recognize the applet element, but don't support Java or don't have Java enabled. It's important to note that developers could also provide this alternate text content between <applet> start and ending tags, as shown. This is a better method than using the alt attribute, because it allows developers to provide additional HTML5 markup in the alternate content. This approach also works in HTML2 or HTML 3.2 browsers that don't yet support this <applet> element, but will still process this text.

An **archive** parameter specifies a comma-separated list of archived files. However, Java developers usually provide one single **jar** (Java archive) file, the standard archive format for Java files. Jar files are created by a jar tool included in the Java SE Development Kit, which you learn how to download and install in the appendices (A through C) of this book.

It is important to note that some browsers don't support an archive parameter, so all necessary JAR files should also be provided as .class files and referenced using a code parameter.

An **align** attribute specifies an alignment for the applet to specify data values of top, middle, bottom, left, right, and baseline. These set applet position with respect to surrounding content on its left and right.

The **align="middle"** in the example aligns the vertical center of the applet with the current baseline. The left and right align values specify a floating applet. In this use-case, an applet is set at the left or right margin; the surrounding content flows around the applet.

The **hspace** and **vspace** parameters allow HTML5 developers to specify horizontal or vertical whitespace, respectively, around an applet. The data value must be in pixels and applies to both left and right sides (or top and bottom) of the applet.

Finally, the **object** parameter (rather than the code parameter) specifies a serialized Java applet, like this:

```
<applet object="serializedJavaAppletName.ser"
        width="1024" height="600"
        alt="Your HTML5 Browser, or OS, does not support Java!"
        codebase="https://www.YourRemoteServerURLgoesHere.net"
        name="appletTagsName" align="middle">
        <param name="permissions" value="sandbox" />
        ALERT: Your HTML5 Browser, or OS, does not support Java!
</applet>
```

When this <applet> tag configuration is encountered, an HTML5 parsing engine creates an applet by deserializing it. This allows an applet to be shipped in a pre-initialized state. When an applet is deserialized, an init() method is not invoked, allowing initialization to be performed on the client side.

The <object> tag is provided for HTML5 to replace the <applet> tag in HTML 4.01 (and previous versions).

Embed Objects in HTML5: The OBJECT Tag

The **<object>** tag defines any **embedded objects** within your HTML5 documents. You can use this element to embed **multimedia assets**, such as digital audio, digital video, Java and JavaFX applets, Active-X controls, Adobe Acrobat PDF documents, and Shockwave Flash applications within your HTML5 documents, websites, and applications. It is interesting to note that you can also use the <object> tag to embed another web page into an HTML5 document. You can also use a child <param> tag to pass parameters to plug-ins that you have embedded using the <object> tag. Images should use the **<img>** tag instead of the <object> tag.

Your <object> elements need to appear inside the <body> element, since they are local objects and not global (<head>) settings. The text between <object> and </object> is alternate text for browsers that don't support this tag. One of the data or type parameters also needs to be specified. The form parameter is new in HTML5, because objects can be submitted in HTML5 forms.

Objects can no longer appear in the <head> tag in HTML5. Table 20-3 describes 17 parameters supported by the <object> tag or element.

Table 20-3. *Seventeen Supported HTML5 <object> Tag Parameters*

Parameter	Parameter Data Value	Object Tag Parameter's Usage
align	top	Specifies an **alignment** of an <object> element to its surrounding elements
archive	URL	Space separated **URL** list to archive of relevant object resources
border	pixels	Specifies a **width for object's border**
classid	class_ID	Defines a **class_ID** value, as set in the Windows Registry, or in the URL
codebase	URL	Defines the **base URL**, referencing where to find the .class code for object
codetype	media_type	The **media type** of the code referred to by the classid attribute
data	URL	Specifies the **URL** for a **data resource**
declare	declare	Defines the object should only be **declared not instantiated** (created)
form	form_id	Specifies the **forms** object belongs to
height	pixels	Specifies the **height** for the object
hspace	pixels	Specifies the **whitespace** on the **left and right** sides of the object
name	name	Specifies the **name** for the object
standby	text	Defines **text value** to display while the object is streaming or loading
type	media_type	Specifies a **media type** for the data specified in the data attribute
usemap	#mapname	Specifies the name of a **client-side image map** to be used with the object
vspace	pixels	Specifies the **whitespace** on **top and bottom** of an object
width	pixels	Specifies the **width** for the object

You can define a basic <object> element using a **type** and **data** parameter to reference the asset data and object MIME type along with a **width** and **height** parameter defining the dimensions for your object canvas, as shown in the following HTML5 markup:

```
<!DOCTYPE html><html><head><title>Acrobat PDF Object Example</title></head>
<body>
 <section id="PDF-ObjectInsertionExample">
  <h1>Adobe Acrobat Object is Inserted Below</h1>
   <object data="abc.pdf" type="application/pdf" name="objectTagName"
```

```
        standby="Loading, please wait..."
        width="1024" height="600">
   <embed src="abc.pdf" type="application/pdf">
    <noembed>HTML5 Browser/OS doesn't support Java object type!</noembed>
   <embed>
  </object>
 </section>
</body>
</html>
```

You can also add a **standby** parameter for a "please wait" message to display while the object is loading. You can use **<embed>** inside of <object> to support legacy browsers! The **<param>** tag is a child tag, which adds parameters to the tags not covered in this chapter. Doing so adds capabilities that don't have to be parameters of the parent tag. Let's take a look at the <param> tag next, before we finish up.

Declaring Parameters: Using the PARAM Tag

The parameter <param> tag is used with the <applet> tag to pass parameters. It is also used with the <object> tag to specify the object parameters, as seen in the previous HTML5 markup example. Table 20-4 describes four <param> tag parameters.

Table 20-4. *Four <param> Tag Parameters*

Param Tag Parameter	Param Tag Parameter's Usage
name	Defines the **name** of the parameter
value	Defines the **value** of the parameter
type	Defines a **media (MIME) type (no HTML5 support)**
valuetype	Defines a **value type** (not supported in HTML5)

Let's use <param> to embed a Java applet using <object>.

```
<!DOCTYPE html><html>
<head><title>Java Object Insertion Example</title></head>
<body>
 <section id="Java-JavaFXObjectInsertionExample">
  <h1>Java or JavaFX Application Object is Inserted Below</h1>
   <object type="application/x-java-applet" name="objectTagName"
           standby="Object is loading, please wait..."
           width="1024" height="600">
     <param name="code" value="classNameHere.class" />
     <param name="archive" value="archiveNameHere.jar" />
     <param name="scriptable" value="true" />
     <param name="mayscript" value="true" />
```

185

```
      ALERT: Your HTML5 Browser or OS doesn't support a Java object type!
    </object>
   </section>
  </body>
</html>
```

Next, let's discuss the rules of thumb on when to use one embedding approach vs. another.

To Embed or Not to Embed: Tag Selection

One of the most active discussion topics regarding HTML5 tags concerns <embed> versus <object> versus <applet> versus <iframe> when it comes to embedding content in HTML5 documents and applications.

The <applet> tag is deprecated, but developers still use it; the other three are part of an HTML5 specification, but each has its own following. You need to discover how each works for your own purposes. These tags are almost as complex as the <canvas> tag and WebGL 2.

Oracle discusses the rules of thumb on its Java 8 website at:

docs.oracle.com/javase/8/docs/technotes/guides/jweb/applet/using_tags.html

Use the <applet> tag if an HTML5 web page is accessed through the Internet. If the HTML5 web page is accessed through a corporate intranet, use the <object> tag or the <embed> tag.

When deploying applets for specific HTML5 browsers, use the <object> tag for Internet Explorer only. Use an <embed> tag for the Mozilla family of browsers. If you must deploy an applet in a mixed-browser environment, follow these guidelines.

When using a pure HTML approach to deploy applets in a mixed-browser environment, note the following regarding IE and Mozilla:

Internet Explorer recognizes the <object> tag and ignores the contents of the **<comment>** tag, as shown in this markup:

```
<!DOCTYPE html><html><head><title>Acrobat PDF Object Example</title></head>
<body>
  <section id="PDF-ObjectInsertionExample">
   <h1>Adobe Acrobat Object is Inserted Below</h1>
    <object data="abc.pdf" type="application/pdf" name="objectTagName"
            standby="Loading, please wait..."
            width="1024" height="600">
     <comment>
```

```
    <embed src="abc.pdf" type="application/pdf">
      <noembed>HTML5 Browser/OS doesn't support Java object type!</noembed>
    <embed>
  </comment>
   </object>
  </section>
 </body>
</html>
```

Mozilla browsers ignore the <object> tag using the **classid** attribute and interpret the contents of a <comment> tag, so consider using the previous PDF example code for HTML5, where an <embed> tag is used inside a <comment> tag in the <object> tag.

The moral of this chapter is to test all of your plug-in assets and applications carefully! Testing is the best way to actually ascertain how HTML5 application and embedded assets ultimately work together.

Summary

In this chapter, you learned about tag support in HTML5 for plugging in or embedding external application or document assets, including the <embed>, <applet>, <object>, and <param> tags. In the next chapter, you explore the HTML5 **template** <template> tag and learn how to use HTML5 templates.

CHAPTER 21

■ ■ ■

HTML5 Frames: Using the <iframe> Tag

Now let's cover tags from the golden days of **HTML**, when **framesets** and **frames** were commonly used to define areas on the screen. One of these frame-related tags, the <iframe> tag, is still in use today. It allows developers to add pages in other websites into an internal frame, or iframe, in their HTML5 design. This is sometimes called **embedding content**, but it is different from the <embed>, <object>, and <applet> elements.

In this chapter, you look at three frame-related tags. Two of these are legacy tags not supported in HTML5; they are not recommended for use. They were used heavily in HTML2 and HTML 3.2, so I am including them here for the sake of completeness. One of the tags, the <iframe> tag, is still supported in HTML5, and that is what we'll focus on for most of this chapter.

In this chapter, you look at the frameset **<frameset>** tag, the related frame **<frame>** tag, and the iframe **<iframe>** tag which is still supported for use in HTML5.

HTML Frame Legacy: The FRAMESET and FRAME Tags

The **<frameset>** tag used to be a popular way in the legacy **HTML** specifications to create areas in a website that would change shape and size as you resized the browser window. As HTML advanced over the years, other tags such as <div> and <span> and CSS elements such as center, auto and fit-content were introduced for doing this, and became the recommended way of doing things. Framesets and frames are not recommended for use in HTML anymore, and that goes tenfold for HTML5, where they are not supported. So, here I cover <frameset> and its child tag <frame> briefly, and then get into <iframe>, which is still supported in HTML5.

The <frameset> tag defines the frame set, which then holds several **<frame>** elements. Each <frame> element holds a separate document, using a src parameter to reference the document source HTTP location.

A <frameset> element specifies the number of columns or rows there are in the frame set, and the distribution of space, using a percentage or pixel value. These indicate the amount of space each frame occupies in the HTML document or website.

© Wallace Jackson 2016
W. Jackson, *HTML5 Quick Markup Reference*, DOI 10.1007/978-1-4302-6536-8_21

If you wanted to validate any page containing frames, be sure that your <!DOCTYPE> is set to either HTML Frameset DTD or to XHTML Frameset DTD.

Table 21-1 shows two frameset tag parameters supported in legacy HTML.

Table 21-1. *Two Frameset Parameters*

Menu Parameters	Menu Parameters' Usage
cols	Specifies the number and size of **columns** in a frameset
rows	Specifies number and size of **rows** in a frameset

Here is an example of how you would create a frame set in HTML **using the <frame> child tag to hold the frame definitions**:

```
<frameset cols="25%,*,25%"> <!-- 25% outer column width, center scales -->
  <frame src="frame_one.html" />
  <frame src="frame_two.html" />
  <frame src="frame_three.html" />
</frameset>
```

Next, let's take a look at the **<iframe>** tag, which shows another HTML5 page in a frame in HTML5.

HTML5 Frames: Using the IFRAME Tag

The **<iframe>** tag defines an **area** in an HTML document design to show a remote HTML page; it's kind of like a portal that encapsulates another HTML document inside of your own HTML5 document, website, e-book, or application designs. An <iframe> tag is in somewhat similar to the <embed>, <object>, and applet tags, but instead of apps or plug-ins, the <iframe> embeds another HTML document design. Technically, the <iframe> tag specifies an **inline frame**, which seamlessly embeds another document within your current HTML5 document. To support browsers that do not support <iframe>, you add text between the opening <iframe> tag and the closing </iframe> tag. You can use CSS3 if you want to style an <iframe> element. For instance, you may want to include scrollbars. This is done by using the CSS3 **overflow** property set to the value of **scroll** in the following CSS3 style:

```
iframe { overflow: scroll; }
```

Table 21-2 shows 11 <iframe> tag parameters. The first six are new to HTML5 and the second five are acceptable parameters in legacy HTML projects, but they are not used in HTML5.

Table 21-2. *Eleven HTML5 iFrame Parameters (six new in HTML 5)*

iFrame Parameter	iFrame Parameter Usage
src	Specifies an **HTTP URL address** of an HTML document to embed in your <iframe> element
width	Specifies the **width** for your <iframe> in pixels
height	Specifies the **height** for your <iframe> in pixels
name	Specifies the **name** for your <iframe> element
sandbox	Enables the **extra set of restrictions** for your content in an <iframe> options include: allow-forms, allow-pointer-lock, allow-popups, allow-same-origin, allow-scripts, and allow-top-navigation
srcdoc	Specifies actual **HTML content** values for the page you want to show in the <iframe>
align	Specifies the **alignment** of an <iframe> according to other surrounding HTML elements
frameborder	Specifies whether or not to display a **border** around your <iframe> element
longdesc	Specifies a **URL** to a page that contains a long form description of the content of an <iframe>
marginwidth	Specifies the **left and right margin** for the content in your <iframe> element
marginheight	Specifies the **top and bottom margin** for the content in your <iframe> element
scrolling	Specifies whether to display **scrollbars** for your <iframe> element. Parameter options include yes, no, and auto

Let's add the Apress website to the HTML5 example using an <iframe> named "apress" that is 800 × 600 resolution. This is accomplished in the following HTML5 markup:

```
<iframe src=http://www.apress.com width="800" height="600" name="apress">
  ALERT: If you can see this message, your browser doesn't support iFrame
</iframe>
```

You can use your **sandbox** parameter to "sandbox" external content for testing. The sandbox attribute enables an **extra set of restrictions**, for content displayed inside of your <iframe>.

When the sandbox attribute is present, it treats your HTML5 content as if it comes from a unique origin. It blocks form submissions and JavaScript execution. The sandbox parameter disables any APIs and prevents any links from targeting another browsing context. The sandbox prevents content from using plug-ins through <embed>, <object>, and <applet>. It also prevents content from navigating to a top-level browsing context and blocks automatically triggered features, such as automatically playing video streams or automatically setting focus to form controls.

The value of the sandbox attribute is simply the keyword **sandbox**, as shown in the following example. All restrictions are applied. Here the Apress website is added to the HTML example by using an <iframe> with a sandbox parameter:

```
<iframe src=http://www.apress.com width="800" height="600" sandbox >
  ALERT: If you can see this message, your browser doesn't support iFrame
</iframe>
```

You could also specify a value for the sandbox parameter, which contains a space-separated list of pre-defined values. This allows you to turn off any of those specific restrictions.

Let's add the Apress website to the current HTML5 example using an <iframe> that allows forms, pop-ups, and JavaScript. This is accomplished in the following HTML5 markup:

```
<iframe src=http://www.apress.com width="800" height="600" name="apress"
        sandbox="allow-forms allow-popups allow-scripts" >
  ALERT: If you can see this message, your browser doesn't support iFrame
</iframe>
```

Rather than the <iframe> tag, some HTML5 developers use the <object> tag with a type=text/html parameter to load external HTML content. Let's revisit this discussion again, as you did in the previous chapter with embed vs. applet vs. object.

Using Object or iFrame: More Discussion

Some HTML5 developers are bound to make the assumption that the <object type="text/html"> element declaration is the same as using an <iframe>, and some may go as far as to assume that <object> is more powerful because it also allows a nesting of <param> (parameter passing) child tags. However, HTML5 developers would be incorrect in making this assumption.

The primary "under the hood" difference is that <iframe> establishes a **real-time link** between your two HTML5 pages, such that it establishes "dynamic updating" between those two servers and the content they establish. Indeed, that **sandbox** parameter, that we looked at in the previous section, proves this out, and the <object> tag does not have this internal "DOM wiring" as it was originally purposed with connecting HTML5 with non-HTML5 content types, and not with "other-HTML5 content" types. This is your primary difference between <object> and <iframe>, and, between <embed> and <iframe> for that matter, if you want to look at something using a blanket, high-level assumption.

The moral of this story is to use <iframe> for real-time embeds of inter-HTML5, real-time linked content, to insert other HTML and HTML5 content (if it is not your intellectual property (IP), be sure to get written permission) into your HTML 5 or HTML 5.1 documents, websites, e-books, iTV Sets, and applications.

Summary

This chapter explained legacy <frameset> and <frame> tags, and support in HTML5 for the <iframe> tag. It discussed embedding differences among the <iframe>, the <object>, and <embed> tags. In the next chapter, you look at the new support in HTML5 for ruby annotations.

■ ■ ■

HTML5 Ruby Annotations: Using the <ruby> Tag

Now let's discuss a brand-new tag in HTML5 that allows developers to provide ruby annotations, which allow you to provide small text helpers for your HTML5 users to help them understand your primary content. Oftentimes this is translation assistance for foreign languages or technical jargon.

In this chapter, you look at three powerful tags in HTML5 that allow you to implement **ruby annotations** content seamlessly for HTML5 content. These include the ruby annotation **<ruby>** tag, the ruby parenthesis **<rp>** tag, the ruby text **<rt>** tag, the ruby base **<rb>** tag and the ruby text container **<rtc>** tag. You'll learn when to use each of the tags and what they allow you to add to your HTML5 content production, publishing, and work delivery process.

Currently, ruby annotations don't have widespread browser support. This chapter is included as a quick reference. That said, ruby annotations are something that many of you want to know about.

Ruby Annotations: The RUBY Tag

A <ruby> tag specifies a ruby annotation. It has *zero* relationship to the popular Ruby programming language! A ruby annotation is a small, extra snippet of text attached to the primary text. It indicates a pronunciation for, or alternate meaning of, the corresponding characters that it is connected to. This kind of annotation is often used in Japanese, Chinese, Korean, or Arabic publications.

You can use a <ruby> tag as a parent container to define ruby annotations by using the <rt> child tag with an <rp> child tags to define the annotation itself. A <ruby> element consists of one character, or a series of characters, which requires the technical explanation, or possibly some pronunciation details.

Inside a parent **<ruby>** tag, you have an **<rt>** tag that contains your pronunciation information. You may also have an optional ruby parenthesis or **<rp>** element. This defines what to show in browsers that do not currently support ruby annotations. The hope is that browser or HTML5 OS manufacturers move quickly to support the ruby annotation convention, because it should be especially useful for consumer electronics devices such as UHD iTV Sets, smartphones, e-book readers, and tablets.

© Wallace Jackson 2016
W. Jackson, *HTML5 Quick Markup Reference*, DOI 10.1007/978-1-4302-6536-8_22

Table 22-1 shows the six ruby annotation tags that are currently supported in HTML5.

Table 22-1. *Six HTML5 Ruby Annotation Tags All Are New in HTML5*

HTML5 Ruby Tag	HTML5 Ruby Annotation Tag's Usage
<ruby>	Defines a **ruby annotation definition (parent)**
<rt>	Defines a **ruby annotation text element (child)**
<rtc>	Defines a **ruby text container (child)**
<rp>	Defines a **ruby annotation parenthesis (child)**
<rb>	Defines a **ruby base text element (child)**
<rbc>	Defines a **ruby base container (child)**

Here's an example of how you use a ruby annotation to define the word **colloquialism** using the primary three HTML5 <ruby> tags, supported across all of the browsers, in the HTML5 markup for a basic dictionary word entry and pronunciation:

```
<ruby>
   <strong>col·lo·qui·al·ism</strong>
     <rp>(</rp>
           <rt>kə'lōkwēə,lizəm</rt>
     <rp>)</rp>
</ruby>
```

The parent ruby tag contains the word colloquialism, and surrounds this word with the semantic **<strong>** tag, to bold it. This shows the user that this is a word that is central to your content, and is the word which is going to be defines using the ruby annotation which follows it in parenthesis.

After this is your **<rp>** tag to add the left parenthesis, and then the **<rt>** tag containing your pronunciation text, and then the <rp> tag again to add the right parenthesis, and then the closing **</ruby>** tag to end the ruby annotation definition.

I am not sure if the publisher is using the UFT-16 character set to publish the book, but here is an example of the Japanese word *Kanji* defined using a <ruby> annotation:

```
<ruby>
  漢 <rp>(</rp>
             <rt>Kan</rt>
     <rp>)</rp>
  字 <rp>(</rp>
             <rt>ji</rt>
     <rp>)</rp>
</ruby>
```

196

If you want to see <ruby> in action mixing together the Japanese *Kanji*, Chinese, Korean, and Arabic examples, you have to look at these online to get an idea as to how ruby annotations work with foreign languages, which each have completely different character sets. Simply enter a search for "ruby annotation example" and you will find some examples. Next, let's cover some of the more complex ruby annotation child tags that allow you to build advanced ruby annotations.

Advanced Ruby Annotations: Ruby Containers

The ruby text container **<rtc>** element can be used as the container for <rt> elements, in more advanced ruby annotations. One or two <rtc> elements may appear inside a <ruby> element to associate ruby texts with a single base text, represented by an **<rbc>** element, which you look at next. No more than two <rtc> tags can appear inside a ruby element. Here is an HTML5 example of the parent-child relationship for these tags:

```
<ruby>
 <rtc>
  <rt>さい</rt>
  <rt>とう</rt>
  <rt>のぶ</rt>
  <rt>お</rt>
 </rtc>
</ruby>
```

The ruby base container <rbc> element serves as the container for ruby base <rb> elements for ruby annotation. Only one <rbc> element is allowed to appear inside of a ruby tag.

This ruby base <rb> element marks up base text. In simple ruby annotation only one <rb> element may appear. In complex ruby annotation, multiple <rb> tags may appear inside an <rbc> element, as is shown in the following HTML5 markup:

```
<ruby>
 <rbc>
  <rb>斎</rb>
  <rb>藤</rb>
  <rb>信</rb>
  <rb>男</rb>
 </rbc>
</ruby>
```

Each <rb> tag is associated with your corresponding <rt> element yielding fine-grained control for ruby annotation. The <rb> element contains in-line elements or character data as its content. The <ruby> element isn't allowed as a child tag because it can only be used as a container tag (i.e., the parent tag).

Once you put these together, you get a complex definition, where the <rbc> construct holds base text for the base language and the <rtc> holds the ruby text definition in the translation language. When rendered, the <rb> text is on the bottom and the <rt> characters are at the top, in a smaller font, defining the <rb> characters using a different language character set:

```
<ruby>
 <rbc>
  <rb>斎</rb>
  <rb>藤</rb>
  <rb>信</rb>
  <rb>男</rb>
 </rbc>
 <rtc>
  <rt>さい</rt>
  <rt>とう</rt>
  <rt>のぶ</rt>
  <rt>お</rt>
 </rtc>
</ruby>
```

Expect ruby annotations to gain support as the HTML5 OS continues to proliferate and HTML5 continues to internationalize due to increased sales of HTML5 iTV Sets and smartphones.

Summary

In this chapter, you looked at the <ruby> tag support in HTML5 for defining ruby annotations, including the <ruby>, <rt>, <rtc>, <rb>, <rbc>, and <rp> tags. In the next chapter, you look at the new HTML 5.1 **OS features** tags, which ultimately allow HTML5 to implement application features, such as **menuing** and **dialogs**.

CHAPTER 23

■ ■ ■

HTML 5.1 Tags: Using Menu and Dialog Design Elements

Finally, let's discuss the tags that are new in **HTML 5.1** that allow developers to add elements such as menu structures and dialogs that are used in HTML5 applications. These have been added because HTML5 is now being used for at least half a dozen major consumer electronics operating systems, including Mozilla's Firefox OS, Canonical's Ubuntu Touch OS, Opera OS, Jolla's Sailfish OS, Google's Chrome OS, and Linux Foundation Tizen OS.

This chapter looks at three powerful tags that are new in HTML 5.1 allowing implementation of **application user interface elements** seamlessly in HTML 5.1 OS content. Note that current browsers may not have implemented these as yet; an exception to this is your **Firefox** browser. This is probably due to Mozilla's aggressive expansion of the Firefox OS worldwide.

The menu **<menu>** tag, a related menu item **<menuitem>** tag, and the dialog **<dialog>** tag are all new. You see how to use these tags and what they allow you to add to HTML5 applications for use on consumer electronics products, such as smartwatches, UHD iTV Sets, e-book readers, tablets, laptops, and smartphones.

HTML5 Application Menu: The MENU Tag

The **<menu>** tag in the new **HTML 5.1** specification creates menuing systems. This works in documents, websites, e-books, and HTML5 applications, though it's necessary only for HTML5 applications, as HTML 5.1 needed to add launch icons, menuing, and dialogs at a minimum to achieve the required user interface elements in order to be taken seriously as an operating system. The underlying Linux kernel provides the rest of those "under the hood" OS features that are necessary.

A <menu> tag can be used to define a list of commands or a menu filled with commands. The <menu> tag is used for context menus, toolbars, or for lists of form controls or command lists.

© Wallace Jackson 2016
W. Jackson, *HTML5 Quick Markup Reference*, DOI 10.1007/978-1-4302-6536-8_23

Table 23-1 shows two <menu>tag parameters supported in HTML 5.1 when it is released in the fourth quarter of 2016, a few months after this reference title is published.

Table 23-1. *HTML 5.1 Menu Parameters Supported in HTML 5.1*

Menu Parameter	Menu Parameter's Usage
label	Defines a **menu label using a text value**
type	Defines a **menu type (list, context, or toolbar)**

Here is an example of how you can create an **empty** pop-up **context** (right-click) menuing structure using the primary HTML 5.1 <menu> tags inside of a standard HTML5 markup structure:

```
<menu type="context" id="emptymenu" label="Click For Sub-Menu">
    <menu label="submenu1">
        <menuitem/>
        <menuitem/>
    </menu>
    <menu label="submenu2">
        <menuitem/>
        <menuitem/>
    </menu>
    <menu label="submenu3">
        <menuitem/>
        <menuitem/>
    </menu>
</menu>
```

Next, let's take a look at the <menuitem> tag, which populate menus or submenus with menu option items.

Populating HTML5 Menus: Using a MENUITEM Tag

The **<menuitem>** tag defines a **command** or a **menu item** that your users select using a pop-up menu (context right-click or list left-click) or a toolbar menu (a graphical menu representation). You can make your <menuitem> commands execute JavaScript functions or DOM API calls by using the **onclick** parameter that we looked at earlier in the book. To give the <menuitem> a text label, you'll use the required label parameter. It is also important to note that the <menuitem> tag is currently supported only in Mozilla Firefox and that even in the Firefox OS and browser, it currently only works for context menus. Expect label menu and toolbar support to arrive shortly!

Table 23-2 shows the seven <menuitem> tag parameters that should be well supported when HTML 5.1 comes out in 2016.

Table 23-2. *Seven HTML5 MenuItem Parameters All New in HTML 5.1*

MenuItem Parameter	MenuItem Parameter Usage
label (Required)	Specifies your **text for your command/menu item**, as it is shown to the users of your menu
checked	Specifies that this command/menu item should be **checked** (selected) when your page loads. Only use this for type="radio" and type="checkbox"
default	Specifies a command or menu item as being your **default** command or menu item
disabled	Specifies that the command or menu item should be **disabled** (greyed-out, and not selectable)
icon	Specifies the **icon URL** for a command/menu item
radiogroup	Specifies the **name of a group of commands** that is toggled when the command or menu item itself is toggled. This is for type="radio"
type	Defines a **menuitem type (check box, command or radio) default is command**

Let's add three <menuitem> tags to a <menu> tag, to show you how this works with the Italian car example.

Since this <menuitem> tag only holds parameters, you can use the **<menuitem parameter-list />** tag format, rather than the <menuitem parameter-list > </menuitem> format, which would also be valid markup, if you prefer to use that markup approach:

```
<menu type="context" id="carmenu" label="Italian Cars">
    <menuitem label="Lamborghini"
              icon="lamborghini_icon.png"
              type="command" />
    <menuitem label="Maserati"
              icon="maserati_icon.png"
              type="command" />
    <menuitem label="Ferrari"
              icon="ferrari_icon.png"
              type="command" />
</menu>
```

You can use the other parameters to add selection check markings, default menu items, disable menu items, radio button groups, and icon graphics, just like menus in advanced operating systems such as Android, Solaris, Windows, Linux, and Macintosh OS/X. HTML5 operating systems that began as browsers should be added to this list, including Firefox OS, Opera OS, Tizen OS, and Chrome OS.

Creating Sub-Menus: Nested MENU Tag Usage

To create a **sub-menu** you would simply **nest** a <menu> tag, as demonstrated in the following HTML5 markup for this example:

```
<menu type="context" id="carmenu">
  <menu label="Italian Cars">
    <menuitem label="Lamborghini"
              icon="lamborghini_icon.png"
              type="command" />
    <menuitem label="Maserati"
              icon="maserati_icon.png"
              type="command" />
    <menuitem label="Ferrari"
              icon="ferrari_icon.png"
              type="command" />
  </menu>
  <menu label="German Cars">
    <menuitem label="Porsche"
              icon="porsche_icon.png"
              type="command" />
    <menuitem label="Audi"
              icon="audi_icon.png"
              type="command" />
    <menuitem label="Volkswagen"
              icon="volkswagen_icon.png"
              type="command" />
  </menu>
  <menu label="American Cars">
    <menuitem label="Chevrolet"
              icon="chevy_icon.png"
              type="command" />
    <menuitem label="Ford"
              icon="ford_icon.png"
              type="command" />
    <menuitem label="Jeep"
              icon="jeep_icon.png"
              type="command" />
  </menu>
</menu>
```

Next, let's take a look at how we can add HTML5 dialogs!

HTML5 Application Dialog: A Dialog Tag

Dialogs are another important component for applications, and a dialog component is just as important for an operating system to support as a menu component or application launch icons. The **<dialog>** tag can be used to define a dialog box or a dialog window. This <dialog> element allows developers to create pop-up dialogs and modal dialogs in a document, e-book, web page, or application. The browsers which currently support this HTML 5.1 tag include Opera or Chrome, but interestingly, not Firefox as yet. Table 23-3 shows the one parameter that is currently supported for the <dialog> tag (element), which specifies that a dialog be open initially.

Table 23-3. *One HTML5 Dialog Parameter That Is New in HTML 5.1*

Dialog Parameter	Dialog Parameter's Usage
open	Defines an initial **open dialog state for dialog**

To create an open dialog with some text information, you would use the following HTML 5.1 markup, using the Italian Cars example using a basic table of car models with standard colors:

```
<table>
 <tr>
  <th>Ferrari<dialog open>Ferrari Cars Are Usually Red!</dialog></th>
  <th>Lamborghini</th>
  <th>Maserati</th>
 </tr>
 <tr>
  <td>Red</td>
  <td>Yellow</td>
  <td>Black</td>
 </tr>
</table>
```

Expect <dialog> support in the other HTML5 engines soon.

Summary

In this final chapter, you looked at the new <menu> and <dialog> tag support in HTML 5.1 for defining HTML5 application components for the upcoming explosion of HTML5 operating systems, of which there are currently half a dozen in use. You looked at the <menu>, <menuitem>, and <dialog> tags, and how to create basic menus and dialogs.

I hope you have enjoyed this *HTML5 Quick Markup Reference* manual as much as I have enjoyed writing it! Best of luck with your HTML5 development endeavors.

■ ■ ■

NetBeans: Set up an HTML5 Integrated Development IDE

Let's pull together your foundation for a highly professional, HTML5-friendly, **NetBeans 8.1** integrated development environment (IDE). Your development workstation is the most important combination of PC hardware and software, allowing you to reach the goal of HTML5-compatible applications development. Let's take an appendix to consider your hardware HTML5 software development workstation needs.

Let's first get all of the tedious setup tasks out of the way. If you already have your workstation configured, you can proceed to Chapter 1 for an overview of HTML. If you already are familiar with HTML, start with Chapter 2.

Everything that you learn over the course of this book needs to be experienced equally by each reader. In Appendix D, you learn where to go to download and how to install several of the most impressive, professional, open source new media software packages on the face of this planet! You are about to "max out" your HTML5, CSS3, and JavaScript development workstation, so be sure to hold on tight and enjoy this virtual download ride!

Create a HTML Development Workstation

The first thing to do after looking at hardware requirements is to **download** and **install** the entire Java software development kit (SDK), which Oracle calls Java SE 8 JDK (Java Development Kit). The NetBeans 8.1 IDE uses the Java 8 SE (Standard Edition) runtime, which is one of the components of the Java Development Kit.

The second thing to do is **download** and **install** the NetBeans 8.1 IDE from www.netbeans.org. The NetBeans 8.1 IDE allows you to develop HTML5-compatible applications with all of the popular programming languages, including C, C++, Java, PHP, Python, JavaFX, Ruby, HTML5, CSS3, ECMAscript, and JavaScript.

After your HTML5 application development environment is set up, you can then download and install new media asset development tools, as outlined in Appendix D. These are used in conjunction with NetBeans for image editing (GIMP) or non-linear digital video editing (Lightworks); visual effects or VFX (Fusion 8); digital audio sweetening or editing (Audacity 2.1.2); i3D modeling and animation (Blender); SVG digital illustration (Inkscape); and even a open source office business productivity suite (Apache OpenOffice).

© Wallace Jackson 2016
W. Jackson, *HTML5 Quick Markup Reference*, DOI 10.1007/978-1-4302-6536-8

This appendix can take your development to an all-new level, showing you how to create the HTML5 development and markup workstation that runs your HTML5 design business.

All of these software development tools come close to matching the primary feature sets of expensive paid software packages, such as those from Apple (FCP-X), Autodesk (3D Studio Max 2016), Adobe (Photoshop, Illustrator, After Effects), Avid (ProTools), and Nuke, and all at *zero* cost to your production company!

Open source software is free to download, install, and upgrade, and it continuously adds features. It's becoming more like professional software every day. You will be completely amazed at how professional open source software packages have become over the last decade or so.

Development Workstations: Hardware Foundation

Since you will put together the foundation of your HTML5-capable application development workstation that will be used for the duration of this book, I want to take a moment to review NetBeans 8's HTML5 development workstation hardware requirements. This is a factor that influences your development performance (speed). This is clearly as important as the software itself, since hardware is what is actually running the software package's algorithms.

Minimum requirements for NetBeans 8.1 IDE include 512MB of memory, 750MB of hard disk space, and XGA (1024 × 768) display.

Now let's discuss what you need to make the NetBeans 8 HTML IDE usable. Let's start with upgrading the 1024 × 768 XGA display to an HDTV (1920 × 1080 at 120FPS refresh rate) or UHD (4096 × 2160 at 120FPS refresh rate) widescreen display. These are now affordable and give you 4 to 16 times the display "real estate" of an XGA display. HDTVs are now $250 to $500 and UHDTV displays are now under $1,000.

I recommend using, at a bare minimum, the **Intel i7** quad-core processor, or, the **AMD 64-bit** octa-core processor. Install at least 8GB of DDR3-1600 memory. I'm using a 64-bit, octa-core AMD 8350, with 16GB of DDR3-1600. Intel also has a hexa-core i7 processor. This would be the equivalent of having twelve cores, as each i7 core can host two threads. Similarly, an i7 quad-core should look like eight cores, to your 64-bit operating system's thread-scheduling algorithm.

There are also DDR3-1800 and DDR3-2133 clock speed memory module components available. A high number signifies fast memory access speeds. To calculate actual megahertz speeds the memory is cycling at, divide the number by 4 (1333 = 333MHz, 1600 = 400MHz, 1800 = 450MHz, 2133 = 533MHz).

Memory access speed is a massive workstation performance factor, because your processor is usually bottlenecked by the speed at which processor cores can access your data (in memory).

With the high-speed processing and memory access going on inside the workstation, it's extremely important to keep everything cool so that you do not experience **thermal problems**. I recommend using a wide, full-tower enclosure with 120mm or 200mm cooling fans (one or two at least), as well as a captive liquid induction cooling fan on the CPU.

It is important to note that the cooler the system runs, the faster it can run, and the longer it will last, so load the workstation up with lots of silent high-speed fans!

If you really want a maximum performance, install an SSD (solid-state drive) as your primary disk drive, where your applications and operating system software load. Use legacy HDD hardware for your D:\ hard drive for the slower data storage (long-term). Put your current project files on the SSD.

I am using a 64-bit Windows 8 operating system, which is fairly memory efficient. The Linux 64-bit OS is extremely memory efficient. I recommend using any 64-bit OS, so you can address more than 3.24GB of system memory.

HTML5 Development Workstation: Open Software

To create your well-rounded HTML5 application development workstation, you'll be installing all of the primary genres of open source software that comprises a professional development workstation. First, you install Java SE 8 and NetBeans 8.1. I also show you how to download GIMP, Lightworks, Fusion, Blender3D, and Audacity, which are also all open source software packages, in case your HTML applications are going to be using a graphical front end. Thus, we'll be putting together a 100% open source workstation for you. I'll also recommend other free software at the end of Appendix D so you can put together the production workstation that you have always dreamed of.

Open source software recently reached the close parallel to the level of professionalism of "paid" development software packages that cost thousands of dollars each to acquire. Using open source software packages like Java 8, NetBeans 8, Blender, GIMP, Audacity, Lightworks, Fusion, OpenOffice, and others, you can put together a free application development workstation and rival paid software workstations that would have cost you thousands!

For those readers who have just purchased their new HTML development workstation PC, and who are going to put the entire development software suite together completely from scratch, we'll go through the entire work process.

Java 8: Installing the Foundation for NetBeans 8.1

The first thing that you want to do is to visit the NetBeans website (`www.netbeans.org`) to find out what you'll need to run this IDE. When you get to the homepage, click the **Download** button, shown on the far right side of Figure A-1.

Figure A-1. *Go to netbeans.org and click Download*

As you can see, there are nine different download options to consider; six support JavaScript, which HTML is based on. I suggest the All version, which supports all of your popular programming languages, all of which HTML works with. If you are wondering why some of these downloads offer 32-bit, and 64-bit, versions, and some do not, as you can see in the bottom of Figure A-2, this is because the ones with both versions have been **pre-compiled**, whereas the other three require a Java 8 JDK to be installed. If you use the All version so that any programming languages you want to use with HTML are supported, you have to first install Java SE 8.

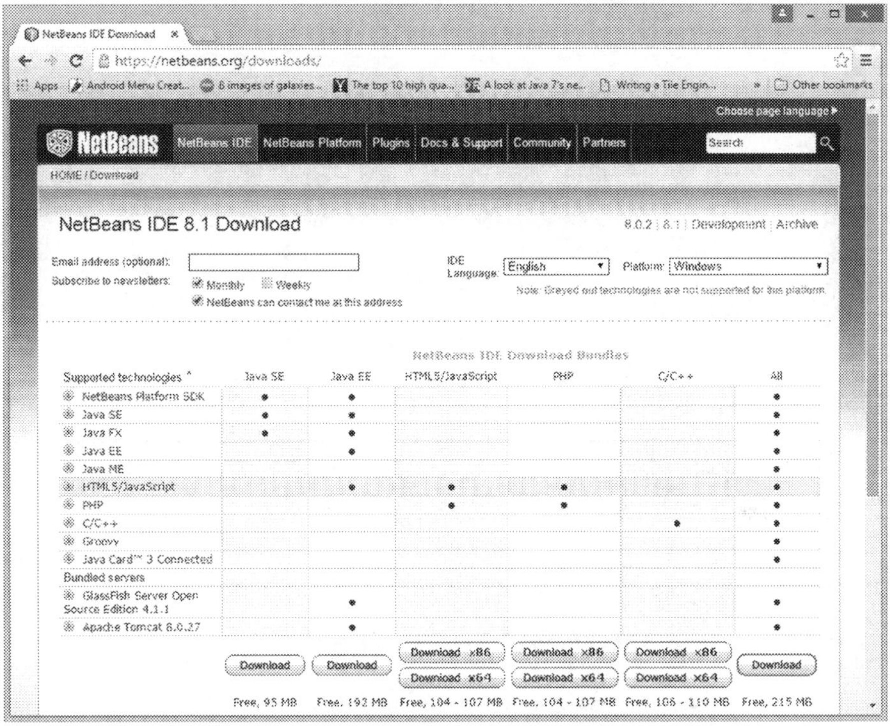

Figure A-2. *Download one of the HTML5/JavaScript IDE versions*

Open Google Chrome and Google "Java JDK" (see Figure A-3). Look for the **Java SE Development Kit 8 - Downloads** search result. Click it to open the Oracle Java 8.

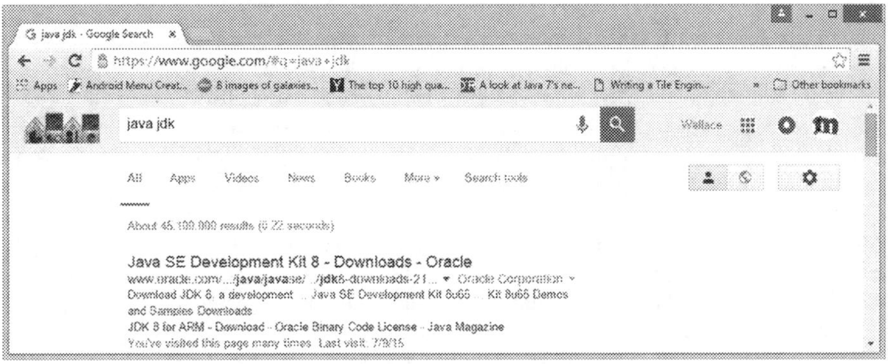

Figure A-3. *Google "Java JDK" and then click the Downloads link*

Go to the Oracle website to download and install the latest Java JDK environment, which at the time of this writing, is Java SE Development Kit 8u77 (see Figure A-4).

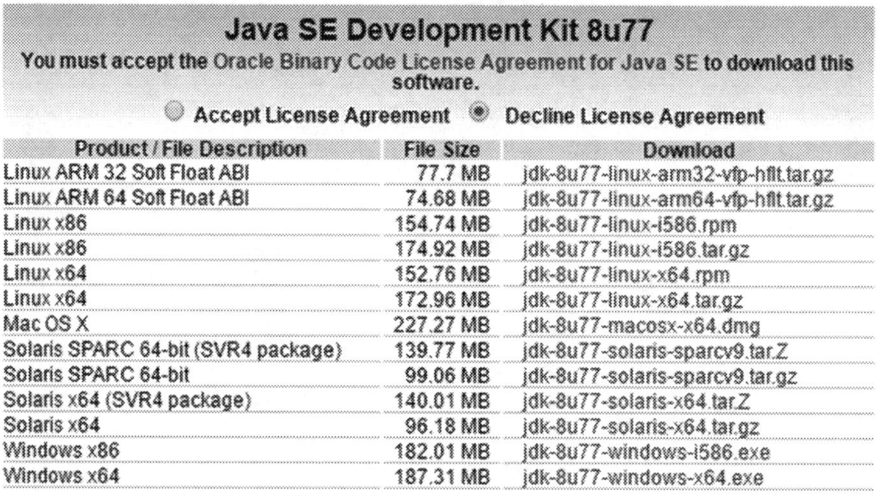

Java SE Development Kit 8u77

You must accept the Oracle Binary Code License Agreement for Java SE to download this software.

◯ Accept License Agreement   ◉ Decline License Agreement

Product / File Description	File Size	Download
Linux ARM 32 Soft Float ABI	77.7 MB	jdk-8u77-linux-arm32-vfp-hflt.tar.gz
Linux ARM 64 Soft Float ABI	74.68 MB	jdk-8u77-linux-arm64-vfp-hflt.tar.gz
Linux x86	154.74 MB	jdk-8u77-linux-i586.rpm
Linux x86	174.92 MB	jdk-8u77-linux-i586.tar.gz
Linux x64	152.76 MB	jdk-8u77-linux-x64.rpm
Linux x64	172.96 MB	jdk-8u77-linux-x64.tar.gz
Mac OS X	227.27 MB	jdk-8u77-macosx-x64.dmg
Solaris SPARC 64-bit (SVR4 package)	139.77 MB	jdk-8u77-solaris-sparcv9.tar.Z
Solaris SPARC 64-bit	99.06 MB	jdk-8u77-solaris-sparcv9.tar.gz
Solaris x64 (SVR4 package)	140.01 MB	jdk-8u77-solaris-x64.tar.Z
Solaris x64	96.18 MB	jdk-8u77-solaris-x64.tar.gz
Windows x86	182.01 MB	jdk-8u77-windows-i586.exe
Windows x64	187.31 MB	jdk-8u77-windows-x64.exe

Figure A-4. *The Oracle TechNetwork Java SE JDK Download website*

The URL is in the address bar in Figure A-4 and opens the download page for Java SE Development Kit, version 8u77.

I put the link here as well, in case you wanted to simply cut and paste it, copy it, or click it to launch:

```
www.oracle.com/technetwork/java/javase/downloads/jdk8-downloads-2133151.html
```

You should pull your scrollbar (on the right side of the webpage) halfway down the page to display the Java Development Kit download links table (see Figure A-4).

Once you click the **Accept License Agreement** radio button on the top-left of this download links table, you'll be able to click the link that you wish to use. If you're on Windows 10 and your OS is 64-bit, use the Windows x64 link, otherwise, use a Windows x86 link. I am using what is described in these links as "Windows x64," which is a 64-bit version of Windows, for my hexa-core Windows 7 and octa-core Windows 10 workstations.

Make sure that you use this Java SE Development Kit 8u77 downloading link, and do not use the JRE download (Java Runtime Edition) link. This JRE is part of JDK 8u77, so you do not have to worry about getting Java Runtime Edition (JRE) separately. In case you are wondering, you do indeed use the Java Runtime Edition to launch and run NetBeans IDE. You use this JDK inside of that software package, to provide the Java core class foundation that can also be used as a foundation for the Android OS Java-based API classes and for Java 8 or JavaFX apps.

Before you run this installation, you should remove your older versions of Java from your Windows Control Panel by using **Add or Remove Programs** (XP) or **Programs and Features** (Windows Vista, 7, 8, or 10), shown selected in blue in Figure A-5.

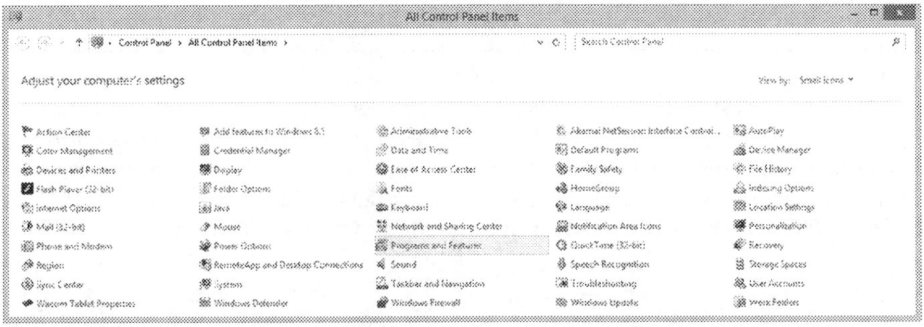

Figure A-5. *Launch your Control Panel* ➤ *Programs and Features*

This is necessary, especially if your workstation is not brand new. We do this so that only your latest Java SE 8u77 and JRE 8u77 are the Java versions that are currently installed on your HTML development workstation.

Select all the older Java versions, right-click each one, and select the **Uninstall** option, as seen in the bottom-right of Figure A-6.

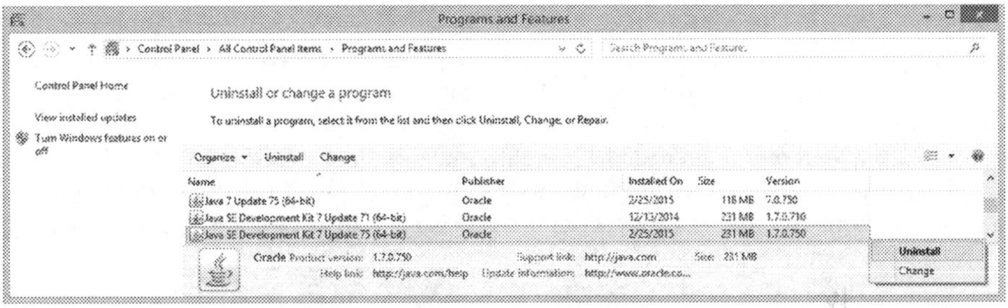

Figure A-6. *Find old versions of Java, right-click and Uninstall*

Once you have done this and downloaded your installation executable, locate it, and install this latest Java SE 8u77 JDK on your system, by double-clicking on the .exe file to launch a Setup dialog, seen on the left-hand side of Figure A-7. You can also right-click your installer file and then select the **Run as administrator** option.

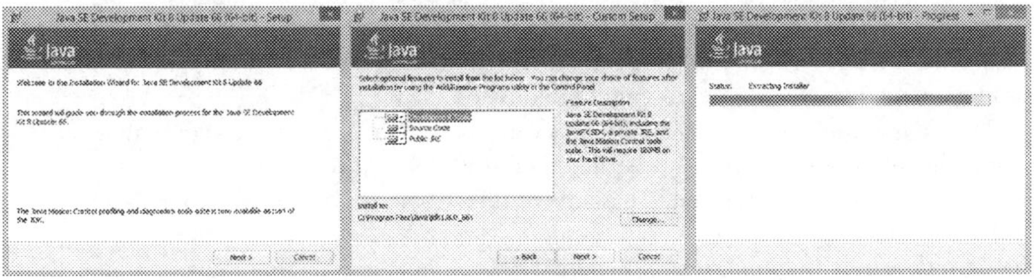

Figure A-7. *Setup, Custom Setup, and Extraction install dialogs*

Click the **Next** button to access the **Custom Setup** dialog, shown in the middle of Figure A-7. Accept the default settings, and then click the **Next** button again, to access the **Extracting Installer** progress dialog seen on the right side of Figure A-7.

Once you've extracted the installation software, you can select a Java JDK software installation folder. Use the default C:\ProgramFiles\Java\jre1.8.0_77 in the **Destination Folder** dialog as shown on the left-hand side of Figure A-8. Actually, the screenshots in Figures A-7 and A-8 were taken when I installed Java 8u66 for my *JSON Quick Syntax Reference* (2016) book; so just use your imagination and turn the 66 into a 77!

Figure A-8. *Destination, Progress, and Complete install dialogs*

JSON is also related to HTML5 development, so if you are interested in this topic, you can find a book of mine on the Apress website. If you enter "Wallace Jackson" in the search bar, it should bring up my books on new media, Java, JavaFX, game development, and Android.

Click the **Next** button, to install a Java Runtime Edition (JRE) edition in the default specified folder. Interestingly an installer won't ask you to specify the JDK folder name for some reason, probably because it wants your Java JDK to always be in a set or fixed (locked in the same location) folder name.

The JDK folder is named C:\ProgramFiles\Java\jdk1.8.0_77. Notice that internally Java 8 is referred to as Java 1.8.0. Thus, Java 6 is 1.6.0, and Java 7 is 1.7.0. This is useful to know if you are looking for Java versions using a search utility, for example, or want to show off your knowledge of legacy Java version numbering.

Once you click the **Next** button, you get the Java **Setup Progress** dialog, shown in the middle of Figure A-8. Once Java 8 is finished installing, you see your **Complete** dialog, which is seen on the right-hand side of Figure A-8. Congratulations! You have successfully installed Java 8!

Remember that the reason that you did not download a JRE is because it is part of this JDK 8u77 installation. The Java 8 Runtime Edition is the executable (platform) which runs the Java software app once it has been compiled into an application and also the latest JRE is needed to run NetBeans 8, which as you now know, is 100% completely written using the Java SE 8 development platform.

Once Java 8u77 or later is installed on your workstation we can then download and install the latest NetBeans 8 software installer from the NetBeans website.

You can also use that same **Programs and Features** (or **Add or Remove Programs**) utility in your Control Panel to remove older Java or NetBeans versions, or even to confirm the success of this latest Java 8 install.

Now you are ready to add the second layer of the NetBeans 8.1 IDE software on top of Java.

NetBeans 8.1: Download the NetBeans HTML IDE

The second step in the process is to visit the NetBeans website (https://www.netbeans.org/sdk/) to download and install the All version of the software (see Figure A-2).

Click the **Download** button found at the bottom of the All column on the webpage. This starts the browser download function, which should put the **netbeans-8.1-windows.exe** file in your Downloads folder.

Find this executable file on your workstation and either double-click it or right-click it, and select the **Run as administrator** option. This opens a **Welcome to the NetBeans IDE 8.1 Installer** dialog, shown on the left side of Figure A-9.

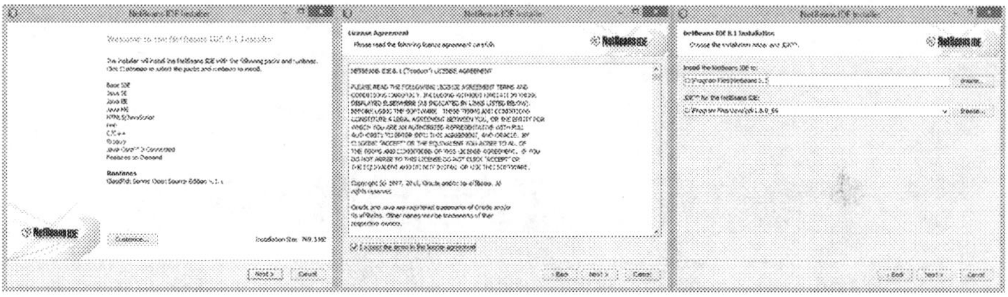

Figure A-9. *NetBeans install Welcome, License Agreement dialogs*

Click the **Next** button and select the **I accept the terms in the license agreement** option, and then click the **Next** button. I accepted the default Windows Program Files folder locations for all software installations, and again, clicked the **Next** button.

This gives you the **Summary** dialog (see Figure A-10), where you select **Check for Updates**, and then click the **Install** button to start the NetBeans 8.1 installation.

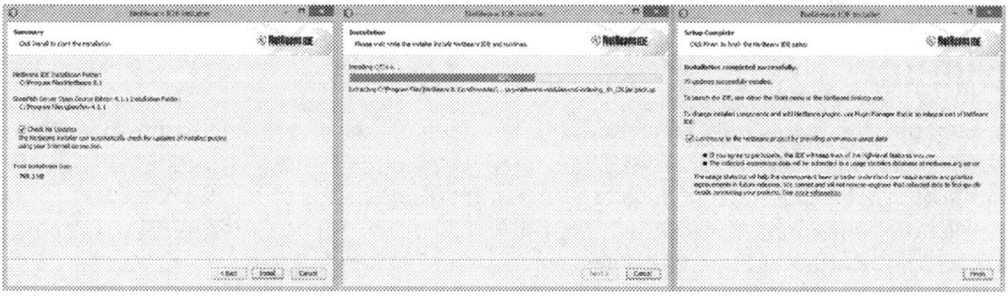

Figure A-10. *NetBeans Summary, Installation, and Complete dialog*

Once the setup is complete, click the **Finish** button. Launch the software to make sure that it works (see Figure A-11). I get into how to use NetBeans 8.1 to create a HTML project in Appendix B.

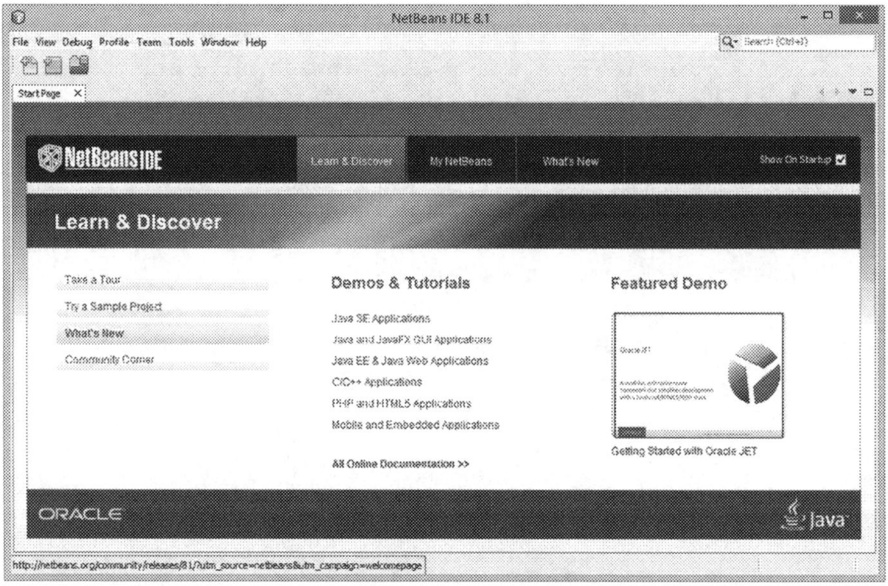

Figure A-11. *Launch NetBeans and explore using Learn & Discover*

If you're going to create new media–compatible HTML applications, you need to get seven more open source packages, so that you can create new media assets referenced by HTML and JavaScript (or Java, JavaFX, PHP, C++, AJAX, JSON, or similar).

These span the new media genres, including digital image compositing, 3D modeling and 3D animation, digital illustration and digital painting, digital audio editing, visual effects (VFX), and digital video editing, and are covered in Appendix D.

Summary

You set up a **NetBeans HTML5 workstation** by downloading and installing the open source **Java 8 JDK** and **NetBeans 8.1** integrated development software to code HTML applications. In Appendix B, you learn **how to set up an Eclipse 4.5.1 Mars HTML workstation in much the same fashion**. I show you how to set up your **IntelliJ IDEA 2016 HTML workstation** in Appendix C if you are an Android Studio 2.2 developer and prefer to use that IDEA instead.

■ ■ ■

Eclipse: Set up an HTML5 Integrated Development IDE

Let's put together your foundation for a professional, HTML5-friendly, **Eclipse 4.5.2** (Mars) integrated development environment (IDE). Your development workstation is the most important combination of PC hardware and software, allowing you to reach the goal of HTML5–compatible applications development.

Let's first get all of the tedious setup tasks out of the way. If you already have your workstation configured, you can proceed to Chapter 1 for an overview of HTML. If you already are familiar with HTML, start with Chapter 2.

I will outline all of the steps to put together an **Eclipse Mars** IDE–based HTML5 content development workstation.

Everything that you learn over the course of this book needs to be experienced equally by each reader. In this appendix, you learn where to go to download and how to install several of the most impressive, professional, open source software packages on the face of this planet!

You're about to "max out" your HTML, HTML5, CSS3, and JavaScript development workstation—so hold on tight and enjoy the ride!

Set up an HTML Development Workstation

The first thing to do after taking a look at hardware requirements is download and install the entire Java software development kit (SDK), which Oracle calls the Java SE 8 JDK (Java Development Kit). **Eclipse 4.5.2**, which is called the **Mars** IDE, uses the Java 8 SE (SE stands for Standard Edition).

The second thing to do is download and install the Eclipse Mars IDE from www.eclipse.org. It allows you to develop HTML-compatible applications using all of the popular programming languages, including Java EE, Java SE, Java Server Faces (JSF), JavaFX, HTML5, CSS3, and JavaScript.

After your HTML5 application development environment is set up, you can then download and install new media asset development tools. These are used, in conjunction with Eclipse Mars, for things such as image editing (GIMP) and non-linear digital video editing (Lightworks), special effects (Fusion), digital audio sweetening, or editing

(Audacity), i3D modeling, rendering, animation (Blender), digital illustration (Inkscape), and a business productivity suite (Open Office). I cover installation of these software packages in Appendix D.

This appendix should take your development to an all-new level, showing you how to create the media development and programming workstation that will run your HTML business.

All of these software development tools, which you'll be downloading and installing, come close to matching all the primary feature sets of expensive paid software packages, such as those from Apple (Final Cut Pro), Autodesk (3D Studio Max), Adobe (Photoshop, Illustrator, After Effects), Avid (ProTools), and all at *zero* cost to your content production company!

Open source software is free to download, install, and upgrade. It is continuously adding features. It's becoming more like professional software every day. You will be completely amazed at how professional your open source software packages have become over the last decade or so.

Development Workstations: Hardware Foundation

Since you will put together the foundation of your HTML5-capable application development workstation, which will be used for the duration of this book, I want to take a moment to review Eclipse Mars' HTML5 development workstation hardware requirements first. This is a factor that influences your development performance (speed). This is clearly as important as the software itself, since hardware is what is actually running the software package's algorithms.

Minimum requirements for Eclipse Mars IDE include 2GB of memory, 900MB of hard disk space, and WXGA (1280 × 768) display.

Next let's discuss what you need to make an Eclipse Mars HTML5 IDE usable. Let's start by upgrading the 1280 × 768 WXGA display to an HDTV (1920 × 1080 at 120FPS refresh rate) or UHD (4096 × 2160 at 120FPS refresh rate) widescreen display. These are now affordable and give you 3 to 12 times the display "real estate" of a WXGA display. HDTVs are now $250 to $500 and UHDTV displays are now under $1,000.

I recommend using, at a bare minimum, the **Intel i7** quad-core processor, or, the **AMD 64-bit** octa-core processor. Install at least 8GB of DDR3-1600 memory. I'm using a 64-bit, octa-core AMD 8350, with 16GB of DDR3-1600. Intel also has a hexa-core i7 processor. This would be the equivalent of having twelve cores, as each i7 core can host two threads. Similarly, an i7 quad-core should look like eight cores to your 64-bit operating system's thread-scheduling algorithm.

There are also high-speed DDR3-1800 as well as DDR3-2133 clock speed memory module components available, as well. A high number signifies fast memory access speeds. To calculate actual megahertz speeds the memory is cycling at, divide the number by 4 (1333 = 333MHz, 1600 = 400MHz, 1800 = 450MHz, 2133 = 533MHz).

Memory access speed is a massive workstation performance factor, because your processor is usually "bottlenecked" by the speed at which processor cores can access your data (in memory).

With the high-speed processing, and memory access, going on inside the workstation while it is operating, it's extremely important to keep everything cool so that you do not experience **thermal problems**. I recommend using a wide full-tower enclosure with 120mm or 200mm cooling fans (one or two at least), as well as a **captive liquid induction** cooling fan on the CPU.

It is important to note that the cooler the system runs, the faster it can run, and the longer it will last, so load the workstation up with lots of ultrawide, silent, high-speed fans!

If you really want a maximum performance, install an SSD (solid-state drive) as your primary disk drive, where your applications and operating system software load. Use legacy HDD hardware for your D:\ hard drive for the slower data storage (long-term). Put your current project files on the SSD.

I'm using a 64-bit Windows 10 operating system, which is fairly memory efficient. The Linux 64-bit OS is extremely memory efficient. I recommend using any 64-bit OS, so you can address more than the 3.24GB of system memory, which is the capacity that's allowed by 32-bit memory addressing schema.

HTML5 Development Workstation: Open Software

To create a well-rounded, HTML5 application development workstation, you'll be installing all of the primary genres of open source software, which comprises a professional development workstation. First, you install Java SE 8 and Eclipse Mars. I also show you how to download GIMP, Lightworks, Fusion, Blender3D, and Audacity, which are all open source software packages if your HTML5 applications are going to be using a graphical front-end. Thus, you'll be putting together a 100% open source workstation for you. I'll also recommend other free software at the end of the chapter, so you can put together the "super" production workstation that you have always dreamed of.

Open source software has reached a close parallel to the level of professionalism of paid software that costs thousands of dollars to acquire. By using open source software packages like Eclipse, NetBeans, Blender3D, GIMP, Audacity, Inkscape, Fusion, Lightworks, and OpenOffice, you can assemble a free application development workstation that rivals paid software workstations!

For those readers who have just purchased their new HTML development workstation PC, and who are going to put the entire development software suite together completely from scratch, we go through the entire work process in this appendix.

Java 8: Installing the Foundation for Eclipse Mars

The first thing that you do is visit the Eclipse website (`www.eclipse.org`). Click the orange **Download** button on the homepage, as seen on the top right hand side of Figure B-1.

Figure B-1. *Go to eclipse.org; click the orange Download button*

As you can see, there is a multitude of download options to consider. One can support JavaScript, which HTML5 is based on. I suggest this Java EE version, which supports all of your popular Java programming languages, with Web applications, each of which HTML works with. Each of the downloads offers 32-bit and 64-bit versions, as you can see in the bottom of Figure B-2. This is because these have been **pre-compiled**, whereas your other NetBeans IDE install required Java 8 JDK to be installed. This tells you that although Eclipse Mars was created with Java SE 8, it is distributed in a Windows Binary format, not in Java ByteCode format, like NetBeans is. You can see further proof of this in Figure A-2, where non-Java versions of NetBeans 8.1 are also compiled out to OS binary format whereas the Java versions use the Java ByteCode format binaries and do not specify a bit-level, as the Java SE 8 environment is doing this for you.

Figure B-2. *Download the JavaEE with HTML5/JavaScript version*

Since HTML5 works with Java 8 just like with JavaScript, let's get the **Java 8 JDK** just to be thorough in our development system coonfiguration work process. If you wanted an **Enterprise Edition** (EE) version of Java 8 then download the Java 8 EE JDK, otherwise, if you are only going to use the HTML5 features, you can simply install the Java SE JDK and not use the Eclipse Java EE features.

Open Google Chrome and Google "Java JDK" (see Figure B-3). Look for the **Java SE Development Kit 8 - Downloads** search result. Click it to open the Oracle Java SE site (see Figure B-4), which is located at

www.oracle.com/technetwork/java/javase/downloads/jdk8-downloads-2133151.html

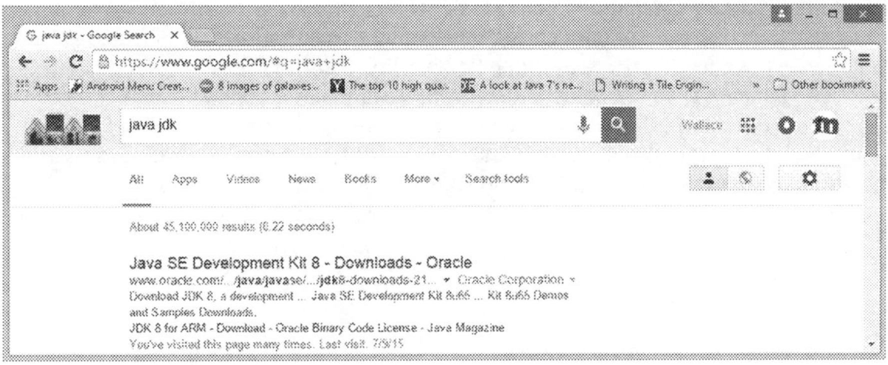

Figure B-3. *Google "Java JDK" and then click the Downloads link*

Java SE Development Kit 8u77
You must accept the Oracle Binary Code License Agreement for Java SE to download this software.

◯ Accept License Agreement   ◉ Decline License Agreement

Product / File Description	File Size	Download
Linux ARM 32 Soft Float ABI	77.7 MB	jdk-8u77-linux-arm32-vfp-hflt.tar.gz
Linux ARM 64 Soft Float ABI	74.68 MB	jdk-8u77-linux-arm64-vfp-hflt.tar.gz
Linux x86	154.74 MB	jdk-8u77-linux-i586.rpm
Linux x86	174.92 MB	jdk-8u77-linux-i586.tar.gz
Linux x64	152.76 MB	jdk-8u77-linux-x64.rpm
Linux x64	172.96 MB	jdk-8u77-linux-x64.tar.gz
Mac OS X	227.27 MB	jdk-8u77-macosx-x64.dmg
Solaris SPARC 64-bit (SVR4 package)	139.77 MB	jdk-8u77-solaris-sparcv9.tar.Z
Solaris SPARC 64-bit	99.06 MB	jdk-8u77-solaris-sparcv9.tar.gz
Solaris x64 (SVR4 package)	140.01 MB	jdk-8u77-solaris-x64.tar.Z
Solaris x64	96.18 MB	jdk-8u77-solaris-x64.tar.gz
Windows x86	182.01 MB	jdk-8u77-windows-i586.exe
Windows x64	187.31 MB	jdk-8u77-windows-x64.exe

Figure B-4. *Oracle TechNetwork Java 8 SE JDK downloads website*

Go to the Oracle website and download the latest Java 8 JDK environment, which at the time of the writing of this book, was Java SE Development Kit 8u77 (see Figure B-4). The URL listed earlier opens the download page for Java SE 8 Development Kit JDK 8u77.

You should pull your scrollbar, on the right side of the page, halfway down the page, to display the Java SE Development Kit 8u77 (or any later version) download links table, as can be seen on the very bottom of Figure B-4.

You can also read the explanation of the new CPU and PSU Java release versions which is located right above the download link table. I'm going to be using the latest Java 8u77 version.

Once you click the **Accept License Agreement** radio button, the links become bold and you are able to click the link that you wish to use. If you are on Windows, and your OS is 64-bit, use the Windows x64 link, otherwise use the Windows x86 link. I am using what is described in these links as Windows x64, the 64-bit versions of Windows, for my Windows 7/8/10 workstations.

Make sure that you use this Java SE Development Kit 8u77 downloading link, and do not use the JRE download (Java Runtime Edition) link. This JRE is part of your JDK 8u77, so you do not have to worry about getting the Java Runtime separately.

Before you run this installation, you should remove your older versions of Java from your Windows Control Panel by using **Add or Remove Programs** (XP) or **Programs and Features** (Windows Vista, 7, 8, or 10), shown selected in blue in Figure B-5.

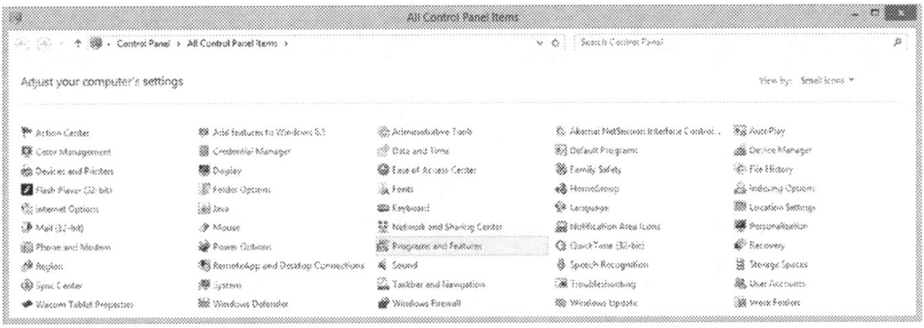

Figure B-5. *Launch your Control Panel ➤ Programs and Features*

This is necessary especially if your workstation is not brand new. We do this so that only your latest Java SE 8u77 and JRE 8u77 are the Java versions that are currently installed on your HTML development workstation. You also do this for any older IDEs that you have (NetBeans, Eclipse, or IntelliJ).

Select all the older Java versions, right-click each one, and select the **Uninstall** option (see Figure B-6). You could also perform this work process before installing other software packages although traditional media production software packages should "replace" older versions automatically, as part of their install process.

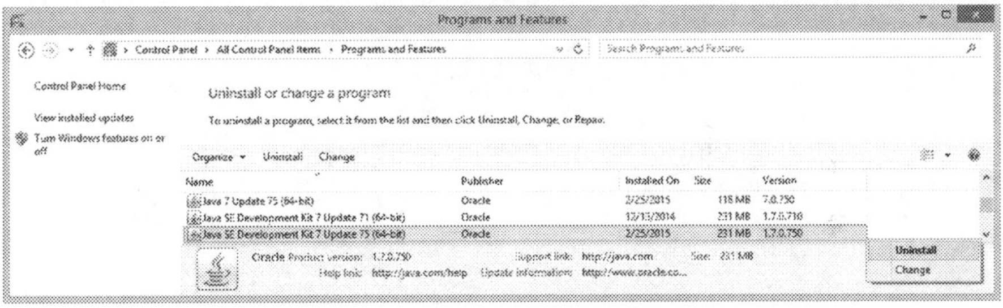

Figure B-6. *Find old version of Java, right-click and Uninstall*

Once you have downloaded your installation executable, install it on your system by double-clicking the .exe file to launch a Setup dialog (seen on the left-hand side of Figure B-7). You can also right-click your installer file and then select the **Run as administrator** option, which gives you better file access so that you have all of those OS "permissions" granted, such as read, write, overwrite, append, or delete, which a installer may need to have access to in order to complete the installation.

Figure B-7. *Setup, Custom Setup, and Extraction install dialogs*

Click the **Next** button to access the **Custom Setup** dialog, shown in the middle of Figure B-7. Accept the default settings, and then click the **Next** button again, to access the **Extracting Installer** progress dialog seen on the right side of Figure B-7.

Once you've extracted the installation software, you can select a Java JDK software installation folder. Use the default C:\ProgramFiles\Java\jre1.8.0_77 in the **Destination Folder** dialog, as shown on the left-hand side of Figure B-8. You have to use your imagination with Figures B-7 and B-8. I created these two screenshots because I was installing Java8u66 for my *JSON Quick Syntax Reference* (Apress, 2016). JSON works hand in hand with HTML5, CSS3, and JavaScript.

Figure B-8. *Destination, Progress, and Complete install dialogs*

Click the **Next** button, to install a Java Runtime Edition (JRE) edition in the default specified folder. Interestingly an installer won't ask you to specify the JDK folder name for some reason, probably because it wants your Java JDK to always be in a set or fixed (locked in the same location) folder name.

The JDK folder is named C:\ProgramFiles\Java\jdk1.8.0_77. Notice that internally Java 8 is referred to as **Java 1.8.0**. Thus, Java 6 is 1.6.0 and Java 7 is 1.7.0. This is useful to know if you are looking for Java versions using a search utility, for example, or want to show off your knowledge of legacy Java SE version numbering.

Once you click the **Next** button, you get the Java **Setup Progress** dialog, shown in the middle of Figure B-8. Once Java 8 is finished installing, you'll finally see your **Complete** dialog, which is seen on the right-hand side of Figure B-8. Congratulations! You have successfully installed Java 8!

Remember that the reason that you did not download a JRE is because it is part of this JDK 8u77 installation. The Java 8 Runtime Edition is the executable (platform) that runs the Java software app once it has been compiled into an application and also the latest

JRE will be needed to run NetBeans 8, which as you now know, is 100% completely written using the Java SE 8 development platform, as well as to work with Android Studio 2.

Once Java 8u77 (or later) is installed on your workstation, you then download and install the latest Eclipse software installer from the Eclipse website.

You can also use the same Programs and Features (or Add or Remove Programs) utility in your Control Panel to remove older Eclipse or Java versions or even to confirm the success of the latest Java 8 install.

Now you are ready to add the second layer of the Eclipse 4.5.2 Mars IDE software.

Eclipse 4.5: Installing the Eclipse Mars HTML IDE

The second step in this process is to install the **JavaEE** version of the software, which you saw in Figure B-2.

Find this executable file on your workstation and either double-click it, or right-click it, and select the **Run as administrator** option. This should open the **Security Warning: Do you want to run this file?** dialog (see Figure B-9).

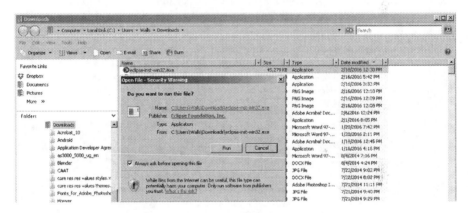

Figure B-9. *NetBeans install Welcome, License Agreement dialogs*

Click the **Run** button to launch the installation. You see the **Eclipse Installer by Oomph** loading screen, as shown in Figure B-10.

Figure B-10. *Eclipse Installer by Oomph loading screen*

Once the installer has loaded into memory, your software version selector dialog appears (see Figure B-11). You want to select the version that supports JavaScript (Web Applications), which is the **Eclipse IDE for Java EE Developers**.

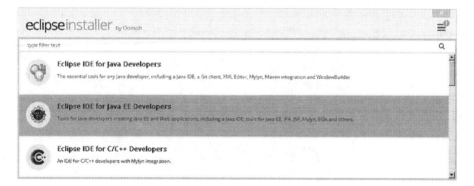

Figure B-11. *Click Eclipse IDE for Java EE Developers option*

In the next **Installation Folder** dialog, accept a default folder name offered by Eclipse and select the **create start menu entry**, and **create desktop shortcut** option (if needed), for your workstation. These are shown on the left side of Figure B-12.

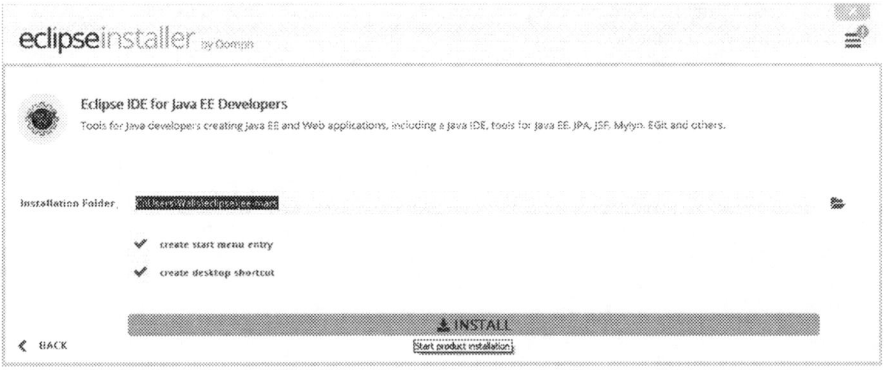

Figure B-12. *Select launch options, default installation folder*

Click the **Install** button, and in your **Eclipse Foundation Software User Agreement** dialog, seen in Figure B-13, select the **I accept the terms in the license agreement** option, after you (or legal department) have reviewed these terms and conditions, which specify what you can and cannot do using this software.

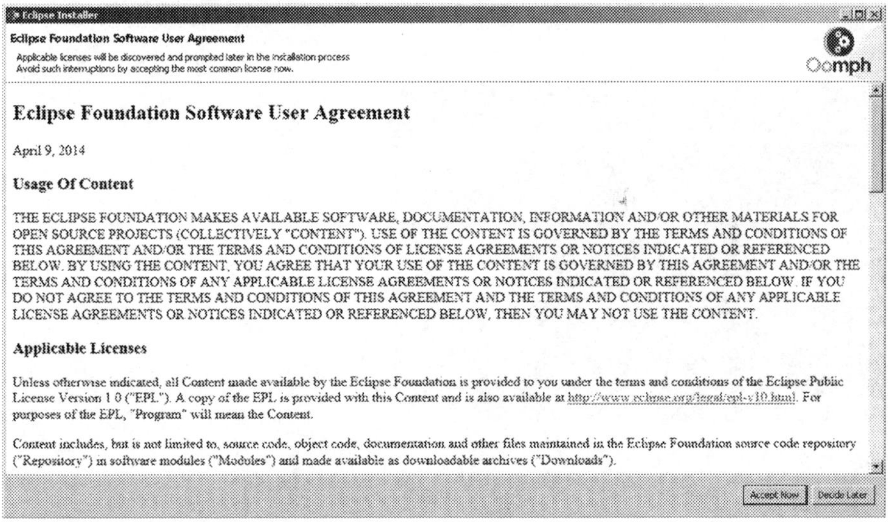

Figure B-13. *Click the Accept Now button to agree to the terms*

Acceptance of the licensing terms and conditions is accomplished by clicking the **Accept Now** button.

225

Once you agree to the terms of your licensing agreement, you get an Installing dialog with a green progress bar (see Figure B-14).

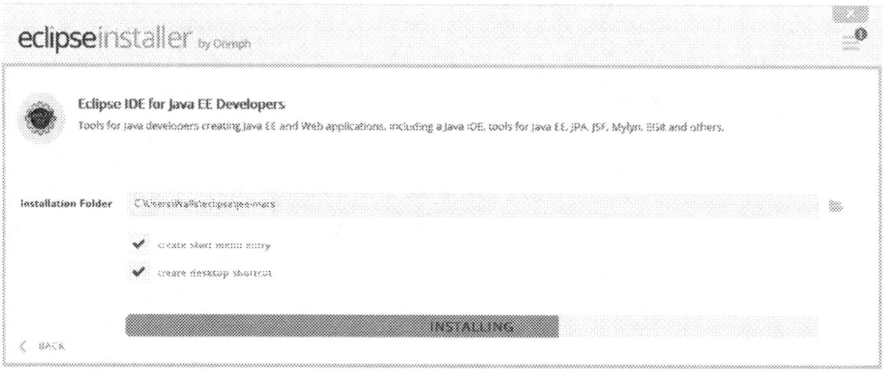

Figure B-14. *Your Installing progress bar can be seen in green*

Once the installation is completed, Eclipse Mars should launch automatically, showing you the branded start-up screen, which can be seen in Figure B-15. This is shown as the software loads into memory from your hard disk drive for the first time.

Figure B-15. *Eclipse Mars launch*

Once Eclipse Mars launches, it displays the **Workspace Launcher** dialog, which prompts you to select your **Workspace** location for your hard disk drive (see Figure B-16).

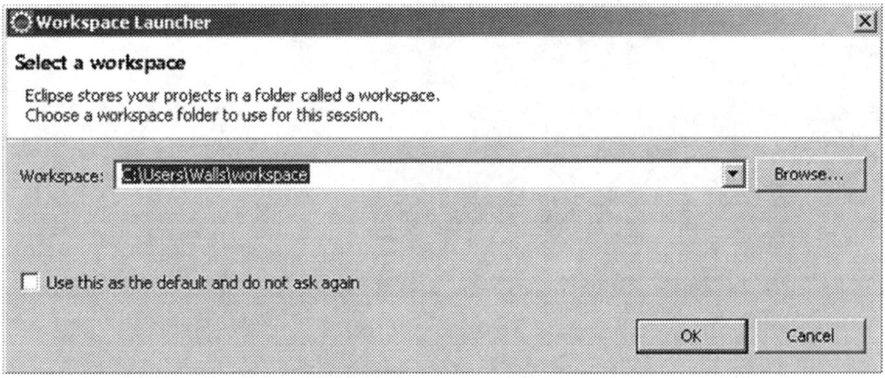

Figure B-16. *Select Workspace folder name for Eclipse projects*

I selected the default C:\Users\Walls\workspace directory as I felt that name was acceptable. As you can see in Figure B-17, if you have a previous version of Eclipse installed, you should get an **Older Workspace Version** dialog, prompting you to update.

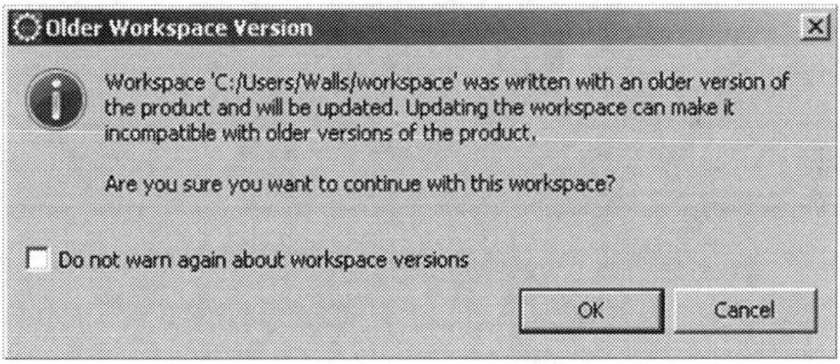

Figure B-17. *Update older version of workspace (if necessary)*

After all of this is complete, Eclipse Mars launches using the Eclipse Mars loading screen (see Figure B-18).

Figure B-18. *Eclipse Mars loading screen*

Figure B-19 shows Eclipse Mars with the sample **FirstApp**.

Figure B-19. *Eclipse IDE on start-up, with FirstApp sample app*

Summary

In this appendix, you set up your HTML5 workstation by downloading and installing open source Java 8 JDK and Eclipse Mars 4.5 IDE software to code HTML5 applications.

■ ■ ■

IntelliJ: Set up an HTML5 Integrated Development IDE

Let's put together the foundation for a highly professional, HTML5-friendly, **IntelliJ IDEA**. Your development workstation is the most important combination of PC hardware and software, allowing you to reach the goal of HTML5 compatible applications development. Let's spend an appendix to consider your hardware and HTML5 software development workstation needs.

Let's first get all of the tedious setup tasks out of the way.

If you already have your workstation configured, you can proceed to Chapter 1 for an overview of HTML. If you already are familiar with HTML, start with Chapter 2.

Everything that you learn over the course of this book needs to be experienced equally by each reader. In this appendix, you learn where to go to download and how to install several of the most impressive, professional, open source software packages on the face of this planet!

You're about to "max out" your HTML, HTML5, CSS3, and JavaScript development workstation so hold on tight and enjoy the ride!

Set up an HTML Development Workstation

The first thing to do after looking at hardware requirements is to download and install the entire Java software development kit (SDK), which Oracle calls: Java SE 8 JDK (Java Development Kit). **IntelliJ IDEA**, which is called the **IntelliJ** IDE, uses Java 8 SE (SE stands for Standard Edition).

The second thing to do is download and install the IntelliJ IDEA from www.jetbrain.org. IntelliJ IDEA (integrated development environment application) allows you to develop HTML-compatible applications with all of the popular programming languages, including Java EE, Java SE, JavaScript, HTML5, CSS3, JavaFX, Android Studio 2, XML, XSL, PHP, and SQL.

After your HTML5 application development environment is set up, you can then download and install new media asset development tools, if you wish. These are used in conjunction with IntelliJ for image editing (GIMP) and non-linear video editing (Editshare Lightworks 12), VFX (Fusion 8), digital audio sweetening, or editing

(Audacity), i3D modeling, renderer, animation (Blender), digital illustration (Inkscape), and even a complete business productivity suite (Open Office).

This appendix should take your HTML development to an all-new level, showing you how to create a media development and programming workstation that runs your HTML business.

All of these software development tools come close to matching all the primary feature sets of expensive paid software packages, such as those from Apple (Final Cut Pro), Autodesk (3D Studio Max), Adobe (Photoshop, Illustrator, After Effects), Avid (ProTools), and all at *zero* cost to your production company!

Open source software is free to download, install, and upgrade, and continuously adds features. It's becoming more like professional software every day. You will be completely amazed at how professional open source software packages have become over the last decade or so.

Development Workstations: Hardware Foundation

Since you'll put together the foundation for your HTML5 application development workstation that is used for the duration of this book, I want to take a moment to review IntelliJ's hardware requirements first. This is a factor that influences development performance (speed). This is clearly as important as the software itself because hardware is what is actually running your software package's algorithms.

Minimum requirements for IntelliJ IDEA include **1GB** of memory, **300MB** of hard disk space, and a **Java 6 JDK**, or higher.

Next, let's discuss what you need to make your IntelliJ HTML IDE usable. Let's start by upgrading your 1280 × 768 WXGA display to an HDTV (1920 × 1080 at 120FPS refresh rate) or UHD (4096 × 2160 at 120FPS refresh rate) widescreen display. These are now affordable and give you 3 to 12 times the display "real estate" of a WXGA display. HDTVs are now $250 to $500 and UHDTV displays are now under $1,000.

I recommend using, at a bare minimum, the **Intel i7** quad-core processor, or, the **AMD 64-bit** octa-core processor. Install at least 8GB of DDR3-1600 memory. I'm using a 64-bit, octa-core AMD 8350, with 16GB of DDR3-1600. Intel also has a hexa-core i7 processor. This would be the equivalent of having twelve cores, as each i7 core can host two threads. Similarly, an i7 quad-core should look like eight cores, to your 64-bit operating system's thread-scheduling algorithm.

There are also DDR3-1800 and DDR3-2133 clock speed memory module components available. A high number signifies fast memory access speeds. To calculate actual megahertz speeds the memory is cycling at, divide the number by 4 (1333 = 333MHz, 1600 = 400MHz, 1800 = 450MHz, 2133 = 533MHz).

Memory access speed is a massive workstation performance factor, because your processor is usually bottlenecked by the speed at which processor cores can access your data (in memory).

With the high-speed processing and memory access going on inside the workstation, it's extremely important to keep everything cool so that you do not experience **thermal problems**. I recommend using a wide full-tower enclosure with 120mm or 200mm cooling fans (one or two at least), as well as a captive liquid induction cooling fan on the CPU.

It is important to note that the cooler the system runs, the faster it can run, and the longer it will last, so load the workstation up with lots of silent high-speed fans!

If you really want a maximum performance, install an SSD (solid-state drive) as your primary disk drive, where your applications and operating system software load. Use legacy HDD hardware for your D:\ hard drive for the slower data storage (long-term). Put your current project files on the SSD.

I'm using a 64-bit Windows 10 operating system, which is fairly memory efficient. The Linux 64-bit OS is extremely memory efficient. I recommend using any 64-bit OS, so that you are able to physically address more than 3.24GB of system memory, which is a limitation with your 32-bit operating system that does not exist once you have upgraded to 64-bit OS, and have that full 64-bits of memory addressing headroom.

HTML Development Workstation: Open Software

To create your well-rounded HTML application development workstation, you'll be installing all the primary genres of open source software that comprises a professional development workstation. First we'll install JavaSE 8u77 and IntelliJ IDEA. I also show you how to download GIMP, Lightworks, Fusion, Blender3D and Audacity, which are also all open source software packages, in case your HTML applications are going to be using a graphical "front end." Thus, we'll be putting together a 100% open source workstation for you. I'll also recommend other free software at the end of the chapter, so you can put together the mega production workstation that you have always dreamed of.

Open source software has reached a close parallel to the level of professionalism of paid software, which costs thousands of dollars to acquire. Using open source software packages like Eclipse, NetBeans, Blender3D, GIMP, Audacity, Inkscape, Fusion, Lightworks, and OpenOffice, you can assemble a free application development workstation that rivals paid software workstations!

I go through the entire work process for those readers who have just purchased their new HTML development workstation PC and who are going to put the entire development software suite together completely from scratch.

Java 8: Installing the Foundation for IntelliJ IDEA

The first thing you do is visit the IntelliJ website (`www.jetbrains.com/idea/`) and then click the black **Download** button in the center of the IntelliJ IDEA homepage (see Figure C-1).

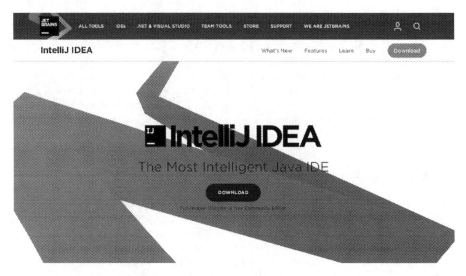

Figure C-1. *Load the jetbrains.com/idea/ and click Download*

As you can see, there are two different download options; but only one that supports JavaScript, which HTML is based on. I am therefore forced to suggest the Ultimate version! This supports all the popular programming languages which work with HTML. If you don't want to purchase IntelliJ IDEA Ultimate, use their 30-day trial version or use NetBeans 8.1 (Appendix A), or use Eclipse 4.5.1 Mars (Appendix B) both of which are free. The two different versions of IntelliJ IDEA are shown in Figure C-2 along with the different programing features they each support.

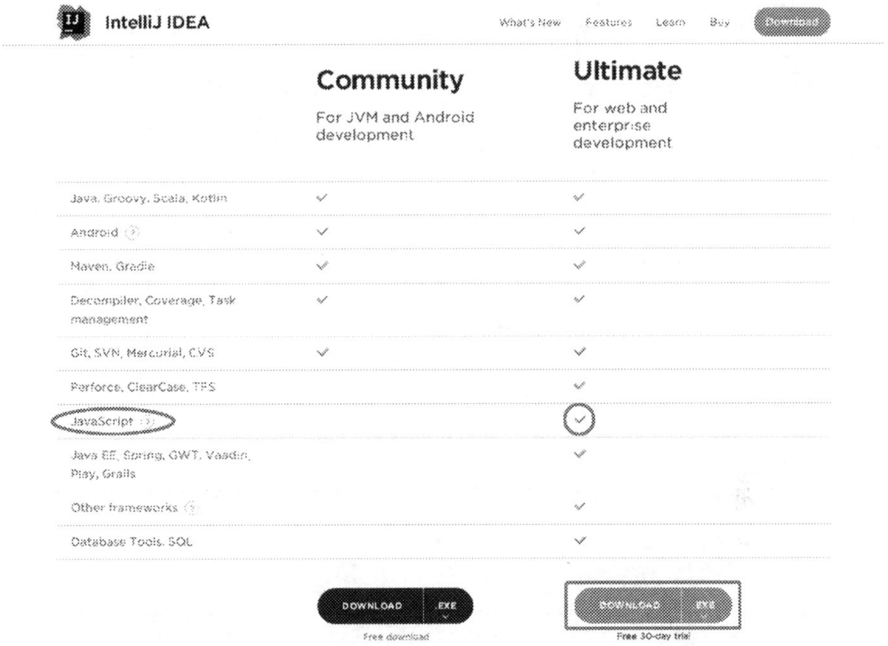

Figure C-2. *Download the IntelliJ Ultimate 30-day trial version*

If you're wondering why the IntelliJ IDEA download isn't offered in 32-bit and 64-bit versions, this is because the IDEs which do this have both versions **pre-compiled**, whereas IntelliJ IDEA requires the Java 6 (or later Java 8) JDK to be installed.

If you want to use the IntelliJ IDEA version, so that any programming languages that you want to use with HTML are supported, you have to first install Java SE 6 or later. In our case, this should be Java 8.

This is very similar to what you will see using NetBeans 8.1 (see Appendix A), as both of these use a Java ByteCode JAR file to run off of, by using the Java Runtime Edition (JRE).

This approach allows the bit-versions to be handled by a JRE bit-version, so be sure to install the correct JDK version, either 32-bit for Windows Vista and XP or 64-bit for Windows 7, 8.1 or 10. Note that there are other bit versions of these OSes and that I am just generalizing here; XP and Vista were 32-bit, and Windows 7, 8, and 10 are 64-bit, due to when they came out.

Download IntelliJ. After that is completed, get the latest Java 8 SE JDK so that you can run IntelliJ.

Open Google Chrome and Google "Java JDK" (see Figure C-3). Look for the **Java SE Development Kit 8 - Downloads** search result. Click it to open the Oracle Java website.

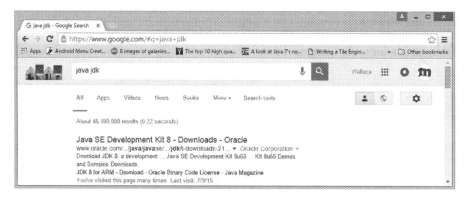

Figure C-3. *Google "Java JDK" and then click Downloads link*

Download and install the latest Java 8 JDK, which at the time I wrote this book was Java SE 8u77, as seen in Figure C-4.

Java SE Development Kit 8u77

You must accept the Oracle Binary Code License Agreement for Java SE to download this software.

○ Accept License Agreement   ● Decline License Agreement

Product / File Description	File Size	Download
Linux ARM 32 Soft Float ABI	77.7 MB	jdk-8u77-linux-arm32-vfp-hflt.tar.gz
Linux ARM 64 Soft Float ABI	74.68 MB	jdk-8u77-linux-arm64-vfp-hflt.tar.gz
Linux x86	154.74 MB	jdk-8u77-linux-i586.rpm
Linux x86	174.92 MB	jdk-8u77-linux-i586.tar.gz
Linux x64	152.76 MB	jdk-8u77-linux-x64.rpm
Linux x64	172.96 MB	jdk-8u77-linux-x64.tar.gz
Mac OS X	227.27 MB	jdk-8u77-macosx-x64.dmg
Solaris SPARC 64-bit (SVR4 package)	139.77 MB	jdk-8u77-solaris-sparcv9.tar.Z
Solaris SPARC 64-bit	99.06 MB	jdk-8u77-solaris-sparcv9.tar.gz
Solaris x64 (SVR4 package)	140.01 MB	jdk-8u77-solaris-x64.tar.Z
Solaris x64	96.18 MB	jdk-8u77-solaris-x64.tar.gz
Windows x86	182.01 MB	jdk-8u77-windows-i586.exe
Windows x64	187.31 MB	jdk-8u77-windows-x64.exe

Figure C-4. *The Oracle TechNetwork Java SE JDK Download website*

The URL is in the address bar in Figure C-4; it opens the download page for Java SE Development Kit 8u77. I put this link here as well, in case you want to simply cut and paste it, copy it, or click it to launch the site:

www.oracle.com/technetwork/java/javase/downloads/jdk8-downloads-2133151.html

You should pull your scrollbar on the right side of the webpage halfway down the page, to display the Java Development Kit 8u77 (or a later version) download links table, as seen at the very bottom of Figure C-4. You should also read the explanation of a new

CPU and PSU Java release versions, located just above the download link table. I'm going to use Java 8u77.

Once you click the **Accept License Agreement** radio button, these links become bold. You should be able to click the links that you wish to use. If you're on Windows and your OS is 64-bit, use the Windows x64 link; otherwise, use the 32-bit Windows x86 link. I am using what's described in these links as Windows x64. This is a 64-bit versions of Windows, for my Windows 10 workstation.

Make sure that you use this Java SE Development Kit 8u77 downloading link, and do not use a JRE download (a Java Runtime Edition) link. The JRE is part of the JDK 8u77, thus you do not have to worry about getting the Java Runtime separately.

In case you are wondering, you indeed use this Java Runtime Edition (JRE), to launch and run your IntelliJ IDE, and you'll use the JDK inside of that IntelliJ software package, to provide the Java SE 8 core class foundation that is used as the foundation for JavaFX and for Android's Java-based API classes.

Before you run this installation, you should remove your older versions of Java from your Windows Control Panel by using **Add or Remove Programs** (XP) or **Programs and Features** (Windows Vista, 7, 8.1, and 10). This is shown selected in blue in Figure C-5. This opens a Windows utility that manages installed software packages and allows you to remove them from your operating system.

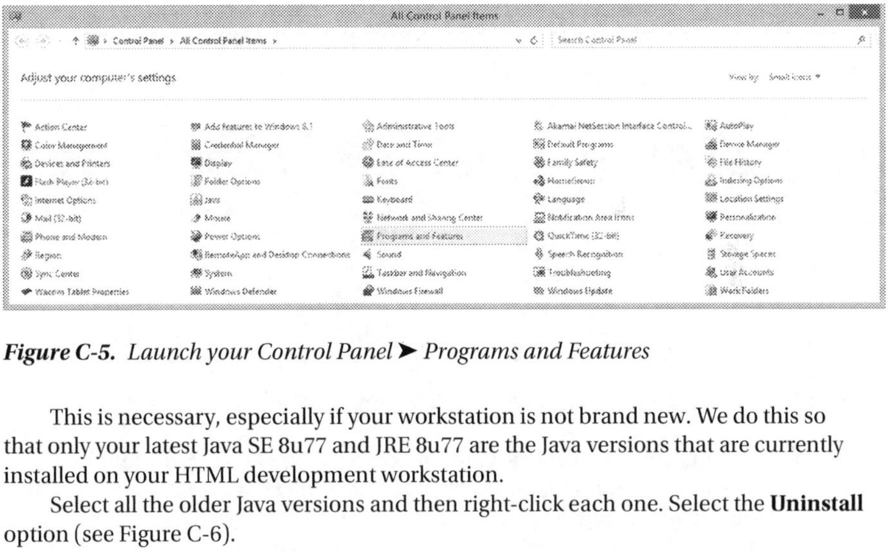

Figure C-5. *Launch your Control Panel ➤ Programs and Features*

This is necessary, especially if your workstation is not brand new. We do this so that only your latest Java SE 8u77 and JRE 8u77 are the Java versions that are currently installed on your HTML development workstation.

Select all the older Java versions and then right-click each one. Select the **Uninstall** option (see Figure C-6).

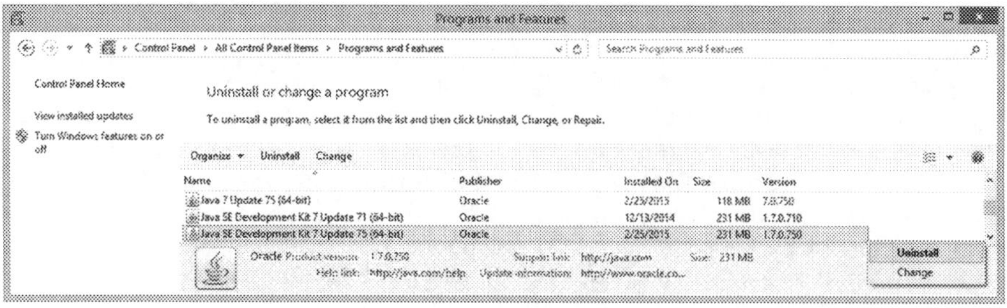

Figure C-6. *Find old versions of Java .right-click .and Uninstall*

As you can see, I am more than one hundred versions old, as I am at Java 7, update 71! If you install different versions of Java SE JDK on your system, they will not replace each other, but instead exist in parallel, or next to each other.

The reason for this is you might have older projects and software (such as IDEs), which use these older versions of Java without crashing. For instance, Android 4.4 and earlier use the Java 6 SDK, Android 5.x or 6.x (64-bit Android) use Java 7 SDK, and JavaFX, and everything else uses Java 8, and soon, Java 9!

Once you have downloaded your installation executable, install it on your system by double-clicking the .exe file to launch a Setup dialog (see the left-hand side of Figure C-7). You can also right-click your installer file and then select the **Run as administrator** option to assure that you have proper files access.

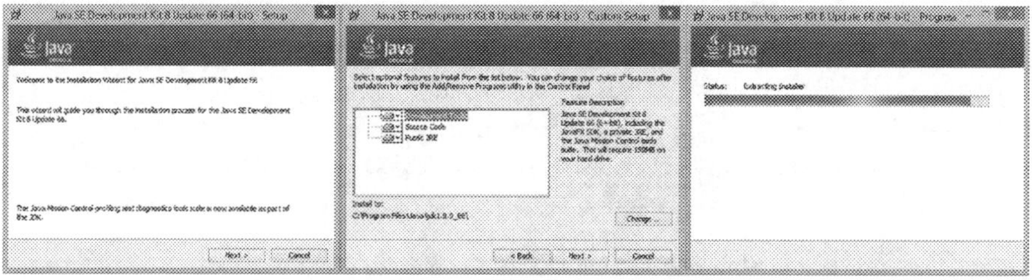

Figure C-7. *Setup, Custom Setup, and Extraction install dialogs*

Click the **Next** button to access the **Custom Setup** dialog, shown in the middle of Figure C-7. Accept the default settings, and then click the **Next** button again, to access the **Extracting Installer** progress dialog seen on the right side of Figure C-7.

Once you've extracted the installation software, you can select a Java JDK software installation folder. Use the default C:\ProgramFiles\Java\jre1.8.0_77 in the **Destination Folder** dialog, as shown on the left-hand side of Figure C-8.

Figure C-8. *Destination, Progress, and Complete. install dialogs*

Click the **Next** button, to install a Java Runtime Edition (JRE) edition in the default specified folder. Interestingly an installer won't ask you to specify the JDK folder name for some reason, probably because it wants your Java JDK to always be in a set or fixed (locked in the same location) folder name.

The JDK folder is named C:\ProgramFiles\Java\jdk1.8.0_77. Notice that internally Java 8 is referred to as Java 1.8.0. Thus, Java 6 is 1.6.0 and Java 7 is 1.7.0. This is useful to know if you are looking for Java versions using a search utility, for example, or want to show off your knowledge of legacy Java version numbering.

Once you click the **Next** button, you get the Java **Setup Progress** dialog, shown in the middle of Figure C-8. Once Java 8 is finished installing, you see your **Complete** dialog (see the right-hand side of Figure C-8). Congratulations! You have successfully installed Java 8!

Remember that the reason that you did not download a JRE is because it is part of this JDK 8u77 installation. The Java 8 Runtime Edition is the executable (platform) which runs the Java software app once it has been compiled into an application and also the latest JRE is needed to run NetBeans 8, which as you now know is 100% completely written using the Java SE 8 development platform.

Once Java 8u77 or later is installed on your workstation you can then download and install the latest IntelliJ software installer from www.jetbrains.com/idea/.

You can also use the **Programs and Features** (or **Add or Remove Programs**) utility in your Control Panel to remove older Java or IntelliJ versions, or to confirm the success of the latest Java 8 install.

Now you are ready to add the second layer of the IntelliJ IDEA software, which runs on top of the Java 8 environment.

IntelliJ IDEA: Download the IntelliJ IDEA for HTML

The second step in this process is to install IntelliJ (see Figure C-2). The download function should have put the **ideaIU-15.0.3.exe** or later 2016 version file into your C:\Users\Your-Name-Goes-Here\Downloads\ folder.

Find this executable file on your workstation and double-click it or right-click it. Select the **Run as administrator** option. This opens a **Security Warning: Do you want to run this file?** dialog, shown on the left side of Figure C-9. The two steps are numbered in red.

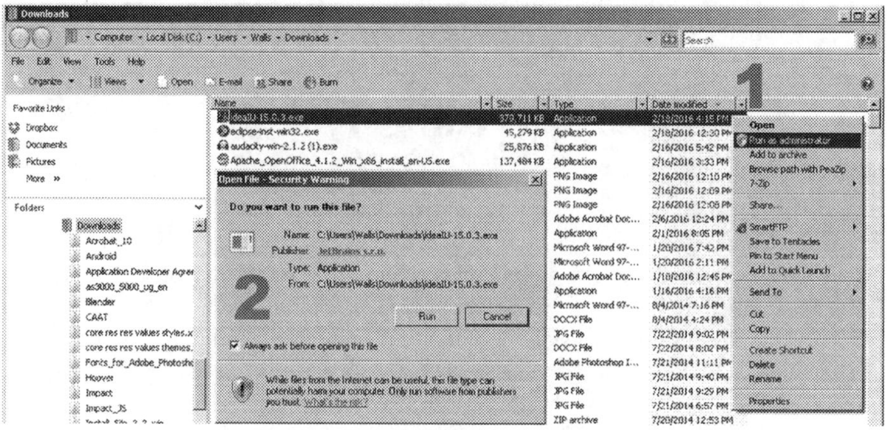

Figure C-9. *Right-click IDEA installer and Run as administrator*

Click the **Run** button and launch the installer. This provides you with the **IntelliJ IDEA Setup Wizard** dialog (see Figure C-10). Click **Next** to continue, as the dialog instructs you and in the **Choose Install Location** dialog, select a default value provided for the **Destination Folder** data field. Click the **Next** button, which allows you to proceed with your install.

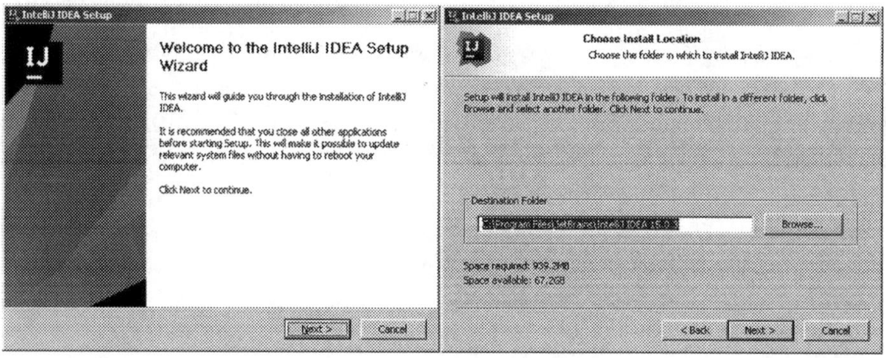

Figure C-10. *Start your install and accept the default location*

In the **Installation Options** dialog, select the shortcuts that you want to have created for you, as well as specifying an association for Java and Groovy files that you wish to have put into your system registry (see Figure C-11). Click the **Next** button to enter the **Choose Start Menu Folder** dialog. Select the default JetBrains Start Menu folder name. Then click the **Install** button to start your installation process.

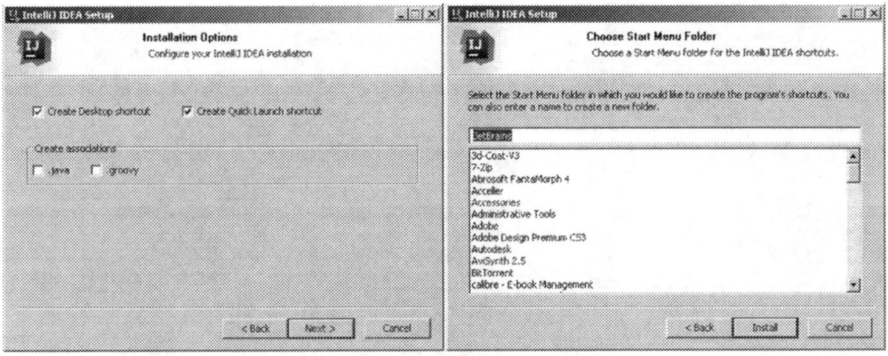

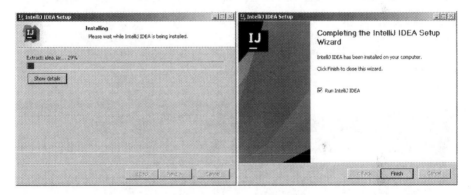

Figure C-11. Select Installation Options, and Start Menu Folder

The **Installing** dialog shows you a progress bar along with the files that are being installed and the percentage of completion, as shown in the left-hand side of Figure C-12.

Figure C-12. Select Run IntelliJ IDEA after install completes

Once the IDEA installation is complete, you see the **Completing the IntelliJ IDEA Setup Wizard** dialog (see Figure C-12). Notice that I have selected the **Run IntelliJ IDEA** option, so I can show you the IDE itself.

Once you click the **Finish** button to exit the install, you see the IntelliJ IDEA 15 loading screen (see Figure C-13). This is shown every time you start IntelliJ IDEA.

Figure C-13. *IntelliJ IDEA 15 software loading start-up screen*

If you have a previous version of IntelliJ IDEA, you can import your previous IntelliJ IDEA version's settings using the Complete Installation dialog, which is shown in Figure C-14.

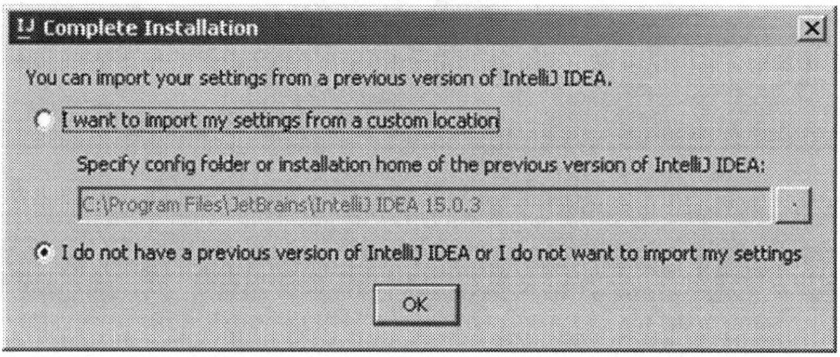

Figure C-14. *Complete Installation dialog*

Once you click the **OK** button, you get the **IDEA License Activation** dialog, shown in Figure C-15. If you want to purchase IntelliJ IDEA click the **Buy IntelliJ IDEA** and enter an **Activation code** into the data field for this dialog. Otherwise, click the **Evaluate for free for 30 days** button on the right.

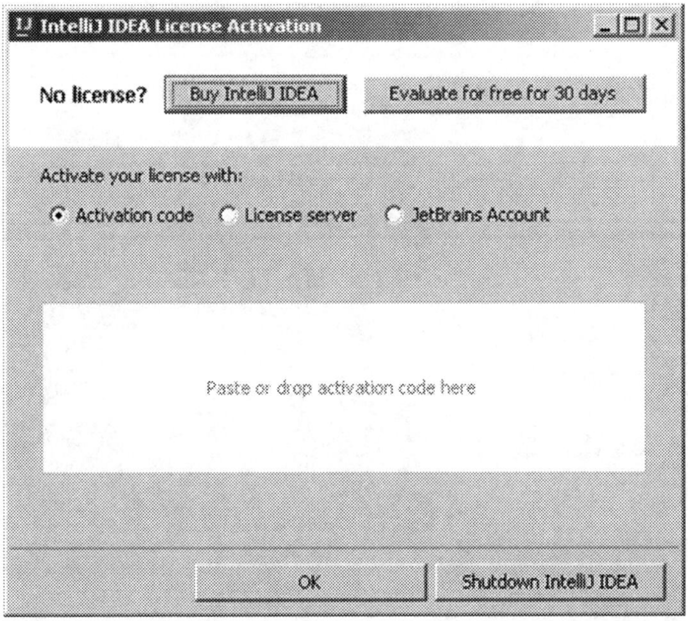

Figure C-15. IDEA License Activation

In the next dialog, click **Accept** to accept the licensing agreement on the JetBrains website's store, so that you can use the IDEA software for your HTML development.

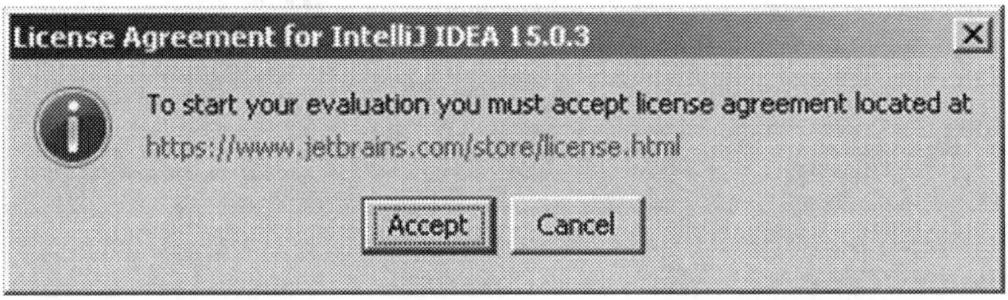

Figure C-16. License Agreement dialog

Accept the default **IntelliJ** UI theme, or choose the dark version, and click the **Next** button, as shown in Figure C-17.

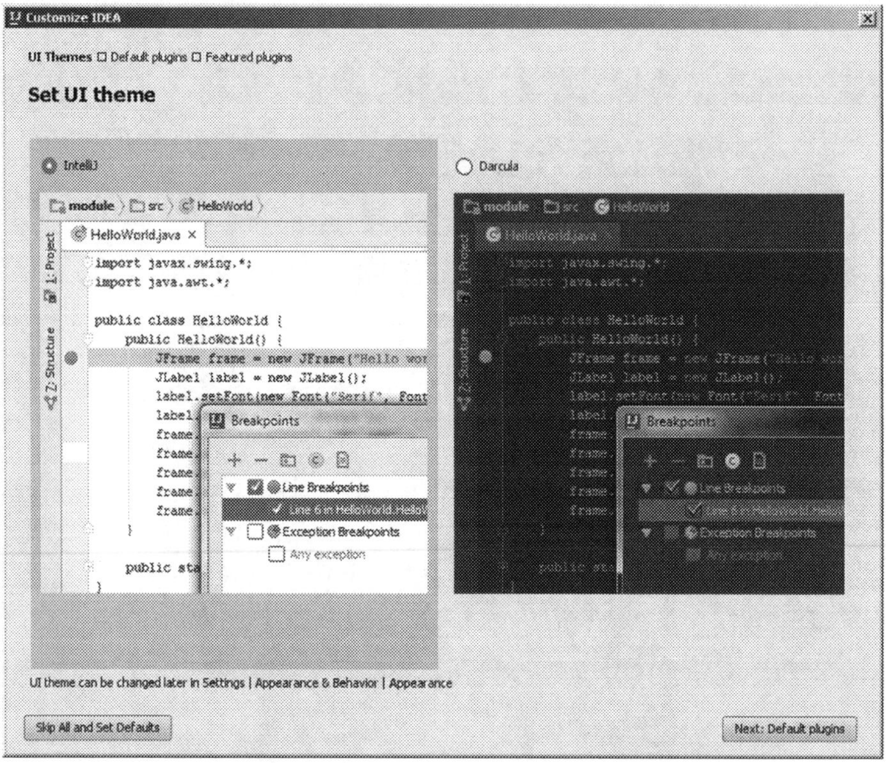

Figure C-17. *IntelliJ Set UI theme dialog*

I left all of the IntelliJ capabilities enabled and then clicked the **Next: Featured plugins** button (see Figure C-18).

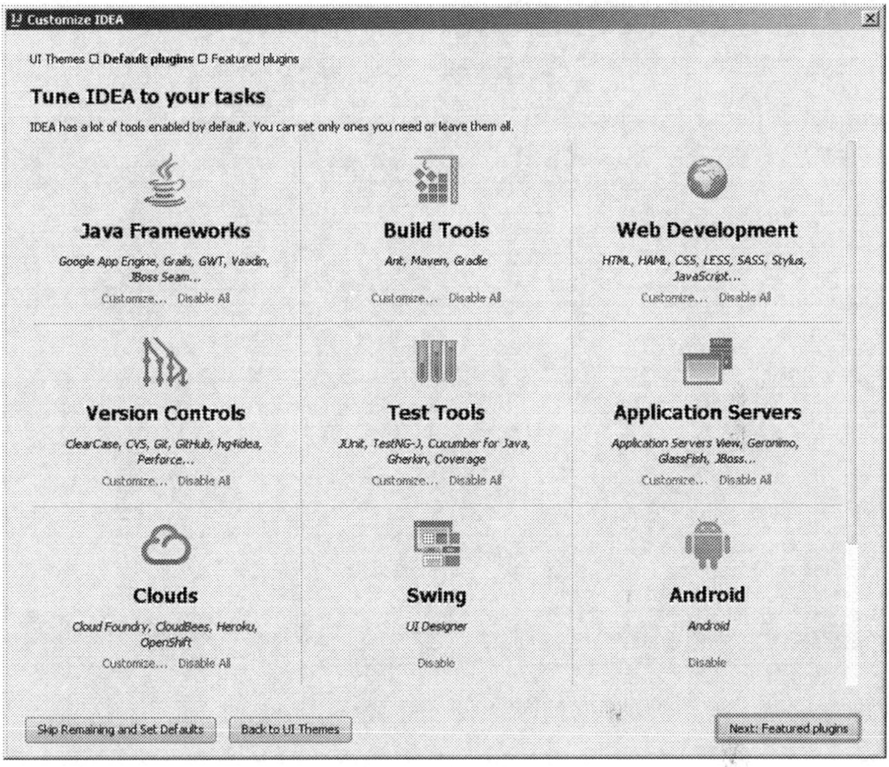

Figure C-18. *Tune IDEA to your tasks dialog*

If there are any featured plug-ins you want to add in to IntelliJ, select them in your **Download featured plugins** screen, seen in Figure C-19 and click **Start using IntelliJ IDEA** button.

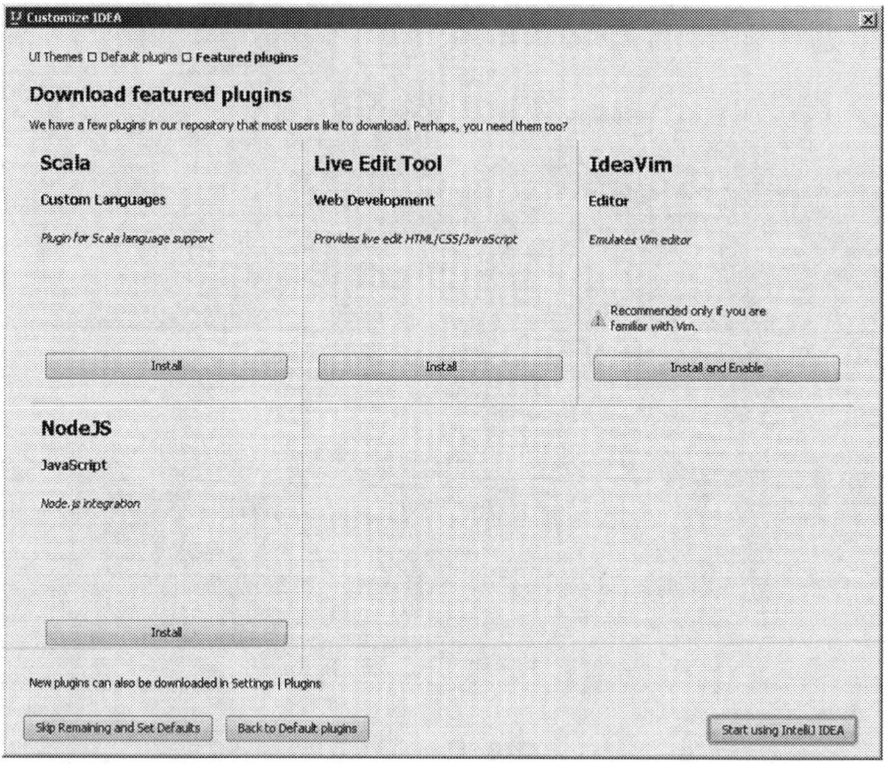

Figure C-19. *Download featured plug-ins dialog*

The first time IntelliJ launches, you get the screen shown in Figure C-20, where you have Create New Project options and configuration and help options. Click the **Create New Project** option highlighted in light blue to create a new empty project to make sure that IntelliJ IDEA is working.

Now you are ready to develop HTML5 applications!

Summary

You set up your HTML5 workstation by downloading and installing the open source Java 8 JDK and the IntelliJ 2016 IDEA software to code HTML5 applications. You can also set up new media content production applications. See Appendix D if you plan to develop multimedia HTML5 applications and documents.

APPENDIX D

■ ■ ■

Multimedia: Set up Your New Media Content Development

Let's put together your foundation for a highly professional, HTML5-friendly, **new media content development workstation**. Your content development workstation is an important fusion of PC hardware and software, allowing you to reach your goal of interactive HTML5 multimedia application development. Let's use this appendix to consider your new media hardware and the software infrastructure needs. You will then have everything you need to develop new media content for Chapter 8 and Chapter 17 of this book, no matter what type of HTML5 application you want to develop for your end users!

Let's get all of these tedious setup tasks out of the way.

If you already have your workstation configured, you can proceed to Chapter 1 for an overview of HTML, or if you already are familiar with HTML, start with Chapter 2.

In this appendix, I outline the steps to put together a multimedia production workstation to work with the IDE HTML5 development workstations that you created in the first three appendices.

Everything that you learn over the course of this book needs to be experienced equally by each reader. Here you'll learn where to download and how to install several of the most professional, open source software packages on the face of this planet. You are about to max out your HTML5 workstation!

Set up a New Media Content Workstation

The first thing to do after looking at hardware requirements is to download and install new media asset development tools, if you wish. These are used in conjunction with NetBeans, Eclipse, or IntelliJ for things such as image editing (GIMP), non-linear digital video editing (Lightworks), special effects (Fusion), digital audio sweetening or editing (Audacity), i3D modeling, rendering, and animation (Blender), digital illustration (Inkscape), and business productivity (OpenOffice). This appendix takes your development to an all-new level, showing you how to create the new media development and HTML5 programming workstation that will run your HTML5 application development business.

© Wallace Jackson 2016
W. Jackson, *HTML5 Quick Markup Reference*, DOI 10.1007/978-1-4302-6536-8

All of these software development tools come close to matching all the primary feature sets of expensive paid software packages, such as those from Apple (Final Cut Pro), Autodesk (3D Studio Max), Adobe (Photoshop, Illustrator, After Effects), Avid (ProTools)—and all at *zero* cost to your production company!

Open source software is free to download, install, and upgrade, and it continuously adds features. It's becoming more like professional software every day. You will be completely amazed at how professional your open source software packages have become over the last decade or so.

New Media Content Production: Hardware is Key!

I want to take a moment to review new media content development workstation hardware requirements. It is a factor that influences your development performance (speed). This is clearly as important as the software itself, since hardware is actually running the software package's algorithms.

Let's discuss what you need to make a multimedia content production workstation usable. You need an HDTV (1920 × 1080 resolution using a 120FPS refresh rate) or UHD (4096 × 2160 at a 120FPS refresh rate) widescreen display. These are affordable and give you 4 to 16 times the display "real estate" of the XGA displays typically utilized. HDTV is now $200 to $400 and UHDTV displays are now well under $1,000.

I recommend, at a bare minimum, the **Intel i7** quad-core processor, or, the **AMD 64-bit** octa-core processor. Install at least 8GB of DDR3-1600 memory. I'm using a 64-bit, octa-core AMD 8350, with 16GB of DDR3-1600.

Intel also has a new hexa-core i7 processor. This is the equivalent of having twelve cores, as each i7 core can host two threads. Similarly, the i7 quad-core should look like eight cores to a 64-bit operating system thread-scheduling algorithm.

There are DDR3-1800 and DDR3-2133 clock speed memory module components available, as well. A high number signifies fast memory access speeds. To calculate actual megahertz speeds the memory is cycling at, divide the number by 4 (1333 = 333MHz, 1600 = 400MHz, 1800 = 450MHz, 2133 = 533MHz).

Memory access speed is a massive workstation performance factor, because your processor is usually "bottlenecked" by the speed at which processor cores can access your data (in memory) which that processor core needs to process.

With the high-speed processing, and memory access, going on inside the workstation while it is operating, it's extremely important to keep everything cool so that you do not experience **thermal problems**. I recommend a wide full-tower enclosure with 120mm or 200mm cooling fans (one or two at least), as well as a captive liquid induction cooling fan on the CPU.

It is important to note that the cooler the system runs, the faster it can run, and the longer it will last, so load the workstation up with lots of silent high-speed fans!

If you really want a maximum performance, install an SSD (solid-state drive) as your primary disk drive, where your applications and operating system software load. Use legacy HDD hardware for your D:\ hard drive for the slower data storage (long-term). Put your current project files on the SSD.

As far as the operating system goes, I'm using 64-bit Windows 10 operating system, which is fairly memory efficient. The Linux 64-bit OS is extremely memory efficient. I recommend any 64-bit OS, so you can address more than 3.24GB of system memory.

New Media Content Development: Open Source

To create a well-rounded, HTML5 application development workstation, you'll install all the primary genres of software needed to create a professional content production workstation. I show you how to download GIMP, Lightworks, Fusion, Blender3D and Audacity, which are also all open source software packages, in case your HTML5 applications use a graphical front-end. Open source software has reached level a parallel to the professionalism of paid software packages that cost thousands of dollars each. Open source software packages offer you a free application development workstation that rivals any paid application development software workstation! Let's get started!

GIMP 2.8: Digital Image Editing and Compositing

The GIMP project offers a professional imaging software package that allows you to do digital image editing. Download this software package from www.gimp.org. GIMP is currently at version 2.8.16, but version 3.0 is just around the corner—a preview (2.9.2) of it is available! GIMP 2.10 should come out just about the time that this book becomes available. The GIMP homepage, with its red download button, is shown in Figure D-1.

Figure D-1. *Go to www.gimp.org to download GIMP 2.8.16*

If you want to learn more about digital image compositing, check out my *Digital Image Compositing Fundamentals* (Apress, 2015) book.

Blender: 3D Modeling, Rendering, and Animation

The Blender Foundation project offers a professional i3D software package called Blender. It allows you to do 3D object modeling, rendering, and animation. Download this software package at www.blender.org. Blender's homepage with its blue download button is shown in Figure D-2.

Figure D-2. *Go to blender.org and download the latest version*

This is a professional-level software package with many of the same features as 3D Studio Max, Maya, XSI, and Lightwave.

Inkscape: Digital Illustration and Digital Painting

The Inkscape Project offers a professional digital illustration software package called Inkscape. It can also do digital painting. Download this software package at www.inkscape.org. Inkscape's homepage with download button is shown in Figure D-3.

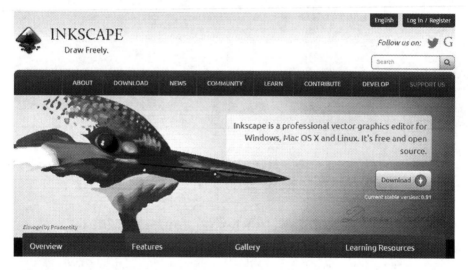

Figure D-3. *Go to inkscape.org and download the latest version*

If you want to learn about digital illustration and painting, check out my *Digital Illustration Fundamentals* (Apress, 2015) and *Digital Painting Techniques* (Apress, 2015) books.

Audacity: Digital Audio Editing and Special Effects

The Audacity team offers a professional digital audio software package called Audacity, which specializes in digital audio editing, sweetening, and special effects. You can download this software package from www.audacityteam.org. The Audacity homepage with its **Download Audacity 2.1.2** link is shown in Figure D-4. Audacity offers many of the same digital audio editing features as professional audio editors. It adds new 64-bit capabilities and professional features every month. The next major version will have a more professional user interface. If you want to learn more about digital audio editing, synthesis, and special effects, check out my *Digital Audio Editing Fundamentals* (Apress, 2015). Digital audio can greatly enhance the user experience with any HTML5 application.

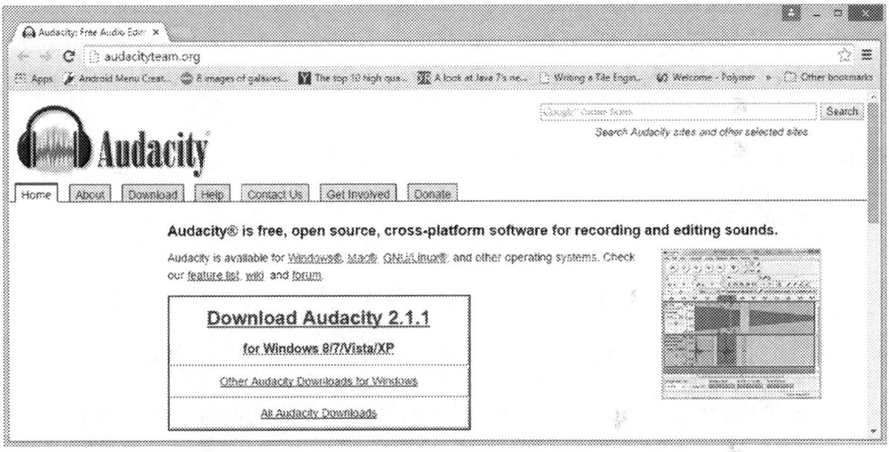

Figure D-4. *Go to audacityteam.org and download version 2.1.2*

Next, let's take a look at the free Fusion 8 VFX package.

Visual Effects: BlackMagic Design Fusion 8.0 VFX

BlackMagic Design's Fusion 8 is a professional visual effects (VFX) software package used in film and television. Download this software package from https://www.blackmagicdesign.com/products/fusion/. Fusion 8's homepage with its blue Download button is shown in Figure D-5. If you want to learn more about VXF pipelines, check out my *Visual Effects (VFX) Fundamentals* (Apress, 2016) book at www.apress.com.

Figure D-5. *Go to blackmagicdesign.com, and download Fusion 8.0*

Next let's take a look at the free digital video editing software package called Lightworks 12.6 from EditShare. This software package has been used to create a large number of feature films. So I'm not just setting you up with any software package, but with software used in professional and commercial projects. That goes for each of the new media software packages I'm having you download and install. We're not messing around in this HTML5 book!

Digital Video Editing: EditShare Lightworks 12.6

EditShare Lightworks is a professional digital video editing software package that includes special effects. Download the software package from www.lwks.com after signing up for the download. Lightworks' homepage and **Downloads** tab are shown in Figure D-6. I recommend 64-bit OS and software so that you can use 8MB of memory. If you want to learn more about digital video editing, optimization, and special effects, check out my Digital Video Editing Fundamentals (Apress, 2016).

Figure D-6. *Go to lwks.com and download Lightworks for your OS*

Office Productivity Suite: Apache OpenOffice 4.1.2

Apache OpenOffice, originally Sun Microsystems' StarOffice, was acquired by Oracle and released as open source. It provides HTML5 content development businesses with professional office and business productivity software support. Download this software package from www.openoffice.com. The Apache OpenOffice homepage with download button is shown in Figure D-7. I recommend 64-bit OS and software so that you can use 8MB of memory.

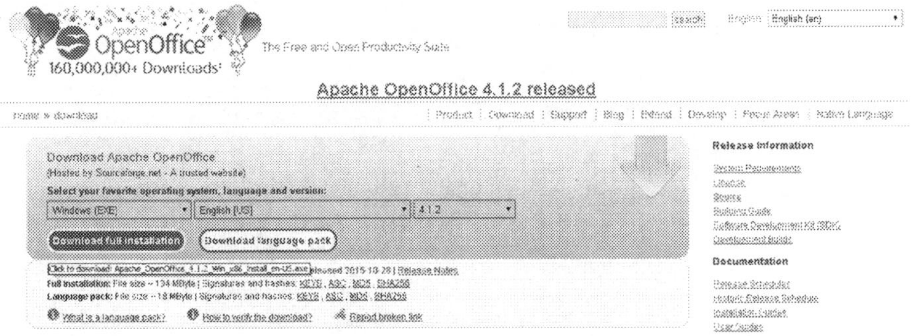

Figure D-7. *Download Apache OpenOffice 4.1.2 at OpenOffice.org*

Summary

In this appendix, you set up your open source **new media content production workstation**. You did this by downloading and installing professional open source new media content development software packages. These included **GIMP**, **Inkscape**, **Blender**, **Lightworks**, **Fusion**, **Audacity**, and the **Open Office** integrated office-productivity suite software.

Index

© Wallace Jackson 2016
W. Jackson, *HTML5 Quick Markup Reference*, DOI 10.1007/978-1-4302-6536-8

Get the eBook for only $5!

Why limit yourself?

Now you can take the weightless companion with you wherever you go and access your content on your PC, phone, tablet, or reader.

Since you've purchased this print book, we're happy to offer you the eBook in all 3 formats for just $5.

Convenient and fully searchable, the PDF version enables you to easily find and copy code—or perform examples by quickly toggling between instructions and applications. The MOBI format is ideal for your Kindle, while the ePUB can be utilized on a variety of mobile devices.

To learn more, go to www.apress.com/companion or contact support@apress.com.